SECRETS
OF THE MAYA

SECRETS OF THE MAYA

from the editors of

ARCHAEOLOGY
M A G A Z I N E

With a Preface by PETER A. YOUNG,
EDITOR IN CHIEF, ARCHAEOLOGY MAGAZINE

HATHERLEIGH PRESS
New York

Secrets of the Maya

The articles in this compilation were previously published in Archaeology Magazine.

Published by Hatherleigh Press
5-22 46th Avenue, Suite 200
Long Island City, NY 11101
Toll Free 1-800-528-2550
www.hatherleighpress.com

Hatherleigh Press books are available for bulk purchase, special promotions and premiums. For more information on reselling and special purchase opportunities, please call us at 1-800-528-2550 and ask for the Special Sales Manager.

Library of Congress Cataloging-in-Publication Data available upon request

Interior design and layout by Corin Hirsch
Cover design by Corin Hirsch

10 9 8 7 6 5 4 3 2 1
Printed in Canada on acid-free paper

ABOUT THE ARCHAEOLOGICAL INSTITUTE OF AMERICA

The Archaeological Institute of America (AIA), publisher of Archaeology Magazine, is North America's oldest and largest organization devoted to the world of archaeology. The Institute is a nonprofit group founded in 1879 and chartered by the United States Congress in 1906. Today, the AIA has nearly 10,000 members belonging to 103 local societies in the United States, Canada, and overseas. The organization is unique because it counts among its members professional archaeologists, students, and many others from all walks of life. This diverse group is united by a shared passion for archaeology and its role in furthering human knowledge.

Contents

Part I:
POLITICS, WAR & SURVIVAL

Part II:
ARTS, RELIGION & CULTURE

Part III:
READING the MAYA PAST

Part IV:
AN ENDANGERED HISTORY

A JOURNEY FROM PREHISTORY INTO HISTORY

by PETER A. YOUNG

SINCE THE FIRST ISSUE OF ARCHAEOLOGY rolled off the presses more than fifty-five years ago, the magazine has been on the forefront of discovery, a privileged witness to the unfolding field of Maya studies. ARCHAEOLOGY was among the first to bring to a wider audience the discoveries of early pioneers in the field, notables such as Matthew Sterling, Floyd Lounsbury, Tatiana Proskouriakoff, and Gordon Willey. Back then, a mere five percent of Maya glyphs had been deciphered. Sites such as Tikal and Palenque, now major tourist attractions, were in the earliest stages of excavation. Today, an estimated 80 percent of the hieroglyphs can be read, and scores of new sites have been discovered with the aid of space-age technology.

The articles in this volume, published within the past sixteen years, further document the phenomenal growth in our understanding of this ancient culture, from its origins in the preclassic cultures of Mesoamerica around 1000 B.C. through its rise and eventual collapse ca. A.D. 1000.

My own personal journey among the Maya began in 1990 when I first encountered the late Linda Schele, a brilliant epigrapher with a flair for communicating the thrill of research and discovery. A humanist, able by dint of superior intellect and long hours poring over Maya glyphs to conceive the world like a Maya, Schele could hold an audience transfixed. During an appearance at New York University, she recounted a moment of professional triumph—the discovery, meticulously cross-checked with scholars the world over—of the celestial origin of the Maya creation myth. "It's like being able to read Genesis in the heavens," she declared. Her enthusiasm was infectious.

Here was a born story-teller, a boon to an editor like myself, in a new job groping for new and interesting material. "The job I seem to have," Schele would later tell contributing editor Richard A. Wertime, "is to provide the public voice, you know, to give people access to the things scholars learn from the archaeology, combine it with the interpretations of the glyphs and imagery, the work of people who study the modern Maya and the approaches of many disciplines, and say to the public, 'Listen, folks, let me tell you a story about a great king.' When Schele died of pancreatic cancer in the spring of 1998, colleagues mourned the loss of her erudition and scholarship. I would miss her stories.

And what stories they were. About kings and royal courts, blood sacrifice, ball games, war and politics, creation myths, music and sports, and much more. "Linda possessed an unbelievable visual memory and saw Maya images through Maya eyes," wrote Gillett Griffin in a profile we published in 1991 (see page 126, *The Glyph Decoder*).

Meanwhile, we were reporting breakthrough work by many of Schele's colleagues, learning, among other things, that far from being devout peasants guided by priest-kings, the Maya were subjects of egomaniacal rulers who warred incessantly, and that a few powerful kingdoms had once built vast empires. Gone were theories of fundamentally unstable entities ruled by kings who were ritually important but politically feeble. In fact, so much was being learned so fast about the identity of warrior rulers and the rise and fall of dynasties that it was soon apparent that Maya culture was fast emerging from prehistory into history.

We also explored the musical sophistication of the ancient Maya, examined videographic detail of artwork no longer visible to the naked eye, compared modern-day Maya religious practices with those of ancient forbears, and asked what could be done to stem the systematic plundering of sites throughout the region.

Profiles of extraordinary scholars added immeasurably to our editorial mix.

We spent time with Leningrad epigrapher Yuri Knorosov, who, incredibly

We've been a privileged witness to the unfolding field of Maya studies.

enough, had helped crack the Maya hiero-glyphic code without ever setting foot on Maya soil. We traipsed through the jungles of Mexico, Guatemala, and Belize with Harvard University's Ian Graham, whose unending crusade to record every known Maya monument has earned him the admi-ration of his colleagues and a place in the constellation of great Mesoamerican explorers. And we spent time with funny and feisty Merle Greene Robertson, who for some four decades had ventured deep into the jungles of Mexico to make invalu-able life-size rubbings of thousands of Maya masterpieces before they are destroyed by looters and time.

Much of our coverage reflects the work of senior editor Angela Schuster, now editorial director of the World Monuments Fund.

Schuster covered annual Maya meetings at home and abroad and made scores of trips to Mexico, Belize, Honduras, Guatemala, and El Salvador to be close to the archaeological action. Her familiarity with the Maya world and the scholars responsible for repeated breakthroughs gave the magazine a critical journalistic edge year after year.

You might say that contributors to this collection of articles have drawn back the curtain of an ancient stage, revealing people and places hitherto poorly understood, sur-passing in their art, spirituality, and political savagery our wildest imagination. ▲

PETER A. YOUNG *is editor-in-chief of* ARCHAEOLOGY *magazine.*

Having dispelled the myth of a model society led by gentle priest-kings, scholars are piecing together a fresh picture of the rise and fall of a complex civilization.

THE NEW MAYA

by T. PATRICK CULBERT

The Maya inscriptions treat primarily of chronology, astronomy...and religious matters.... They tell no story of kingly conquests, recount no deeds of imperial achievement...indeed they are so utterly impersonal, so completely nonindividualistic, that it is even probable that the name glyphs of specific men and women were never recorded upon the Maya monuments.

—SYLVANUS MORLEY
The Ancient Maya (1946)

WHEN ARCHAEOLOGY DEBUTED IN 1948, the views of Sylvanus Morley and J. Eric S. Thompson, the leading Mayanists at the time, prevailed. The majority of the Maya, they believed, were devout peasants who practiced slash-and-burn agriculture and lived in small, sparsely populated settlements on the outskirts of temple precincts. They were guided by priest-kings, gentle men without egos, devoted to prayer and temple building. This utopian view of Maya civilization persisted until a new generation of scholars took to the field on the heels of the Second World War.

Unlike their predecessors, concerned only with temples and tombs, postwar archaeologists wanted to study the lives of common people, whose labor had built the great sites. In the early 1950s, Tulane, Harvard, and the University of Pennsylvania, among other institutions, undertook the first systematic mapping of large portions of sites like Tikal in the Petén region of Guatemala. These projects revealed thousands of small structures surrounding pyramid complexes, proving that Maya cities were bustling metro-polises, not vacant ceremonial centers reserved for a priestly class.

Following the gradual decipherment of the hieroglyphs, which began in the 1960s with the pioneering work of Tatiana Proskouriakoff of the Carnegie Institution and Russian epigrapher Yuri Knorosov, the mystical, spiritual society the ancient Maya were thought to have enjoyed began to crumble. Though decipherment of Maya inscriptions is far from complete—epigrapher Peter Mathews of the University of Calgary estimates that 60 percent of the hieroglyphs can now be read with some certainty—we know the names of those responsible for the great buildings and of those buried in royal tombs. What is clear from the inscriptions is that Maya rulers were not devoted to esoteric matters and calendar keeping, but rather to self-aggrandizement. Egomaniacs all, they warred incessantly and sacrificed prisoners to build prestige.

Based on settlement pattern analysis, archaeologists estimate that by the Late Classic, ca. A.D. 600, Maya population had reached a density of 600 people per square mile across a 36,000-square-mile area in the forested lowlands of northern Guatemala and adjacent parts of Mexico and Belize. This is a staggering figure, comparable to the most heavily populated parts of rural China today. Slash-and-burn agriculture alone could not have supported populations this dense. To feed the multitudes, the Maya had to turn to new agricultural techniques that included shortening the fallow cycle to put more land under cultivation, terracing, and cultivating

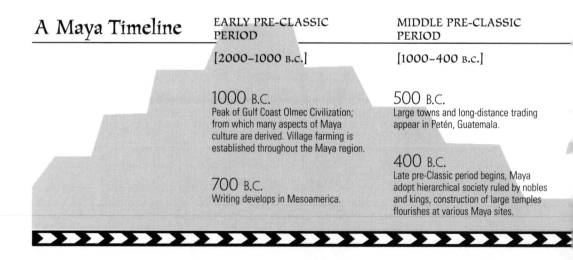

A Maya Timeline

EARLY PRE-CLASSIC PERIOD

[2000–1000 B.C.]

1000 B.C.
Peak of Gulf Coast Olmec Civilization; from which many aspects of Maya culture are derived. Village farming is established throughout the Maya region.

700 B.C.
Writing develops in Mesoamerica.

MIDDLE PRE-CLASSIC PERIOD

[1000–400 B.C.]

500 B.C.
Large towns and long-distance trading appear in Petén, Guatemala.

400 B.C.
Late pre-Classic period begins, Maya adopt hierarchical society ruled by nobles and kings, construction of large temples flourishes at various Maya sites.

the wetlands that make up 40 percent of the southern lowlands. The exact mix of techniques used is still a matter of debate.

Population estimates also figure in our interpretation of the mid-ninth-century Maya collapse. We now know that populations grew at an exponential rate for centuries, peaking around A.D. 750. Within a few decades, however, both urban and rural populations plummeted. By 850, two-thirds of the people living in the southern lowlands were gone, and most of the remainder disappeared by 1100. Archaeologists agree that to point to any single factor as the cause of the collapse would be naive. Most concur that centuries of uninterrupted growth put the Maya in a perilous position from which almost any disaster—drought, erosion, or social disorder—could have triggered a decline.

There has been a recent surge of interest in household archaeology aimed at informing us about the lives of nonelite people. The vast majority, perhaps 90 percent, of the Maya populace was devoted to some level of agricultural production, but there is increasing evidence of specialization in the manufacture of everyday items such as pottery. There are also indications of a middle class of specialists whose status was above that of full-time farmers.

Some of the most exciting work is in the area of Maya political organization, made possible by continued progress in hieroglyphic decipherment. In the 1970s, it was generally thought that a few great Maya cities served as the centers of regional states. By the late 1980s, many scholars began to view the very large centers as city-states with limited areas of political control. A minority argued for larger political units. Epigraphers Simon Martin and Nikolai Grube have discovered phrases within inscriptions that indicate hierarchical relationships among Maya rulers of different cities (see page 28, *Maya Superstates*). They see Late Classic history as a competition between two superpowers, Tikal and Calakmul, a massive site in Mexico just to the north of the Guatemalan border. In a masterful political strategy, Calakmul amassed allies in the sixth and seventh centuries who

LATE PRE-CLASSIC PERIOD	EARLY CLASSIC PERIOD	
[400 B.C.–A.D. 250]	[A.D. 250–600]	

200 B.C.
Appearance of writing in Maya Zone, rise of carved, dated monuments.

A.D. 292
Stela 29, earliest dated monument at Tikal.

A.D. 400
Maya highlands fall under domination of Teotihuacan. Maya elite culture spreads throughout central lowlands.

100 B.C.
The city of Teotihuacan is founded and becomes the cultural, religious and trading center of Mesoamerica.

A.D. 378
Tikal conquers Uaxactún.

A.D. 426
Yax K'uk'Mo' establishes first dynasty at Copán.

attacked Tikal and greatly diminished its power. Not until a new ruler (known as Ruler A) took the Tikal throne in 682, after his father had been captured and sacrificed by one of Calakmul's allies, did Tikal begin to recover. Ruler A's major accomplishment was to capture and sacrifice the ruler of Calakmul. He went on to build the two giant temples at the ends of Tikal's great plaza and a number of the other buildings at the site today.

The late Linda Schele probably did more than anyone to bring the results of Maya hieroglyphic decipherment to public and professional attention. In a series of books with various coauthors, Schele vividly presented the lives and world view of the ancient Maya. Like a growing number of Mayanists in recent years, she focused on ideology as a mainspring for society. The Maya view of the universe underscored the actions of powers and principalities, and the ruler, as mediator between subjects, gods, and ancestors, maintained the universe. Her most recent book, *Code of Kings*, "recounts" the funeral of Palenque's Pakal (A.D. 603–683), whose tomb in the Temple of the

Inscriptions is perhaps the most famous of all Maya royal burials.

Some scholars have taken a more materialistic view of Maya rulers. Ideology, they say, could be manipulated to suit the purposes of those in power and was backed with spears for those who chose not to believe. We now know that war was commonplace in the Classic period and that it was accompanied by the capture and sacrifice of prisoners amid much fanfare. But were sacrifices the chief reason that the Maya went to war or were they simply the ceremonial trappings of campaigns motivated by the desire for tribute and territory? Perhaps the two were inextricably linked.

Despite differences in opinion and approaches inherent in the wide variety of disciplines involved in the study of the Maya, it is possible for scholars to integrate their data in an effort to understand these ancient people. Copán in western Honduras, the first major Maya site to be extensively excavated since the decipherment of hieroglyphic writing, provides an example of a happy marriage of archaeology, epigraphy, and art history. Research by a variety of

LATE CLASSIC PERIOD

[A.D. 600-900]

A.D. 450
Tikal dominates the central lowlands, and has established economic and cultural ties with Teotihuacan.

A.D. 600
Population has increased throughout the lowlands. Large polities increasingly involved in warfare.

A.D. 683
Hanab-Pakal dies and is buried in the Temple of the Inscriptions at Palenque.

A.D. 692
Teotihuacan is burned and destroyed during the fifty-year period ending on this date.

A.D. 749
Smoke-Monkey of Copán dies.

CA. A.D. 750
Long-standing Maya alliances begin to break down, trade between Maya city-states declines, and inter-state conflict increases.

institutions and investigators has been under way for more than 30 years. ARCHAE-OLOGY has provided information about not only the site itself, but the whole Copán Valley, along with indications of ecological stress that resulted in the erosion of the surrounding hillsides, which may have contributed to the site's eventual abandonment.

At the main site, archaeological investigations and the study of inscriptions and iconography have provided a vivid image of elite life and a history of victories and defeats. Most stunning, perhaps, of all the discoveries are those that have been made in the tunnels dug into centuries of early construction underlying the Temple of the Hieroglyphic Stairway and the Acropolis. Just a few years ago, it was thought that the early fifth-century ruler Yax K'uk Mo' (Blue Green Quetzal Macaw), repeatedly acknowledged by later kings to have been the founder of the Copán dynasty, was either mythical or a vaguely remembered leader of a small village that once stood at the site. How wrong these guesses were. Deep beneath the Acropolis, archaeologists have uncovered buildings dating to the time of his reign, including a stela erected by his son and a small temple containing what are probably the remains of Yax K'uk Mo' himself.

Even with the enormous advances that have been made in the last few years, there are a multitude of questions still to be answered. We need to know far more about how commoners, who supplied food for the upper classes and labor for building the great structures, were integrated into the larger social picture. Was most land held privately by individuals or families, or communally by neighborhoods or villages, a proportion of whose production was collected as taxes? Or were there great estates held by Maya nobles, farmed by serfs or corvée labor? And what of the religious life of the commoners? Even in small groups of structures there are flat-topped pyramids that were once topped by perishable religious structures. Were the ceremonies that took place there simply a small-scale reflection of those performed in the great temples, or were there whole cults largely confined to poorer people? Were the ceremonies conducted by local lineage heads, or by "parish priests" who came to conduct rites that demanded special training

POST-CLASSIC PERIOD

[A.D. 900-1500]

A.D. 899
Tikal is abandoned.

A.D. 900
Classic period ends, and the Post Classic begins, marked by the collapse of the southern lowland cities; Maya cities in the northern lowlands continue to thrive.

A.D. 1000
Northern lowlands dominated by Chichén Itzá.

A.D. 1441
Mayapán is abandoned.

A.D. 1500
The first epidemic of smallpox or another European disease invades Yucatán, killing thousands of native Maya.

or an equivalent of ordination? The crux of these questions is the extent to which the lives of the majority of the Maya population were separate from those of the upper classes in kind as well as in degree.

It no longer seems profitable to look at each site in isolation. Beyond the great cities, there are hundreds of Maya sites, and neighborhoods within large sites, of intermediate size that have stone temples and palaces whose construction involved considerable investments of labor, but which lack the inscriptions that would tell us about their ties to the great rulers. Those who governed these sites were certainly elite, but who were they? Were they members of the great royal families, sons and cousins who had been granted small domains in the hinterlands? Or were they local lords, ruling areas that had belonged to their families long before the mighty became mighty? We know from the inscriptions that ruling families visited each other, intermarried, and fought. But if there were long-distance alliances and enmities, how did they work? How strong were superpowers such as Calakmul and Tikal? Texts suggest that rulers in allied cities acknowledged the authority of the great centers, but how dependent they were is still unclear. Did they participate willingly in political campaigns or did superpower lords have to beg, wheedle, or threaten them into joining their causes? Answers to these questions can only come from research by investigators with different interests.

Today, Maya sites attract crowds of tourists. Roads are being opened to previously inaccessible sites such as Calakmul and Uaxactún. While the environmental impact of the new roads is a matter of concern, tourism may be far easier on the landscape than cutting and burning the forest for agriculture, as is currently being done. The Classic Maya collapse may be an example of the price paid for mismanaging the environment. Those concerned with managing the remaining tracts of tropical forest would do well to learn from the experience of this ancient people. ≜

COLONIAL PERIOD

[A.D. 1500–]

A.D. 1519
Hernán Cortés lands on Cozumel island and begins exploring Yucatán.

A.D. 1525
Cortés meets King Kan-Ek' at the Itza capital of Tayasal during his trip across Maya country to Honduras.

A.D. 1542
The Spanish establish a capital at Mérida in Yucatán over the ruins of Tiho.

A.D. 1697
The Spaniards conquer the Tayasa Itzá, the last independent Maya kingdom.

A.D. 1839
American diplomat and lawyer John Lloyd Stephens and English topographical artist Frederick Catherwood begin a series of explorations, revealing the magnificence of the ancient Maya civilization to the world.

PART I:

POLITICS, WAR & SURVIVAL

1

SCRIBES, WARRIORS & KINGS

The Lives of the Copán Maya

by WILLIAM L. FASH, JR. and BARBARA W. FASH

YAX PAC, SMOKE-IMIX-GOD K, 18-RABBIT, SMOKE-Monkey, Smoke-Shell—the very names suggest a world so foreign as to defy our understanding of it. Yet in recent years Mayanists have made astounding progress in understanding the dynasties of these early Maya rulers. Classic Maya culture, in fact, is fast emerging from prehistory into history. Now as never before, noble lineages can be traced, specific individuals can be identified, and the lives of great rulers can be tracked with surprising accuracy. Complementary studies of Maya land use, settlement patterns, population growth, and the lives of ordinary citizens have shed light on the people who lived in the urban subdivisions, or wards, and in the Maya countryside.

Nowhere are these developments proving more revealing than at the site of Copán, a Classic period (at Copán A.D. 250–900) Maya city and ceremonial center in western

Honduras. Copán is the most artistically embellished of all the great Maya sites. Inscriptions on a variety of objects—free-standing sculptures such as stelae and altars; temple panels and stairways; portable objects including incense burners, ceramics, and artifacts made of bone, shell, and other materials—give us the dates of important milestones in the lives of the principal protagonists of Classic Maya history. The Copán inscriptions are the most abundant and diverse of any center in the Classic Maya world, detailing the lives not only of the kings, but of other prominent members of society such as the scribes, warriors, and representatives or statesmen of the communities that made up this particular realm.

The overall objective of our research at Copán is to understand how its rulers responded to changing political and economic conditions. By combining insights into the ancient Maya's material world with an understanding of their art and written language, the multidisciplinary teams studying Copán have produced a body of knowledge well beyond the results achievable by individual scholars. The work at Copán is not unique in this respect. Such collaborative or "conjunctive" efforts, as they are known in the field, increasingly typify research throughout much of the Maya world.

Particularly exciting are recent discoveries concerning the last several rulers in the Copán dynasty and the deteriorating economic and social conditions they faced in the eighth and ninth centuries. The Copán Valley was ultimately the victim of overpopulation and overdevelopment. By the end of the reign of Yax Pac, Copán's sixteenth dynastic ruler (reigned A.D. 763–820), so much of the forest was cut down to provide new lands for settlement and agriculture, for cooking fuel and building materials, that the entire valley was thrown out of ecological balance. Earlier investigations of the Copán Valley, particularly the work of Pennsylvania State University researchers, have demonstrated that at the end of the Classic period there was extensive soil loss and depletion, massive erosion, long-term decline in rainfall, and probably a number of highly communicable diseases. All these factors resulted in the dispersal of the population residing in the Copán urban core. The population of more than 20,000 could not be supported by lands available locally. Copán was eventually abandoned as a major ceremonial center.

We now believe that Copán reached the apex of its political power under its twelfth ruler, Smoke-Imix-God K. Epigraphers David Stuart and Linda Schele have shown that the famous hieroglyphic stairway at the site was built in his honor by Smoke-Shell, Copán's fifteenth ruler. Smoke-Shell's intention in constructing it was to commemorate the glorious days of Smoke-Imix-God K's reign as a way of expunging the memory of the capture and decapitation of Smoke-Imix's successor, 18-Rabbit. The written record left by Smoke-Imix, one of the most complete of any Copán ruler, is inscribed on nine preserved stelae and on as many hieroglyphic altars. These inscriptions record his accession on February 8, A.D. 628 (16 days after the death of the eleventh ruler, Butz' Chan), and his death on June 18, 695. This reign was the longest in the recorded history of the site and one of the most eventful. Besides consolidating power in the valley and proclaiming his might through the dedication of five stelae at the entrances to the Copán Valley, Smoke-Imix seems to have been successful even farther afield. According to David Stuart, an altar at the site of Quirigua, a Maya settlement some 30 miles away, informs us that Smoke-Imix was present at the inauguration of a Quirigua ruler, indicating that he had some sort of alliance with or held hegemony over this neighboring community.

Ongoing excavations in the site-core of Copán also suggest that Smoke-Imix contributed mightily to the buildup of the Acropolis; huge buildings dating to his reign have been discovered in the tunnels excavated into every major building in the Acropolis. Indications are that he was also a warrior. On one of the last monuments dedicated to him, Stela 6, Smoke-Imix is portrayed in full warrior regalia, wearing in his headdress the goggle-eyed Jaguar Tlaloc commonly associated by scholars with war and warriors. Atop the several Tlaloc heads that appear on this stela is a symbol (the "year" sign) identified by the Mayanist

Tatiana Proskouriakoff in 1973 as a badge of warriors among the Classic Maya. Tlaloc heads bearing such motifs also burst forth from the serpent heads of his "ceremonial bar," that quintessential symbol of authority carried by all the rulers depicted in the stelae at Copán.

Smoke-Imix also seems to have been a successful scribe, since he left more inscribed monuments detailing historical, religious, and geographical data than any other Copán ruler. Scribes were more important among the Late Classic Maya than scholars once believed: they recorded calendrical and astronomical data, religious tracts, tribute lists, literature, and historical data. Esteemed for their knowledge and skills, scribes were members of the upper class who not only wrote, but also painted and supervised the carving of sculptures.

The position of scribe, moreover, appears to have been hereditary at Copán. A lavish tomb discovered beneath the hieroglyphic stairway in 1989 seems to have been the burial place of a royal scribe who was one of

18-Rabbit and the Smoke Kings

Epigraphers read Maya inscriptions and texts by deciphering the three major types of hieroglyphs presently known: dates, verbs or "event glyphs," and subjects. The subjects are generally the protagonists of the dated events, particularly on the monumental inscriptions of the Classic period. In other cases, the subject is the actual object itself—a stela, altar, incense burner, or ceramic vessel. In many cases the verbs and subjects can be "translated" into the ancient Maya language, since hieroglyphic experts are now able to "read" the phonetic elements.

The first clue to deciphering the glyphs came from the phonetic "alphabet" recorded by the six-

teenth-century Yucatec scribe for Bishop Diego de Landa's Relación de las Cosas de Yucatán. *Innovative scribes often substituted different signs which had the same phonetic value, providing invaluable clues by which epigraphers can proceed from the known (Landa) signs to the unknown (previously undeciphered) signs. A syllabary has been developed, and new readings are constantly being suggested and tested by scholars. In the case of the names of kings, such as Copán's 18-Rabbit, Smoke-Shell, and Smoke-Monkey, epigraphers use nicknames or neutral descriptive terms derived from how a particular glyph looks.*

Smoke-Imix's younger sons, or at the least a close confidante of the king's. This royal scribe had the greatest number of funerary offerings and the greatest effort and care lavished upon the construction of his funerary chamber of anyone unearthed in 100 years of archaeological investigations at Copán. Analysis by Rebecca Storey, a physical anthropologist at the University of Houston, showed that despite his 35 to 40 years of age, his body showed no signs of arthritis or heavy work, indicating that he had led a relatively tranquil life. A boy whose dental condition indicated that he suffered from ill health or poor nutrition, and who was therefore most likely a commoner, had been sacrificed so that he might accompany the scribe into the underworld. Found in the scribe's tomb were remains of a bark-paper book or "codex," red pigment in numerous paintpots, and a pot decorated with the image of the patron god of scribes. The investigation of a scribe's palace in Las Sepulturas, known as Structure 9N-82, showed that at least one scribal lineage in the valley attained sufficient social status in the late eighth century to have a hieroglyphic bench or throne inscribed in its honor and elaborate sculptures carved on its facade. An earlier (ca. A.D. 450) burial at the same site contained remains of a codex and may represent the founder of this scribal line.

Just as scribes were socially important and highly visible in ancient Maya culture by virtue of the inscriptions and artwork they produced, so too were Maya warriors, at least during the Late Classic period (A.D. 600–900). It was assumed until recently that martial themes were not a principal part of the pictorial and hieroglyphic repertoire at Copán. Discoveries over the past ten years make it necessary to reevaluate our views on this subject and lend credence to the idea that warfare was indeed a major part of the Late Classic Maya political landscape. Indeed, an abundance of warrior imagery indicates the high social status of warriors. In 1979, investigations of the structure on the Acropolis known as Temple 18, directed by Claude F. Baudez of the Proyecto Arqueologico Copán, Phase I, resulted in the reassembly of the sculptural mosaics in a series of portrait panels, two of which show Yax Pac, Copán's sixteenth ruler, brandishing a lance and shield in a public display of his prowess as a warrior. Many other examples of Late Classic art show figures carrying and wearing ropes, often engaged in procuring victims for sacrifice.

Warfare was a major part of the Maya political landscape.

Ironically, the long and fruitful reign of Smoke-Imix was followed by a calamitous one that foreshadowed Copán's eventual demise. The thirteenth ruler of Copán, known to us as 18-Rabbit, was captured by a rival ruler from nearby Quirigua and decapitated—a disastrous event for a society that regarded its ruler as divine or nearly divine.

The hieroglyphic stairway and temple on top of the pyramid were built, as noted earlier, by Smoke-Shell, Copán's fifteenth ruler, in an effort to reaffirm the failing glory of

Who's Buried in Margarita's Tomb?

Archaeologists excavating the richest tomb ever found at the ancient Maya city of Copán in Honduras were surprised to discover that its occupant was a woman. Discovered in 1993, the Margarita tomb, named after the temple-platform in which it was built, was originally thought to be that of Ruler II, Copán's first great builder and the son and successor of Yax K'uk' Mo' (Green Quetzal Macaw), who founded the Copán dynasty in A.D. 426.

Composed of two vaulted masonry chambers with a long entrance passage, the crypt contained the remains of a 50-year-old woman covered with thousands of shell pendants and jade ornaments, earflares, and beads, along with burnt offerings of birds, turtles, and fish. The remains and offerings, resting atop a stone bier, were covered with cinnabar and hematite.

Embedded in the third tier of Copán's multilayered Structure 16, the 1,500-year-old Margarita tomb was designed to remain accessible for many years, its entrance passage lengthened with each addition. "We have archaeological evidence that this tomb was reentered on several occasions, possibly to conduct rituals," says University of Pennsylvania archaeologist Robert J. Sharer. "There are indications in the tomb that these cere-monies included fire and burning incense." According to Harvard University epigrapher David Stuart, texts from Maya sites, including Seibal and Piedras Negras, contain references to reentering tombs for burning rituals.

"After the remains had decomposed," adds Sharer, "still more red pigment was sprinkled over the bones, an act that may have involved the renewal of life forces symbolized by the blood-colored substance. Moreover, it appears that many of the offerings were rearranged after a partial collapse of the building, possibly caused by an earthquake."

Who could have been worthy of such veneration? "She may in fact be Ruler II," said Sharer, "or the wife or a relative of Yax K'uk' Mo'." To answer this question University of New Mexico physical anthropologist Jane Buikstra is analysing DNA from the remains to determine the relationships between the people buried in the various tombs beneath Structure 16. Female rulers are known several centuries later from Palenque in Chiapas, Mexico, and Naranjo in Guatemala. Until now there was no evidence of this tradition at Copán. "Whoever the lady was," says Sharer, "she was long venerated and no doubt played a pivotal role in Copán's ruling dynasty."

—ANGELA M.H. SCHUSTER

the Copán dynasty following 18-Rabbit's capture and decapitation. But Smoke-Shell's claims to glory appear to have been more propaganda than fact. Here the archaeological record helps us. The fact is that the fill used to support the stairway and facades of this building was the weakest we have found in the site-core at Copán: dry earth and stones were used rather than mud mortar, materials that were poorly or incompletely consolidated. We surmise that the economy was so weak and the level of workmanship so poor that Smoke-Shell's builders could not construct a lasting edifice. We know from sixteenth-century accounts that the population paid tribute to the ruling class in various ways—one of which was construction work. Ill health and a lack of willingness on the part of workers may account for some of the poor workmanship. It is also possible that the poor quality of construction reflects a lack of support from Smoke-

Shell's nobles. It is ironic, in any case, that the only major stairway that collapsed was the one the last Copán kings most hoped to be everlasting.

Other evidence of weakening royal command emerges during the reign of 18-Rabbit's immediate successor, Smoke-Monkey, Copán's fourteenth ruler. Smoke-Monkey, it appears, was a relatively self-effacing ruler who either turned to his noblemen for help in making decisions or who found his noblemen in political ascendancy whether he liked it or not. Evidence for Smoke-Monkey's possible weakness comes from the absence of stelae commemorating his reign and from the only building that can be identified with his rule. This relatively small building, Structure 22A, may have served as a *popol na*, or community house (where regional leaders met to confer and make decisions) because it was built next to an important temple on the Copán Acropolis— a location characteristic of the popol na in Maya culture. The telling evidence consists

of ten mat designs originally placed on all four sides of Smoke-Monkey's building; popol na means literally "mat house" in Colonial period dictionaries of the Maya language. These dictionaries also refer to such a structure as a "community house" and "the officials' house." Nine men known as *holpop* ("he at the head of the mat") are represented on the facade of this building; we believe that there were nine such representatives who met with the kings to make decisions and deliberate about social problems.

We also know, now, who some of the leaders from Smoke-Monkey's reign were. One author of this article (Barbara Fash) recently succeeded in reassembling portions of nine of the sculptural portraits and their associated glyphs from Smoke-Monkey's building. These seated figures depict the holpops of the most important wards of Smoke-Monkey's kingdom being given a permanent place of honor on the building that served as his council of state. This council would have helped shore up the confi-

Tomb of King Snake Gourd

Exploratory excavations in a 96-foot-high pyramid at the Late Classic Maya site of Ek Balam (Black Jaguar) in northern Yucatán have yielded the remains of a king known as Ukit-Kan Lek (Snake Gourd) who reigned over the city from ca. A.D. 790–835. Discovered by Victor R. Castillo and a team from Mexico's Instituto Nacional de Antropología e Historia, the tomb contained 22 ceramic vessels, one of which bore the king's name, jade pieces, obsidian blades, and inscribed conch shells.

While the walled city of Ek Balam has been known to archaeologists since the late nineteenth century, systematic excavation and consolidation have been undertaken only during the past 15

years. A decade of work by William M. Ringle of Davidson College and George J. Bey of Millsaps College has revealed more than 100 structures and a complex network of sacbeob, or roads, and evidence of some 2,000 years of occupation from the Middle Preclassic to the Colonial period.

The construction sequence of Structure 1, as the pyramid containing the tomb is known, is not fully understood. Located on the site's acropolis, the six-level structure is built atop at least four earlier buildings. Conservation of the bones and artifacts is expected to take at least three months.

—ANGELA M. H. SCHUSTER

dence of the Copán polity in the years following 18-Rabbit's defeat.

SIGNIFICANTLY, THE LEADERS COMMEMO-rated on Smoke-Monkey's Structure 22A are identified not by their personal names, but rather by the name of the ward they represented. This institutionalized set of jurisdictions and representatives implies that Late Classic Maya political organization was beginning to move beyond the confines of kinship ties to more institutionalized forms of government that cut across traditional family lines and interests.

Such a decentralized—almost "derulerized"—approach to government is particularly significant from an evolutionary perspective, for it points to the concurrent weakening of the personal authority of the king and the emergence of political statehood.

We cannot say, at this point, whether Smoke-Monkey's political strategy of sharing power with his regional leaders was successful or not; he died within three years of completing his building, and was succeeded by a ruler of a decidedly different cast. This was Smoke-Shell, Copán's fifteenth ruler, who poured all of his efforts into the refurbishment of the pyramid and temple and into the building (uniquely his innovation) of the world's largest hieroglyphic stairway. This monument emphasized the glory days (and rulers) of the Copán polity prior to the disastrous loss of 18-Rabbit, and in the process lent legitimacy to Smoke-Shell himself as the sole inheritor of the supernatural and secular power of the Copán throne. The need for such a monument may have arisen either because he had reconsolidated the

support of his subordinates or because he was reacting against the growing power and influence of those formerly subordinate families.

Again, the archaeological record throws some light on the matter; the structural weakness of the fills beneath the stairway and the rest of the building suggest that Smoke-Shell was operating from a position of relative weakness. Of the temple surmounting the pyramidal substructure, all that remains is the floor and the basal courses of two of its walls—hardly a fitting tribute to a man as powerful as Smoke-Shell claimed to be. Earlier Acropolis constructions all have tremendously strong fill; in fact, it is only because of the strength of those fills that we are able to tunnel into them. The contrast with the poor materials and workmanship on the stairway is stark, and is surely not attributable to chance.

The same sad story was to be repeated by Smoke-Shell's successor, Yax Pac, the long-lived sixteenth ruler of Copán. Dozens of texts record Yax Pac's glorious succession to power on July 2 in A.D. 763. Dozens more adorn buildings, incense burners, and other objects from throughout his 58-year reign. Yet, in the end, he apparently turned to the same strategy as Smoke-Shell, because the tallest pyramid in his version of the Acropolis, Structure 16, shows warrior and sacrifice imagery. Investigations directed by Ricardo Agurcia of the Instituto Hondureño de Antropología e Historia have recovered six different types of Jaguar Tlaloc war images that adorned this structure, as well as grisly skulls, ropes for binding captives, and warriors complete with shield and lance. And again, the fill of the final phase construction

Copán: A Site of Almost Overwhelming Complexity

Copán presents us with some special problems as well as special opportunities. The civic and ceremonial center of Copán, known as the Principal Group, is now an archaeological park encompassing 15 acres; it contains dozens of monumental structures, several major pyramid-temples, many smaller structures, and freestanding stelae and altars. Three other enclaves, mainly residential, bound the Principal Group on the east, west, and north. They are known as Las Sepulturas, named for a number of tombs found there; El Bosque, so called for the forest that covers it; and Comedero/Salamar, local names for the gently sloping land in front of the hill from which the ancient Copánecs quarried their stone. These three areas, about one square mile of settlement, comprise the urban "core" of the nine-square-mile area that constitutes the Copán Valley.

The principal obstacle to studying the site is the ruined state of Copán's ancient buildings. The relative paucity of limestone in the Copán Valley meant a scarcity of lime plaster, the basic building agglutinate used in most lowland Maya sites. As a result, stones and mud mortar were used for fill inside the large structures at Copán; even the well-hewn facade stones were joined with mud. Lime plaster was reserved for sealing the floors, terraces, and roofs of the buildings, as well as for periodic "white-washings" (often in dazzling colors) to seal and protect the buildings and their sculptural ornamentation from rainwater. After the Principal Group was abandoned in the ninth century A.D., the lime plaster began to crack. Larger vegetation became established, and the destructive force of successive earthquakes together with the tropical elements reduced the buildings to rubble. Some structures were destroyed or looted in the succeeding centuries; beautiful sculptures were carried off, and grave robbers plundered buried tombs of their offerings. Ironically, earlier archaeologists compounded the confusion by stacking up the fallen facade sculptures from various buildings in piles, still scattered throughout the site.

So hopelessly did they jumble this wealth of sculpture that the great Mayanist Tatiana Proskouriakoff once described it as "a gigantic jigsaw puzzle in stone." No concerted effort was made to study the sculpture until the Carnegie Institution expeditions to Copán (1935–1941, 1946–1947).

Today more than 20,000 fragments of architectural sculpture are being studied by the Copán Mosaics Project, whose staff of nine professionals includes specialists from Honduras, Guatemala, Germany, and the United States. In this cooperative effort insights and detective work are pooled, and specialists in each field—archaeology, art history, epigraphy, and architectural restoration—are constantly prodding one another to answer new questions and explore new areas they would not have considered if they were working on their own.

The Copán Mosaics Project is dedicated to assisting the Instituto Hondureño de Antropología e Historia in the conservation, study, and (where possible) reassembling and interpretation of the architectural sculpture at the site. The Project was founded in 1985 by the authors of this article and Rudy Larios, with Robert Sharer, Ricardo Agurcia, and E. Wyllys Andrews V joining later as co-directors. Epigraphers Linda Schele and David Stuart have been involved in the fieldwork and analysis from its inception. Other teams have worked outside the Principal Group, including ongoing projects directed by William Sanders and David Webster of the Pennsylvania State University, and one led by Wendy Ashmore from Rutgers University.

The objectives of the Mosaics Project include building new storage and laboratory facilities for the long-term conservation and analysis of the sculptural material. We hope to use the lively communicative imagery of the stones as clues to better understand how Copán's central authorities ideologically adapted to changes as political and economic conditions in the Copán Valley altered.

We are now limited by the fact that all the build-

COLLEEN POPSON

This large stone head represents one of the two largest human sculptures at Copán, both of which depict Pauahtuns, mythological earth-bearers. Sculpted during Yax Pahsaj's reign (A.D. 763–820) to adorn the north facade of Structure 10L-11, they symbolize the ruler's divine authority and connection with the cosmos.

ings completely excavated and studied date only to the eighth and ninth centuries A.D. This represents only a portion of the Classic Maya era, which at Copán spans the period from A.D. 250 to 900, and an even smaller part of Copán's entire settlement history, which began in roughly 1000 B.C. By tunneling into the Acropolis structures, however, we have gained valuable insights into the form and function of the earlier versions of these important edifices. The large Maya structures we see today are often the outermost of a nest of preceding smaller ones.

Despite such complexities and our limited knowledge, we are aided by the significant fact that at Copán no two buildings were ever decorated with the same ornamental program or bore the same set of visual messages. By digging previously untouched parts of a given structure, we can determine that building's sculptural motifs—the "signature" of that particular edifice. We can then cull the other examples of those motifs—carved in the same size, style, and depth of relief—from the piles of sculptures stacked up by earlier archaeologists. We first followed this procedure in excavating the four sides of the pyramidal substructure of the famous hieroglyphic stairway of Structure 10L-26 in the heart of the

Principal Group, and subsequently employed it in our investigation of the extant buildings of the East Court of the Copán Acropolis. The monumental hieroglyphic stairway—one of the best-known of Copán's features—comprises the largest single hieroglyphic inscription of the Precolumbian Americas. The Peabody Expedition excavated the steps of this stairway at the turn of this century, and the Carnegie Institution completed the restoration in the late 1930s.

It is astounding how much we can learn when everything is taken together—the historical and ideological data encoded on the sculptures, the contextual information that archaeology has revealed—especially when we consider that earlier students of the site more or less gave up on the mosaic sculptures because of their quantity and disorder. Indeed, the interpretive significance of the archaeological context and the sculptural data recovered through our methods has proved compelling enough that the endeavor has received considerably more financial, institutional, and Honduran governmental support over the years. We have gained major new insights into Classic Maya ideology and statecraft through this "conjunctive" or interdisciplinary approach.

is very weak, resulting in the near-total collapse of the building atop the pyramid.

Even more telling evidence of Yax Pac's attempt to belie his weakness by building impressive monuments can be found on an altar positioned on the main axis of Structure 16. Here Yax Pac had his sculptors carve likenesses of himself and his 15 royal predecessors. The figures were arranged in such a fashion that he is shown receiving a baton of office—that is, the right to rule—from none other than Yax K'uk Mo', the founder of the Copán dynasty, who reigned in the early fifth century A.D. In dedicating this altar, Yax Pac sacrificed 15 jaguars, their bones identified through osteological analyses by Diane Ballinger of Indiana University. Jaguars are associated with Maya warriors and royalty, and we surmise that one animal was sacrificed for each of Yax Pac's royal ancestors. The most important of the ancestors, the founder Yax K'uk Mo', was given a distinctive set of badges or symbols by Yax Pac's sculptors. He is depicted with the Tlaloc eye and a rectangular shield, indicating that he was a warrior

and a provider of victims for sacrifice.

Yax Pac, then, was legitimating not only his right to rule, but also his militaristically and sacrificially oriented means of maintaining authority. The irony is that although we have found Yax K'uk Mo's longest-surviving temple and stela, and numerous posthumous references by subsequent rulers up to Yax Pac's reign, there is no evidence among these to suggest that Yax K'uk Mo' was a warrior, let alone a follower of the Jaguar Tlaloc war cult.

The sculptural monuments have afforded us much more information about political history than we could ever hope for at a site that had no texts. Moreover, the work in the Acropolis has confirmed earlier study of the valley settlements that revealed the importance of the interaction of the valley nobles with the Late Classic kings.

At present, then, we have before us the possibility of discerning the political organization of this ancient Maya state on a level of detail never before possible. We look forward to our ongoing work. ≜

2

UNCOVERING A ROYAL TOMB IN COPÁN

Rescue excavations after Hurricane Mitch yield a ruler's burial.

by ANGELA M.H. SCHUSTER

A MAYA ROYAL TOMB FILLED WITH SPLENDID JADE offerings and painted ceramics is the latest in a series of recent discoveries in the Copán Valley of western Honduras. The tomb, located in a settlement area halfway between the Copán Acropolis and the modern town of Copán Ruinas, was brought to light during rescue excavations prompted by extensive redevelopment in the wake of Hurricane Mitch, which struck Central America in late October 1998.

"We were surprised by the tomb discovery," says Seiichi Nakamura, director of the Integrated Program for Conservation of the Copán Archaeological Park, who began conducting test excavations in an area prior to the construction of a new road that would link the town of El Florido on the Guatemala border to Copán Ruinas. "Before we began our work it was thought there was very little in terms of Prehispanic remains in the area."

Nakamura and his team began working in May of 2000 in the settlement area known as quadrangle 10-J on the Copán site map. By August, they had found some 20 structures, only one of which had been visible above ground, and 11 offering caches and 35 burials within a group of structures dominated by a building known as 10J-45. Included in the caches were ceramic vessels, spondylus shells, and jade figurines. The most elaborate of the offerings was a stone vessel covered in red paint found within a stone cache box. Known as offering 7, the cache contained a set of seashells and jade pendants oriented to the four cardinal directions used by the ancient Maya. It was not until September, however, that Nakamura found the burial with which the offerings were associated, deep within Structure 10J-45.

The pattern of the new-found burial echoes that of the Early Classic (A.D. 400-600) royal tombs excavated on the Copán Acropolis. The roof is vaulted and the interior chamber was made of worked tuff covered in stucco and painted red. The deceased (or his or her bones) had been placed on a flagstone funerary platform, supported by six stone pedestals, with his or her head to the east. Numerous ceramics had been placed beneath the burial platform, which had been covered in red pigment, possibly hematite. The ceramics, says Nakamura, place the construction of the tomb in the sixth century A.D.

Among the most magnificent of the offerings were two large jade pectorals. One, 9.5 inches long, is carved with the image of a god in the Early Classic style. The other, 8 inches long, is carved with the "mat" design, suggesting that the tomb's occupant may have served as *ah pop*, "a man of the mat," a title reserved for Copán's rulers. Both pectorals had been perforated transversally so they could be worn on the chest.

Although the analysis of the human remains, offerings, and soil samples recovered from the tomb is not yet complete, it is clear from the archaeological context of the tomb that once it was buried, it was not disturbed, since it was under the stucco floor of a subsequent building phase. According to Nakamura, the building appears to have been used as a shrine for several generations; the stucco floor was scorched in a number of places, marks left by incense burners. He also notes that Copán's stelae 5 and 6, dedicated in the mid-seventh century by the city's twelfth king, Smoke Jaguar, were erected just 500 and 1,000 feet north of Structure 10J-45. Moreover, the figure on stelae 6 appears to be looking toward the 10J-45 group. "This," he says, "may be more than pure coincidence."

"The pectorals, along with the pattern of the burial and its associated offerings," says Nakamura, "suggest that the individual buried there may have been one of the kings from the Copán dynasty. If a king or queen's

> Among the most magnificent of the offerings were two large jade pectorals.

tomb was placed outside of the Acropolis," he adds, "it will require us to rethink our traditional interpretations of the sociopolitical organization of Copán. This discovery could possess huge significance for all studies of Maya occupation at the site."

Initially, Constructora Nacional de Ingenieros, the company hired to build the new road, paid for the rescue project, hoping to have the area free for construction within a short period of time. Given the nature of the finds, however, funding for the site's excavation has been assumed by the Instituto Hondureño de Antropología e Historía (IHAH); the Honduran government has halted construction of the road, diverting it away from the new-found archaeological zone. Nakamura and his team will return to the site to investigate the other burials and offering caches. ▲

3

MAYA SUPERSTATES

How a few powerful kingdoms vied
for control of the Maya Lowlands
during the Classic period

by SIMON MARTIN and NIKOLAI GRUBE

RESPLENDENT IN JAGUAR PELTS, QUETZAL PLUMES,
and helmets fashioned in the form of fantastic
beasts, Maya warriors set out for battle on a day
often ordained by the position of Venus in the predawn sky.
Led by rulers dressed as gods, they sought to capture and
sacrifice their enemies in a reenactment of sacred myths.
According to many scholars, such religious beliefs motivated all Maya warfare. Our epigraphic research suggests
that far too little attention has been paid to more pragmatic
goals, that wars were also fought to conquer and control
rival kingdoms.

The first clue to understanding Classic period political
organization came in 1958 when Mayanist Heinrich Berlin
identified what he called emblem glyphs. Found in inscriptions throughout the southern Maya Lowlands, these glyphs
consist of a main sign, usually placed in the lower right,
attached to two smaller elements. Berlin noticed that while

the smaller elements remained relatively constant, the main sign changed from site to site. Emblem glyphs from Tikal in the Petén region of northern Guatemala had a main sign representing a knot of hair, while those from Palenque in Chiapas, Mexico, were based on a highly stylized bone. Berlin proposed that the main signs identified individual cities, their ruling dynasties, or the territories they controlled. Among Berlin's more interesting discoveries were four emblem glyphs—those of Copán, Tikal, Palenque, and an unknown city represented by a snake's head grouped together in an inscription on Stela A at Copán in western Honduras. Following Berlin, both Thomas Barthel of the University of Tübingen and Joyce Marcus of the University of Michigan proposed that these cities were the capitals of four large and powerful states, each aligned with one of the cardinal directions. In search of archaeological data bearing on this interpretation, Richard E.W. Adams of the University of Texas, San Antonio, examined the relative size of cities throughout the Maya region. Although many of the smaller cities had their own emblem glyphs, both Marcus and Adams concluded that they were not independent political entities but constituent provinces of larger regional states.

More recent archaeological research has failed to turn up compelling evidence to support this view. Moreover, breakthroughs in the decipherment of hieroglyphs during the past decade have greatly expanded our understanding of the Maya political world, suggesting quite a different interpretation. We now know that emblem glyphs are titles of Maya kings describing each as the *k'ul ahaw* or "divine lord" of a kingdom whose

name appears as the main sign of the glyph. By charting the distribution of emblem glyphs, Peter Mathews of the University of Calgary has created a map of the Lowlands during the Classic period, revealing some 40 separate kingdoms.

Taken by themselves, emblem glyphs demonstrate that all Maya rulers laid claim to an identical political rank, regardless of the size or population of their cities. This decentralized picture has led many scholars to believe that Maya kingdoms, even major ones such as Tikal and Palenque, were fundamentally unstable entities ruled by kings who were ritually important but politically feeble. This view is compatible with the interpretation of Maya warfare as a small-scale, predominantly ritual activity. Surviving inscriptions appear to support this notion since they rarely if ever record conquests in which one state absorbs another—more evidence, it would seem, that Maya kingdoms were too weak to engage in territorial expansion.

Yet such reconstructions have always failed to explain why some cities are vastly larger than others. Were such disparate units really equals? The idea that central authority within larger kingdoms was ineffectual is undermined by the scale of their public works—massive pyramids, defensive earthworks miles in length, and great networks of internal roadways—which would have required centralized planning and the control of substantial manpower. But perhaps the most compelling evidence for a higher level of political organization comes from new information we have uncovered within a body of glyphic data that has often been overlooked.

Political relationships between subordinates and their superiors within individual kingdoms were expressed by the use of possessive terms. Thus *sahal*, a rank or office held by key lieutenants of a king, could be transformed into the possessive form u-sahal, "the sahal of." The glyphs also tell us that the same dominant-subordinate relationship existed between kings of different states, where the highest rank of *ahaw*, "lord or ruler," comes into play. By adding the prefix *y, ahaw* becomes *y-ahaw*, "the lord of," in effect "his vassal."

Further evidence for hierarchy between states is found in passages recording the accession of kings. Some of these statements contain a secondary phrase giving the name and emblem glyph of a foreign ruler. This phrase is introduced by a verb clause that epigraphers have long glossed as "under the auspices of," though we now believe that it should be translated as *u-kahiy*, literally "it was done by him."

Emblem glyphs shed light on the hierarchy between states.

If we combine the appearance of the *y-ahaw* and *u-kahiy* phrases with Classic period texts documenting other forms of diplomatic exchange such as royal visits, gift-giving, joint ritual activity, and marriage, we find that hierarchical contacts are part of relationships spanning several generations. Some kingdoms are consistently more dominant than others and seem to be manipulating the affairs of weaker ones. This analysis is supported by inscriptions describing conflicts. Wars are only rarely recorded between states that usually share political ties, and

politically allied kingdoms tend to share the same adversaries. Together such patterns suggest that there were groupings of states during the Late Classic period (ca. A.D. 600–900). As the *y-ahaw* and *u-kahiy* phrases indicate, kingdoms within such groups did not share power equally, tending rather to fall under the influence of a few especially powerful states. Who were these superstates?

Because of their size and the richness of their architecture, cities such as Palenque, Copán, and the Highland site of Toniná have long been seen as dominant forces in their regions. Along the banks of the Usumacinta River, which separates Mexico and Guatemala, the political situation appears to have been more complicated. There, the iconographic and hieroglyphic record suggests that Piedras Negras held a number of other states in somewhat unruly submission, including for a time its upstream neighbor, Yaxchilán. Inscriptions throughout the area, however, contain references to larger cities in the Petén, where the most populous and influential kingdoms were located.

Tikal emerged as a great center during the Early Classic period (ca. A.D. 300–600). Inscriptions from this time, however, concentrate on chronological and genealogical information, and tell us little about political affairs. *Y-ahaw* relationships with Bejucal and later Motul de San José indicate that nearby kingdoms were closely tied to Tikal, while persistent relations with Uaxactún suggest that this kingdom was also associated with

Tikal. Evidence that Tikal's Early Classic influence extended well beyond the Petén comes from inscriptions on Stela 6 and Altar 21 at Caracol in Belize, which record the accession of the Caracol king *Yajaw Te' K'inich* in 553 under the patronage of a Tikal ruler. Within a few years, however, the relationship between these two kingdoms had disintegrated. Altar 21 records conflict between the two, possibly an attack on Caracol in 556, and a defeat of Tikal at the hands of another kingdom, whose name is now illegible, in 562.

No dated monuments were erected at Tikal during the next 130 years, but inscriptions from other sites in the region tell us that Tikal was diplomatically isolated and at war with every one of its major neighbors—without exception, all either allies or vassals of the kingdom of Calakmul.

Discovered in 1931 deep in the rainforest of southern Campeche, Mexico, Calakmul has been one of the most remote and least visited of all Maya sites. Excavations by William J. Folan, of the Universidad Autonoma de Campeche, and more recently by Ramón Carrasco, of the Instituto Nacional de Antropología e Historia, have revealed a great metropolis. With more than 6,000 structures it is the largest Classic Maya city yet recorded. Impressive even in Preclassic times, its core is dominated by the largest concentration of palace-type buildings in the Maya area, and is surrounded by a substantial system of artificial reservoirs. Though its monuments are badly eroded, it has 115 stelae, more than any other Maya site. Because of the poor preservation of so many monuments it has been extremely difficult to identify Calakmul's emblem glyph.

Inscriptions uncovered in the past two years, however, seem to confirm its association with the enigmatic snake-head glyph, a proposal first put forward by Joyce Marcus in the early 1970s.

Calakmul first comes to prominence in the glyphic record at the close of the Early Classic period, when in A.D. 546 a ruler of Naranjo acceded to the throne "by the doing of" a Calakmul king. This relationship, however, had clearly fallen apart by 631, when Caracol joined Calakmul to defeat Naranjo. Calakmul also attacked Palenque twice, once in 599 and again in 611—campaign treks of some 150 miles. Much of Calakmul's political maneuvering seems to have been directed against Tikal, which it attacked in 657. Its influence over the Lowlands is further attested by its involvement in the accession of two rulers from the distant kingdom of Cancuén in 656 and 677 and two kings at El Perú (dates unknown). From y-ahaw expressions, we know that Calakmul rulers were overlords to *Malah Ka'an K'awil*, Ruler I of Dos Pilas, around 648, and to his grandson Smoking Squirrel, king of Naranjo, beginning in 693. They had ties with Caracol and Dos Pilas and formed marital alliances with El Perú, Yaxchilán, and Naachtún. They were also involved in rituals associated with the designation of heirs at Dos Pilas—relatives of the Tikal royal family—and probably Yaxchilán. There are signs that even the regional power Piedras Negras was not beyond Calakmul's influence, and one especially difficult phrase dated 514 may describe an *y-ahaw* relationship between these states.

By the latter part of the seventh century, Calakmul was the most powerful kingdom in the Maya Lowlands and the hub of an extensive network of affiliated and vassal states. Despite its preeminence it was unable to subdue its great rival Tikal, whose new king, *Hasaw Ka'an K'awil*, was soon to strike a crucial blow. According to an inscription on a lintel in Tikal Temple I, Tikal defeated Calakmul on August 5, 695, and probably captured and killed its king, the great Jaguar Paw. Tikal went on to wage successful wars against two of Calakmul's closest associates, El Perú in 743 and Naranjo the following year. As if in celebration of these triumphs, Tikal embarked on a century-long building program, producing most of the major architecture seen at the site today.

Despite Tikal's rejuvenation, the days of superstates and large political groupings were numbered. Diplomatic exchange between the largest centers all but disappears from the written record by the mid-eighth century. Significantly, the decline of these networks marked the first sign of a wider political breakdown, as previously silent cities began to claim their own royal dynasties and warfare intensified. Within a century or so political disintegration and mounting environmental stress—overpopulation, diminishing resources, and possibly drought—had triggered the collapse of Classic Maya civilization in the southern Lowlands.

The picture that is emerging is neither one of a centralized administration of regional states nor one of a political vacuum populated by weak ones. Instead it would appear that a few powerful kingdoms held lesser ones in their sway, a system not unlike others seen throughout ancient Mesoamerica. Maya kingdoms never achieved the degree of centralization of the fifteenth-century Aztec Empire, but their structure and political strategies offer some interesting parallels. The Aztec Empire was a loose confederation of subjugated kingdoms and smaller empires. Its conquests were not consolidated by military occupation or administered from the capital Tenochtitlán; defeated local lords were usually restored to their offices and allowed to rule their states without further hindrance. Their successors were often sanctioned by the Aztec emperor in ceremonies that invite comparison with the *u-kahiy* events of the Classic Maya. The major consequences of Aztec conquest were economic, in the form of tribute payments, and political, in the transformation of local leaders into vassals of the emperor. Once their military prowess had been proved, the Aztecs were often able to intimidate other states into acquiescence without further use of force. We suspect that the Classic Maya conformed to a similar pattern—a complex environment of overlords and vassals, kinship ties and obligations, where the strong came to dominate the weak. ≜

4

MAYA PALACE UNCOVERED

Extensive palace found at the Maya site of Cancuén in Guatemala's Petén region

by ANGELA M. H. SCHUSTER

ARCHAEOLOGISTS WORKING DEEP IN THE JUNGLE of highland Guatemala in 2000 uncovered the remains of an enormous Maya palace built nearly 1,300 years ago. Found at the site of Cancuén, which means "Place of Serpents," on the Río Pasion in the Petén region, the three-story palace covers some 270,000 square feet and has more than 170 rooms built around 11 courtyards. Its solid limestone masonry walls are six feet thick in places. According to inscriptions, the palace was commissioned by a king, T'ah 'ak' Cha'an, who reigned in the mid-eighth century.

A preliminary survey of the building, undertaken by Arthur Demarest of Vanderbilt University in Nashville, Tennessee, and Tomás Barrientos of the Universidad del Valle in Guatemala City, has revealed a complex labyrinth of rooms and passageways, many with 20-foot-high corbel arches. The palace was surrounded by the houses and workshops of artisans. Adjacent areas had been paved.

Cancuén flourished during the Classic Period (A.D. 300–900), reaching its apogee in the early seventh century, when it controlled much of the southern Petén. The site prospered from its monopoly of trade in jade, pyrite for making mirrors, and obsidian for blade production. Within the workshop area archaeologists uncovered a 35-pound chunk of jade that artisans had been chopping away to make amulets and beads and impressive quantities of pyrite. "Cancuén," says Demarest, "had a distinct advantage in being located at the Río Pasion's head of navigation, the first place the river's waters are navigable after it flows out of the highlands; waterfalls and rapids providing a scenic backdrop to the ancient city."

"Clearly the city's inhabitants were wealthy," he adds, noting that even artisans, whose remains have been found under the floors of houses just south of the palace, had teeth inlaid with jade—a practice generally reserved for royalty—and had been buried with numerous ceramic figurines and elaborate headdresses.

The city was ruled by one of the Maya world's oldest dynasties, one that was established sometime around A.D. 300. The city formed a number of powerful alliances with neighboring kingdoms in the Late Classic period. Inscriptions indicate that a lord from Calakmul in Campeche, Mexico, officiated at the investitures of two Cancuén kings in A.D. 656 and 677, and, according to

> ## The site prospered from its monopoly of the jade, pyrite and obsidian trades.

Guatemalan epigrapher Federico Fahsen, an inscription at the nearby site of Petexbatún records a marriage between a Dos Pilas prince known as To K'in K'awil and a Cancuén princess, Ix Chac K'awil Ix Cancuén Ahau, sometime in the A.D. 730s. "We are just now beginning to work out Cancuén's relationship to surrounding cities," says Fahsen, cautioning that decipherments made so far are preliminary. Demarest and his team estimate that at its height it had a population of several thousand people. The site was abandoned in the mid-ninth century.

Cancuén was first visited by archaeologists in 1905, but dismissed as a minor Maya city. In the 1960s it was surveyed by graduate students from Harvard University who discovered the palace remains. Their sketches and maps, however, underestimated both the size of the palace and the extent of the ancient city; its architecture is obscured by dense vegetation. To date, Demarest and his team have mapped some three square miles of urban development. They will return to begin excavation of the palace, a project they expect to take more than a decade.

The site is at the center of one of the last stands of tropical rain forest in the Petén, complete with howler monkeys, wooly anteaters, and rare birds. Excavators hope to establish the area surrounding the site as an ecological preserve. ⬟

5

LIFE & DEATH IN A MAYA WAR ZONE

Within a Yucatán pyramid lie
the grim traces of a violent change
in rulership—the remains of a
slaughtered royal family.

by CHARLES SUHLER and DAVID FREIDEL

WE FOUND BURIAL 24 QUITE BY ACCIDENT, having walked over it for weeks as we worked on the west face of a 1,700-year-old pyramid on the North Acropolis of Yaxuná, a Classic Maya site in northern Yucatán. Near the end of the 1996 field season, Don Bernardino, one of our field crew, noticed a small hole near one of the trenches. We peered in and saw a large corbel-vaulted chamber, its floor covered in fine, pale dirt—a sealed royal tomb.

We were already two weeks into the excavation of the burial of an Early Classic king in an adjacent pyramid, the first sealed royal tomb in northern Yucatán discovered by archaeologists. Finding a second was an embarrassment of riches for one season, but manageable. We immediately began digging.

The tomb chamber was a little more than six feet long and less than five feet wide, with a stairway at one end leading to its entrance. Forensics expert Sharon Bennett cleared the sediment away, revealing a pile of human bones and polychrome ceramic vessels. We suspected that the bones were those of sacrificial victims placed in the antechamber of a king's burial, like those found at the entrance to the late seventh-century tomb of Pakal at Palenque in Chiapas. But where a second chamber should have been there was nothing.

At the bottom of the pile of bones were the remains of the tomb's principal occupant, a male more than 55 years old. He had been decapitated, his head tossed atop the heap of bodies. The contorted positions of many of them suggested they had been thrown down the stairs. Near his shoulders was an obsidian blade for bloodletting; near his feet, the charred remains of a polished white shell crown. This type of royal headdress, known as a *sak-hunal* or "white oneness," usually consisted of a white cloth band adorned with greenstone talismans. Near the crown we found a small burnt jade carving of a quetzal bird, presumably a jewel from a diadem.

The bones of an adolescent girl and a young woman, neither of whom had borne children, flanked the man's skeleton. Each also wore a *sak-hunal*. The bones of an infant lay in the girl's lap; the young woman cradled a doll-like goddess effigy in her left arm. Other artifacts in the tomb included jade jewels, carved bones, small mosaic

pieces, and little pots and pitchers from a set used to prepare ritual enemas. Altogether, the tomb contained the remains of 11 murdered men, women, and children.

We wondered who these people were and why so many had been placed in a tomb chamber usually reserved for a single person. Then it dawned on us. We had stumbled onto the dark side of Maya history. Like the murder of the Romanovs after the Bolshevik Revolution, the sacrifice of the royal family in burial 24 had accompanied a violent change in rulership.

LOOKING OUT OVER THE LOW SCRUB forest and green, fallow fields surrounding the site today, it is hard to imagine the nobles, warriors, merchants, and artisans who once lived in the dense scatter of buildings here. Ten miles south of Chichén Itzá, Yaxuná was founded sometime in the Middle Preclassic, ca. 500 B.C. The largest known pyramid in Yucatán dating to that period anchors the city's southern end. Fifty miles inland, Yaxuná was a waystation on an overland trade route linking the peninsula's central cities—Calakmul, El Mirador, and Nakbé—with the salt beds of the north coast. The site had natural wells for water, level ground for crops, and abundant surface stone for construction. Until the rise of Chichén Itzá in the eighth century A.D., Yaxuná was the largest city in the central northern lowlands. Its strategic location, however, was not without drawbacks, for Yaxuná became a valuable pawn in the power struggles of the Lowland Maya world.

We came to Yaxuná in 1987 looking for evidence of urban warfare dating to the time of Chichén Itzá's rise to preeminence. Little did we suspect that more than a decade of work would yield signs of no fewer than six deliberate destruction events between the fourth and thirteenth centuries. Nowhere was this more apparent than in the charred building remains, broken pottery, and desecrated burials in the site's North Acropolis. The event that ended the lives of those found in burial 24, dated to the late fourth or early fifth century A.D., is the earliest known in the long sequence of violent acts of conquest.

Most of the damage can be linked to two major wars: a panpeninsular struggle between Tikal, in the Petén region of Guatemala, and a site represented by a snake-head emblem glyph, quite possibly Calakmul in southern Campeche, in the fourth, fifth, and sixth centuries; and a conflict that pitted Chichén Itzá against an alliance of Puuc cities to the west and Cobá to the east, during the ninth and tenth centuries.

Data collected during earlier surveys and excavations at the site suggested that Yaxuná had little if any relationship with Chichén Itzá. George Brainerd of the University of California, Berkeley, who excavated the site during the 1940s and 1950s, was surprised by its apparent lack of Sotuta ceramics, typified by red slatewares and large, wide-necked, black-on-cream vessels, which were produced in abundance at Chichén Itzá. Yaxuná did, however, have links with many other cities of the northern Yucatán. Earlier in this century Mayanist J. Eric S. Thompson had noted the presence at Yaxuná of several Puuc-style buildings, recognizable by their distinctive columned facades, suggesting that the site had strong ties to cities such as Uxmal, Sayil, and Kabah, 70 miles to the west. A 60-mile *sacbé*, or stone causeway, linking Yaxuná with Cobá to the east was built at the beginning of the seventh century.

Warriors from Cobá had seized Yaxuná at the beginning of the Late Classic, ca. A.D. 600. We found destroyed public buildings dating to this period, as well as Cehpech ceramics typical of Cobá and the Puuc cities in the fill just above the destruction layer. Justine Shaw, one of our graduate students, believes that the new overlords must have harnessed most of the local labor for construction of the *sacbé*, since few new structures were built at the site during this time. For the rest of the Late Classic, Yaxuná appears to have remained a frontier outpost of Cobá.

We believe that in the ensuing Terminal Classic period, at the beginning of the ninth century, Cobá strengthened its relationship with the Puuc cities in an attempt to consolidate its control of the peninsula. As a crucial link between Cobá and its allies, Yaxuná was quickly refurbished. Rather than building anew, however, its rulers simply refaced existing structures, ignoring their original Preclassic or Early Classic designs. By the late ninth century, however, Chichén Itzá had defeated the alliance. We believe that the magnificent set of murals adorning Chichén Itzá's Temple of the Jaguars depicts this victory.

We knew from earlier surveys that there were no obvious fortifications at Yaxuná. We did hope to find evidence of urban warfare and conquest in a change of ceramics from the Cehpech of Cobá and the Puuc cities to the Sotuta types of Chichén Itzá. We began excavating the remains of a small Puuc-style palace on the North Acropolis in 1992. A

three-room structure decorated with a columned facade and reliefs with war symbolism, including shields and battle standards, the palace had been built midway up the south face of an Early Classic pyramid. As we cleared the area in front of it we realized that the palace had been deliberately destroyed. Ornamental blocks had been pulled from its facade. Beneath and around them were thick concentrations of smashed vessels with lug handles mixed with marl, a white limy dirt. We had seen such destruction years earlier during excavations at the Late Preclassic site of Cerros in Belize. James Garber, Robin Robertson, Maynard Cliff, and other colleagues from that project described this type of destruction as a termination ritual, a reverential release of sacred power undertaken prior to the construction of a new temple over an old one. At Cerros, evidence of these rituals included concentrations of intentionally smashed ceramic vessels, typically loop-lugged jars, buried in layers of distinctive white marl banked against the walls of platforms and pyramids.

As we cleared the debris from the exterior of the palace, James Ambrosino, another of our graduate students, began excavating the interior. During the 1995 field season, he had discovered the remains of a noblewoman entombed beneath the floor of the palace's west room. In her right hand she held pieces of a small metal mirror inlaid with mosaic, a symbol of accession to high office. Her burial, however, had been violated, apparently during the destruction of the palace; debris and white marl had fallen into the tomb. The bones of her upper torso and head had been scattered, and her burial offerings smashed. Some of the stonework had been removed, causing the masonry roof to cave in; the tomb had then been set on fire.

In the palace destruction debris we found, for the first time at Yaxuná, Sotuta ceramics and green obsidian knife blades characteristic of Chichén Itzá. We surmised from this that warriors from Chichén Itzá had destroyed the palace and the tomb. We began to suspect that we were dealing with an urban battlefield, and that this termination ritual was an act of war, rather than reverence.

AS THE EXCAVATION PROGRESSED, WE attempted to define the relationship between the palace and the pyramid against which it was built. Behind the palace we encountered the remains of an Early Classic temple atop the pyramid. A pair of offering vessels had been placed in a trench dug through its floor, a black-slipped jar in the western end and a red-slipped jar in the eastern. The black jar had a black stone ax jammed inside it, beneath which was a set of bright greenstone jewels. The red jar had a lid of worked pottery and contained a single greenstone portrait jewel depicting a god or a king, a large square plaque made of red spondylus shell, and several shell and jade beads. The offerings had been sealed in the trench and a dance platform built atop the temple remains. It was during the excavation of a terrace extending from the dance platform that we came upon burial 24. The tomb chamber had been built over a portion of the central stairway that once led up to the Early Classic temple. Stratigraphically, the cached vessels and burial 24 belonged to a single destruction–construction event.

As soon as we discovered the tomb, we understood the significance of the ax over the jewels in the black pot. In Maya glyphs, an image of an ax is read *ch'ak*. As a verb, it is *ch'akah*, to ax or decapitate and, more generally, to destroy, as in *ch'akah kun*, to ax or destroy a seat of power. A related concept is *ch'aktel*, scaffold, which can be spelled with the ax glyph. Classic Maya imagery indicates that both decapitation sacrifices and royal accessions were performed on scaffolds. We suspect that such a scaffold may have been built atop the dance platform.

Red shell of the kind used to make the beads found in the red cache vessel is called *k'an* in Mayan. This word means precious and, more generally, the color yellow, but *k'an* also names the birthplace of the resurrected Hun–Nal–Yeh, the primordial Maya maize god. According to some versions of the Maya creation story, Hun–Nal–Yeh, after being beheaded by gods of the underworld, was reborn from his own severed head as a handsome young man, dressed by beautiful girls for triumphal dancing. That the sacrifice of those in burial 24 may have signaled the birth of a new dynasty at the site is an intriguing speculation.

Who would have murdered Yaxuná's royal family during the late fourth or early fifth century? Our excavations yielded a number of tantalizing clues. The cache vessels are of a

New Stela at Tikal

A stela bearing a portrait of K'an Ak (Precious Peccary), the twelfth ruler of Tikal, has been found at the Classic Maya site, the first stela found there in more that 30 years. Discovered within the southwest corner of Structure 5D-29 on the site's North Acropolis, the stela shows the king holding a serpent bar, a Maya sign of rulership, and flanked by portraits of his father and grandfather. The figures are accompanied by a badly eroded text of some 90 glyphs, which begins with a dedicatory date of June 20, A.D. 468, and tells of events in K'an Ak's life, including his accession on August 24, A.D. 458, 15 days after the burial of his father Sian Ka'an (Stormy Sky).

According to Guatemalan epigrapher Federico Fahsen, the monument, known as Stela 40, was most likely carved by the same sculptor responsible for the well-known Stela 31 depicting Sian Ka'an. "While the text of Stela 40 lacks the fine quality of Stela 31, the carved portraits are superb," says Fahsen.

The monument was found last summer by a team of excavators led by Juan Antonio Valdés, director of Guatemala's Instituto de Antropología e Historia. Stela 40 is now on display at the Tikal National Park.

—ANGELA M.H. SCHUSTER

type known from the city of Oxkintok 75 miles to the east, but unknown at Yaxuná except in this set of offerings. We know that Oxkintok was an ally of Tikal during its Early Classic expansion into the Maya lowlands (see page 28, *Maya Superstates*), based on similarities in ceramic assemblages from the two sites dating to this period.

From inscriptions carved on monuments at Tikal and its northern neighbor, Uaxactún, we know that the king of Tikal, Toh-Chak-I'Chak, and his comrade-in-arms, K'ak'-Sih, conquered Uaxactún in A.D. 378. Artifacts typical of the central Mexican site of Teotihuacan found at Tikal and images of K'ak'-Sih and Yax-Ain, Toh-Chak-I'Chak's son, dressed as Teotihuacano warrior kings lead us to believe that Tikal defeated its enemies because it was closely allied with Teotihuacan. K'ak'-Sih is portrayed on stela 5 at Uaxactún wearing the animal tails and balloon headdress of the Tlaloc-Venus war cult practiced at Teotihuacan. Atop his headdress is a macaw, a symbol that also occurs on a painted vessel from Yax-Ain's tomb, which shows the ruler as a Teotihuacan war god, Waxaklahun-U-Bah-Kan.

VESSELS FOUND IN YAXUNÁ BURIAL 24 include some made in Teotihuacan style. A ceramic plate found atop the king's burnt crown bears the portrait of a lord dressed in a red macaw costume and wearing the animal tails of the Tlaloc-Venus war cult. The goddess effigy cradled by the young woman in the tomb bears the same step-fret facial markings as the Teotihuacan Great Goddess. We suspect that the executioners placed these items in the tomb to show their own sources of authority and affiliation with the Tikal-Teotihuacan alliance.

A defaced and broken monument known as Yaxuná stela 1, found by Brainerd not far from the Early Classic temple, also depicts a lord in Tlaloc-Venus war regalia strikingly similar to the portraits of Yax-Ain on Tikal stela 31. It is possible that stela 1 was commissioned by the man responsible for the deaths of those in burial 24, and that the monument may have stood in front of a vaulted gallery constructed in association with the dance platform and terrace along the western side of the pyramid. Several years ago ceramicist Dave Johnstone of SMU found a broken monolith with a *k'an* glyph carved on it in the ballcourt south of the North Acropolis. The stone was of the same color, dimensions, and finish as monoliths used to construct the staircase built in association with the dance platform, terrace, and gallery. The *k'an* glyph might have been part of a victory text carved into the staircase risers.

Why should Yaxuná matter to the alliance? Slowly but surely a picture is emerging of a panpeninsular war in the Maya Lowlands of the Classic period, one that pitted two confederacies, one led by Tikal some 220 miles south of Yaxuná and the other by Calakmul 170 miles to the south, against each other. Yaxuná's North Acropolis and Calakmul's main plaza are mirror images of each other, leading us to suspect that these two sites were allies. If that was the case then Yaxuná would have been a prime target for Oxkintok, an ally of Tikal and Teotihuacan.

We do not know how long the conquerors held onto the city, but the dance platform, terrace, and gallery that they built were destroyed during a later conquest, perhaps when Cobá seized the city at the beginning of the seventh century. The gallery vault was brought down, the staircase disassembled, and the stela thrown down and smashed. Whoever did it was careful not to disturb burial 24. We suspect that the conquerors were avengers of the sacrificed king and his entourage.

We know that the warfare did not end with the sacking of the Puuc palace by warriors from Chichén Itzá in the ninth century. Recent excavations in a nearby pyramid have yielded the remains of a middle-aged man who died a violent death. Ceramics found near his grave suggest that he was sacrificed by warriors from Mayapán sometime in the early thirteenth century, a time when that site was taking control of the northern Yucatán.

In the stratigraphy of the Puuc-style palace and Early Classic temple, long-term patterns of urban warfare are archaeologically visible, and include episodes of deliberate destruction and construction, desecration and dedication. Classic texts tell the story of the winners in these struggles. Evidence such as that gleaned from Yaxuná may yet reveal the story of the losers, giving us a more balanced understanding of Maya history. ≜

6

A MIGHTY MAYA NATION

How Caracol built an empire by
cultivating its "middle class."

by ARLEN F. CHASE and DIANE Z. CHASE

B Y THE CLOSE OF THE SEVENTH CENTURY A.D.
the lowland Maya settlement of Caracol had
become one of the most populous cities in the Precolumbian world. The 65-square-mile metropolis was home
to more than 120,000 people whose stone and thatch
dwellings stood amid lush gardens on terraced hillsides and
valleys. At the northern edge of a high plateau, three large
plazas surrounded by pyramids, palaces, administrative
buildings, and ballcourts formed the heart of the city, from
which paved roads extended to distant suburbs. Caracol had
grown from a modest town to a bustling city in the span of
a century (ca. A.D. 550-650). Its people enjoyed a prosperity
unparalleled in the Mesoamerican world. Military victories
over rival cities, such as Tikal, Naranjo, and Ucanal, had
assured political preeminence over some 4,500 square miles
of territory. What led to Caracol's rapid development and
unique place in Maya history? More than a decade of excavation by our team from the University of Central Florida

has yielded some surprising answers.

Caracol is located in the remote rain forest of the Cayo District of western Belize. Discovered in 1937 by a laborer in search of timber, it attracted the attention of Linton Satterthwaite of the University of Pennsylvania, who in the 1950s drew and photographed most of the site's carved stelae and altars and produced a site plan depicting 78 structures. A. Hamilton Anderson, the first archaeological commissioner of Belize, excavated three tombs as part of the University of Pennsylvania project and undertook two additional short seasons of excavation in the mid-1950s. In 1980 a terrace system was briefly studied by Paul Healy of Trent University in Ontario.

At the start of our work in 1983 we expected to find a midsized Classic Maya city typical of the Southern Lowlands, where major monuments and buildings would be concentrated in the heart of the city, beyond which would lie only scattered settlement. Three years into the project we realized that Caracol was quite different from other Lowland Maya cities. We knew there were more than 78 structures; what we had not expected was a settlement so large and dense that our mapping teams would have difficulty finding the site's outer limits. Unlike Tikal and Calakmul, Caracol had been laid out on a radial plan much like Paris or Washington, D.C. Luxury goods, such as jadeite pendants, eccentrically shaped obsidian objects, and exotic shells, that are confined to the ceremonial precincts of other sites, were found throughout the city. Vaulted masonry tombs, traditionally believed to have been reserved for royalty, were discovered not only in temples and pyramids, but also in humble residential units. Clearly some sort of social policy had been at work here that was unique in the Maya world.

We know from excavations on the outskirts of Caracol that a few scattered hamlets had been established there by ca. 900 B.C. For nearly a millennium the population remained relatively stable. By the first century A.D. monumental architecture was under construction, indicating that the site's elite had the ability to mobilize labor and resources. The Temple of the Wooden Lintel on the eastern side of one of Caracol's main plazas achieved its final form around A.D. 70. Deposits found in the core of this building contained jadeite, shells from the Pacific, and cinnabar, attesting participation in an extensive trade network. By the second century A.D. Caracol had built its most impressive edifice, which we named Caana, Maya for "Sky House," a massive platform atop which temples, palaces, and other buildings were erected. Adjacent to it stood the plastered pyramids and shrines of the Eastern Acropolis, where a woman who had died ca. A.D. 150 was buried. In her grave were 34 pottery vessels and a mantle made of more than 7,000 shell and jadeite beads and fringed with cowrie shells and tapir teeth, indicating the prosperity enjoyed by some of Caracol's early inhabitants.

Caracol was quite different from other lowland Maya cities.

During the next four centuries Caracol grew steadily in size and population. Outlying settlements such as Cahal Pichik and Hatzcap Ceel, five and six miles away, were annexed and eventually incorporated into the expanding city. Construction continued in the central plazas, where even more high-status burials—in front of the Temple of the Wooden Lintel, in the Southern Acropolis, and on the summit of Caana—suggest the site was becoming increasingly prosperous and extending its trade contacts. The placement of yet other tombs in small household shrines suggests that ordinary citizens were beginning to take part in ritual activities normally reserved for the elite, a social development that would accelerate with the passage of time, setting the stage for Caracol's Late Classic success.

According to hieroglyphic inscriptions found on an earlier structure within Caana, on several carved stone monuments, and on a building stairway at Naranjo 25 miles to the northwest, the city embarked on military campaigns throughout the Southern Lowlands in the mid-sixth century. The inscriptions tell us that Caracol defeated Tikal, one of the region's most powerful cities, in A.D. 562, during the reign of Yajaw Te' K'inich (Lord Water), and then consolidated its political position by defeating Naranjo and, presumably, a host of minor centers under the king's son K'an II. Naranjo was annexed in A.D. 631, possibly to have better control over tribute coming from Tikal. Naranjo and Caracol may even have been connected by a long causeway, parts of which have been detected on Landsat photographs. Strategic alliances were also formed with the ruling families of several key cities, most notably

Calakmul to the north. By the mid-seventh century Caracol had become the seat of a small empire, collecting tribute from many of its former rivals and their allies.

In the century following the victory over Tikal, Caracol's population swelled from some 19,000 to more than 120,000—nearly double the maximum estimated population for either Tikal or Calakmul. Even four to five miles from the city center, as many as 2,500 people inhabited each square mile, a population density unparalleled in the ancient Maya world. To maximize the land's agricultural potential, thousands of miles of stone terraces were built and hundreds of reservoirs created.

The city also embarked on a massive building program that included expansion and refurbishment of many principal monuments, including Caana and the Central, Eastern, and Southern acropolises, as well as the construction of a road system linking the city center to outlying areas. As Caracol grew, it absorbed many settlements, sometimes converting their plazas and temples into administrative centers. In some cases new centers were established in previously unoccupied areas, stimulating the development of new residential zones for the site's burgeoning population. The new settlements were connected to the core of the city by additional roads, facilitating the management and economic integration of the area. The road system also permitted rapid mobilization of Caracol's army, whose victories provided tribute labor to expand the city and strengthen its resource base.

Residential areas at Caracol consisted of *plazuela* units—groups of variously sized dwellings generally built on the north, south, and west sides of a central courtyard or small plaza. These units may have been occupied by members of extended families. Many courtyards had squarish structures on their eastern sides that served as shrines and family mausoleums. These ranged from simple wood-and-thatch structures on small platforms to masonry edifices atop pyramids. Inside both platforms and pyramids were vaulted tombs, many containing the remains of more than one individual, along with polychrome ceramic vessels, shell accessories, and ceramic incense burners used in rites venerating the dead.

Residential units with eastern shrines are found throughout the Southern Lowlands, but not as often as at Caracol, where they make up about 60 percent of all dwelling groups recorded to date. Distances between units vary from 150 to 450 feet, depending on the location of terraced fields and the steepness of the terrain. Conspicuously absent in Caracol's outlying settlement areas are housing units grouped around connecting plazas, a common residential feature at Tikal and Copán. The absence of such units may reflect tight control over town planning.

While differences in material culture and life-styles surely separated the upper and lower levels of Maya society, the gap between them seems to have been substantially bridged at Caracol. The distribution of vaulted masonry tombs and the presence of luxury items in the simplest residential units suggest that the people here were somehow sharing the wealth. Moreover, as the Late Classic period progressed more and more of the site's inhabitants appear to have enjoyed the "good life." Any gap in quality of life that may have existed between elites and commoners rapidly closed as a sizeable "middle class" developed. Nowhere is this more evident than in Caracol's mortuary practices. We have excavated 213 burials at the site, 86 of which were in vaulted masonry chambers, many in the eastern shrines of the *plazuela* units. Most of these chambers have passages allowing reentry to bury additional family members, to remove bone relics of ancestors, or to perform funerary rituals. Some tombs were emptied and reused. The newly dead were sometimes placed on wooden palettes. The bundled bones of ancestors would also be put in the chambers with offerings of shell, jadeite, and pottery. Incense was burned in front of the shrines, where offerings, including specially made ceramic vessels containing human fingers amputated in rituals, would be deposited.

Aspects of Caracol's burial practices are unlike those known from other Maya sites. The placement of more than one person in a single grave is relatively common at Caracol, occurring in 42 percent of its Late Classic burials. At Tikal less than two percent of Late Classic burials contain the remains of more than one person; the practice is even less common at other Southern Lowland sites. The widespread distribution of masonry tombs and their occurrence in *plazuela* units of all sizes attests their importance to the population. Though more are sure to be found as the investigation of the site progresses, the number of vaulted tombs encountered to date, some 120, already far exceeds the number found at Tikal, where only 23 have been discovered, most dating to the Early Classic period.

At Caracol we have found eight Late Classic tombs with texts on red-painted

Tikal Temple V Gets a Facelift

Visitors to the Maya site of Tikal in the Petén region of Guatemala will notice bright yellow tarps gracing the face of Temple V. Built sometime between A.D. 600 and 700, the 190-foot-high pyramid is the second tallest of the site's monumental buildings. Beneath the tarps, excavations carried out by Oswaldo Gomez of Guatemala's Instituto de Antropología e Historia (IDAEH) revealed a royal tomb containing the remains of a man and several ceramic incense burners. Conservators are now reconstructing the temple's staircase so that visitors to the site will be able to scale the pyramid. Until the restoration, what had been an elegant staircase in antiquity was little more than a mound of rubble. The reconstruction is part of a ten-year campaign, undertaken by a team led by Juan Antonio Valdés, director of IDAEH.

—ANGELA M.H. SCHUSTER

stucco panels and red-painted capstones. These texts, providing either the date of the chamber's consecration or the date of an individual's death, are usually associated with Caracol's royalty. Inscriptions alone, however, do not necessarily suggest elite status: since texts are found on a variety of artifacts from nonelite burials.

One of the more telling indicators of Caracol's shared wealth is the frequency of inlaid dentition, a cosmetic modification interpreted elsewhere as signifying high social status. Only a few individuals with teeth inlaid either with jadeite or hematite are found at most Maya sites. At Caracol we have studied the remains of more than 50 people with inlaid teeth, nearly all of which date to the Late Classic period. This is more than twice the number of such individuals found at the Southern Lowland sites of Tikal, Seibal, San José, Uaxactún, and Altar de Sacrificios combined. People with inlaid teeth were buried throughout Caracol in both elaborate tombs and simple graves, suggesting that all levels of society had access to this cosmetic practice.

Ceramic incense burners and specially made ceramic cache vessels, considered elite items at many Maya sites, also seem to have been widely used at Caracol. Incense burners are found throughout the city and in a greater variety of contexts than at other Maya sites. We have found complete incense burners on the stairways of residential groups and in seven tombs, all dating between ca. A.D. 450 and 700. This contrasts with Tikal, where incense burners are largely found in association with the site's central plaza. Ritual offerings traditionally associated with elite ceremonial structures at other Maya sites are found in nearly all of Caracol's *plazuela* units, often buried in the courtyard areas in front of the eastern shrines. Many of these deposits date from ca. A.D. 550 to 700 and form a major part of the ritual paraphernalia associated with Caracol's veneration of the dead. The most common ritual deposits consist of small bowls placed rim-to-rim and found either empty or containing the bones of human fingers, from both adults and children. We believe that fingers were removed from the living as part of funeral rituals and in rites venerating the dead. In most cases only one digit was removed. One such cache, however, contained bones from 22 fingers in a single set of bowls. Virtually every excavated *plazuela* unit contained at least one cache of this type.

In Late Classic *plazuela* groups we have found more than 50 large, lidded urns, most with modeled or painted faces. A dozen such urns contained obsidian carved in exotic shapes; others held pyrite mirrors, *Spondylus* shells, and pieces of malachite. Caches in pottery vessels with faces and those with finger bones were also found in the Central and the Eastern acropolises, indicating that high status residents of Caracol were sharing in society-wide rituals.

Caracol's rapid development was surely related to its social policies, presumably initiated prior to its known military conquests. To manage people effectively, the city's leaders encouraged a form of social cohesion that stressed the development of a distinctive identity rooted in ritual activity and bolstered by prosperity. This system worked for more than three centuries. Then, after A.D. 800, the people began to abandon the policies that had integrated them. Luxury items are found only in palaces, suggesting that the rich and powerful kept such goods to themselves. Simultaneously, outlying populations discontinued common ritual practices. About A.D. 895 much of the core of Caracol was burned, by whom we do not know. The Late Classic investment in road and field systems, however, continued to benefit residents of the outlying areas. For another 150 years they farmed the fields much as they always had and made occasional offerings in the abandoned central buildings. By A.D. 1100 Caracol's social identity was gone, and all vestiges of the once mighty nation had been engulfed by the rain forest. ≜

7

TROPICAL TIME CAPSULE

An ancient village preserved in volcanic ash yields evidence of Mesoamerican peasant life.

by PAYSON D. SHEETS

THE ERUPTION BEGAN WITH BLASTS OF STEAM as hot basaltic magma made contact with the nearby river. Scalding vapors, gases, and ash were spewed across the countryside. Within days, the village was buried under more than 15 feet of ash. Warned by the steam explosions, its people had fled, but their architecture, tools, crops, and landscape were preserved for all time.

The excavation of this settlement, in the Zapotitan Valley of central El Salvador, has provided a rare opportunity to understand what peasant life was like in southern Mesoamerica 1,400 years ago, even to the point of knowing the food the villagers ate, the polychrome pots they served it in, the crops they grew in their gardens, and the size and construction of their dwellings and civic buildings. Because the villagers' possessions remained where they left them, we can answer questions that nobody would have even thought to ask. We had no idea, for example, that people in the region lived so well 14 centuries ago.

Until recently, most archaeological projects in Mesoamerica have ignored or neglected the common people, focusing instead on elite palaces, temples, and tombs. Recent research at Copán in Honduras, however, has focused on all social classes on a regional basis. Peasant houses there were gradually abandoned and stripped of artifacts. Exposed to rain, sun, and wind, these dwellings have badly deteriorated; only the outlines of the platforms on which they were built and occasionally some stubs of walls can be seen. Our Salvadoran village would have faced a similar fate had it not been for the protective layer of volcanic ash.

Named Cerén after the Spanish family that colonized the area in the eighteenth century, the village was buried between A.D. 585 and 600. It appears that the eruption began at night. The presence of digging sticks and other agricultural tools in the dwellings suggests that it occurred after the farmers had returned from their fields but before they had gone to bed, since we found no mats rolled out on the benches in the innermost rooms of the houses. The villagers apparently escaped the gases and ash; we have found no evidence that any of them perished during the eruption. Toward the end of our 1990 season, we did find a hollow cavity that we thought might have been formed by the body of a victim; within the cavity were three human teeth. We later determined that the hollow was caused by a collapsed thatched roof. Our workers informed us that in El Salvador peasants throw their loose teeth on the roof of their

houses for good luck. It seems they were doing the same 1,400 years ago.

The Zapotitan Valley had been buried by an earlier, more massive eruption. In A.D. 175 the volcano Ilopango (25 miles east of Cerén) erupted, covering the valley with three feet of white, acidic ash. The blast killed most of the area's vegetation, polluted water supplies, and led to the abandonment of the valley for two or three centuries. Pottery studies indicate that Cerén was settled by people moving back into the area, probably in the fifth century A.D. The village became one of dozens of local ceremonial, political, and economic centers.

THE SITE WAS FIRST DISCOVERED IN 1976 by a bulldozer operator who was leveling ground for a platform on which to put up grain silos. Seeing that his bulldozer had cut the corner of a building buried by volcanic ash, he notified the national museum in San Salvador. Unfortunately, a museum archaeologist, thinking the site was of recent vintage, allowed the bulldozing to continue, thereby destroying a number of structures. Two years later I was in El Salvador with a team of students from the University of Colorado conducting an archaeological survey of the Zapotitan Valley. Local people told me of the discovery. A few hours of excavating revealed only prehistoric artifacts. Radiocarbon dates proved that some of them were 1,400 years old. I requested and received permission to undertake a full-scale excavation. During five field seasons, we have uncovered 11 buildings within a quarter-mile-square area, and we know the whereabouts of a dozen more. Ground-penetrating radar has detected an additional dozen or so structures.

Village architecture at ancient Cerén was quite sophisticated. We were surprised by the variety of buildings, by their reinforced earthen walls, corner columns, lattice windows, sturdy roofs, lintels, cornices, and the like. We did not know that they were also building adobe walls. Civic buildings, perched on large earthen platforms to keep them dry in the rainy season and to make them look imposing, had thick walls with bold cornices and overhanging roofs that offered protection from rain. Two such buildings and perhaps a third faced a 60-foot-square plaza that was probably used for announcements and political functions. A sauna served as a place for physical and spiritual cleansing. Its walls, decorated with a cornice, supported a graceful earthen dome that was protected by a thatched roof on wooden beams and poles. This dome was a major discovery since many architectural historians have assumed that domed architecture was a European import.

We found that dwellings were more resistant to earthquakes than civic buildings. The walls of most households were reinforced with vertical wooden poles set in the floor and interlaced with horizontal poles tied to wooden roof beams. Each household built separate structures for kitchens, storehouses, and rooms for sleeping and family activities such as eating and making clothes, pottery, and chipped-stone tools. Most roofs extended beyond the walls, providing protected space for storing sun-dried adobe bricks, manufacturing thread, and grinding maize.

We were astonished to find more than 70 ceramic vessels in a household that we had deemed among the poorest because it had

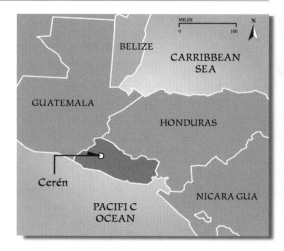

small, poorly constructed rooms compared to those of other households. Some of the vessels were for cooking; others were for storage of grains and items such as sea shells (used for beads), pigment, and miniature metates (used for grinding pigment). Some, elegantly polychrome painted, were used to serve food and drink. Even the most utilitarian vessels were decorated with swirls and parallel lines traced in a wet slip before firing. This household was not wasteful; the handles of large broken jars were mounted in the earthen walls and used for hanging sleeping mats and room partitions. Residents also owned many plain and elaborately painted gourds that served as storage and serving vessels. They used obsidian knives and stored them in thatch roofs over doorways or porches. We found jade axes for woodworking, spindle whorls for making thread, grinding stones for corn processing, pottery vessels for cooking, and deer antlers for husking maize.

The villagers ate better and had a greater variety of foodstuffs than their descendants. Traditional families today eat mostly corn and beans, with some rice, squash, and chiles, but rarely any meat. Cerén's residents ate deer and dog meat. Corn was the most abundant crop, as it is today, and they stored it in great quantities. They also harvested three varieties of beans, as well as squash, chiles, and cacao. Villagers collected avocados, palm fruits and nuts, and achiote (a spice made from the ground seeds of the annatto tree that gives food a rich taste and a yellow-red color). Also found in the gardens were the remains of manioc, medicinal plants called *macoyas* that settle an upset stomach and also yield fine fibers for thread, and *maguey (Agave)*, grown for its strong fibers, which were processed and woven into two-ply twine and rope. With the exception of maguey, which sprouts unpredictably, all crops were planted in neat (north-south and east-west) rows, on top of small earthen ridges, with one species per row.

Cerén residents also had better access to clean water. The nearby Río Sucio (Dirty River) is well named. It is now polluted by chemicals from a paper mill and a tannery upstream. Thatching materials such as grasses and palm were used in the past, but are scarce in the area today. The ancient residents had access to vesicular basalt for making grinding stones, and obsidian for cutting and scraping tools. Households today still use basalt grinding stones, but to save time people often pay to have corn ground commercially. Cutting tools are now made of imported steel, costing substantially more than the ancient people's obsidian blades.

The sixth-century residents used great amounts of hematite and limonite to decorate pottery and buildings. In addition to these pigments, they used a brilliant red cinnabar pigment (mercuric sulfide) and a ground metamorphic greenstone to decorate gourds. Various artifacts, like a deer-skull headdress used in religious ritual, as well as two religious buildings were painted white, using volcanic ash mixed with a binder.

Cerén offers an extraordinary window into the past. Working here is exhilarating, but it is sad that the quality of Salvadoran life has declined so dramatically in the last two centuries. For hundreds of years this country had a relatively stable population. In the mid-nineteenth century, however, Europeans and Americans established haciendas, growing coffee and sugarcane for export. They also brought sanitation and medicine, thus lowering the death rate, which was convenient for landowners since there were more laborers for agricultural work. But in time the land became overpopulated. The country's twentieth-century history has been one of increasing poverty, malnutrition, and civil war. Villagers who work at Cerén generally live in small adobe or fired-clay brick houses that are more prone to earthquake damage than their ancestors' sturdier constructions. Their dwellings are sparsely furnished, and they have few personal possessions and little food stored in their houses. We found no evidence of cockroaches and the workers pondered how wonderful it must have been to live without them.

The Cerén site is important to modern-day Salvadorans. Their forebears successfully adapted to their environment, farming the fields, storing food, and building comfortable, earthquake-resistant homes. They are proud of their ancestors' accomplishments, and are pleased that the world is now learning about them. ▲

8

THE ART OF GARDENING

Eating well at a Mesoamerican Pompeii

by JAMES WISEMAN

FOOD GROWN AT THE SIXTH-CENTURY SITE OF Cerén, a rural village on the southern periphery of the ancient Maya world (see Plate 1), was at least as varied as that enjoyed by nobility at the great Maya center of Copán, according to David Lentz of the New York Botanical Garden and other scientists who have been studying the site's botanical remains, recovered in great quantity and in an excellent state of preservation. The rich palaeoethnobotanical record is matched by the preservation of the architecture, artifacts, and even the house gardens of this ancient site in the Zapotitan Valley of what is now El Salvador. The ancient village was sealed in time on an August evening ca. A.D. 595, when the Loma Caldera volcano erupted and, over a period of a few days or weeks, buried it in 12 to 19 feet of volcanic ash and other debris (see page 48, *Tropical Time Capsule*). Caught by surprise not long after their evening meal, villagers fled their homes, leaving their dishes unwashed and their sleeping mats still rolled up and stored in the rafters, a snapshot of catastrophe, like the remains of Pompeii buried by the eruption of Vesuvius in A.D. 79.

The ash from the first of 14 successive eruptions at Cerén was only about 100 degrees Celsius (the second surge was about 550 degrees Celsius), and thus preserved plants in the fields, burying them before they disintegrated. As the organic material deteriorated, it left cavities with impressions of the original plants. Following the example of Pompeii's excavators, archaeologists at Cerén forced liquid plaster into the cavities as they discovered them and, after it had hardened, dug away the ash to expose a plaster cast of the original form. At Pompeii, the procedure was first used in 1864 by Giuseppe Fiorelli, who created astonishing casts of people buried by ash. Tormented facial expressions were clear on many, and the outlines of clothes were preserved on some. Wilhelmina Jashemski, professor emerita at the University of Maryland, used a similar procedure in her brilliant study of plants growing in the gardens of Pompeii and Herculaneum, thereby providing a direct precedent for the work at Cerén, where forms have been recovered and reconstructed from root tips to leaf points. Excavators have left the casts of plants in place protruding from the raised ridges in which seeds were sown 14 centuries ago. Meanwhile, they are studying ancient Maya methods of planting gardens and fields. No other site in the New World has offered such an opportunity.

Payson D. Sheets, professor of anthropology at the University of Colorado at Boulder, is director of the Cerén project. We discussed his work during a visit last fall to Boston, where he gave a superb lecture on the history of the site for the Boston society of the Archaeological Institute of America and the Department of Archaeology at Boston University. Sheets has identified an agricultural strategy at Cerén that he calls "zoned biodiversity," that is, the creation of specific planting zones for particular species. For example, fields were commonly planted with maize, with two to five plants along a ridge about three feet apart; the ridges themselves were separated by almost three feet, so that beans and squash could be planted between them. Sheets noted that many stalks of maize, planted early in the rainy season, had matured and were doubled over, presumably intentionally, so that rain would wash over the husks without wetting the ears of corn; the nutrient flow would have been cut off to allow the kernels to dry; and birds would have had greater difficulty getting at the corn. Some young stalks, he said, represent a second planting late in the rainy season, pointing to August as the likely month of the volcanic eruption.

Zoned biodiversity was practiced on a smaller scale in house gardens, where each ridge system was normally devoted to a single species. A garden just east of the kitchen in one household complex has a ridge devoted to manioc for half its length and *piñuela*, a flowering plant requiring only a limited water supply, for the other half. The *piñuela* was probably used as a cure for upset stomachs and diarrhea as it is today in traditional Salvadoran homes. *Macoyas* (flowering plants of still unidentified varieties) were planted in rows two and five, and *piñuela* again in rows three, four, and six. Another household garden was devoted to some 70 *maguey* plants (see Plate 2), as *Agave ameri-*

cana is usually known in Latin America; they are also called century plants in North America. These plants could not be cultivated in rows, Sheets pointed out, "because maguey sprouts from the roots of older plants." The agave was a particularly important crop because its leaves could be depulped to produce strong fibers for twine and cord, exemplified by a piece of braided twine found in place around part of an agave. According to Sheets, about five such plants could have provided the fiber needed for a normal household; the produce from this garden may have supplied as many as a dozen families. Agave was used in Mexico in Precolumbian (and later) times for making a fermented alcoholic drink called pulque, and is still used in the manufacture of tequila. When I asked Sheets if there was any evidence for pulque making at Cerén, he replied that the Central American agave was much smaller than the Mexican variety, and there was no evidence for its use as a beverage in this part of Mesoamerica in antiquity. He added that all the examples at Cerén had fully grown flower clusters, and so could not have been used for making an alcoholic drink, since the liquid for pulque or other drinks must be extracted before the flowers bloom. On the other hand, he noted that finely ground maize could have been used to make a fermented drink known as chicha, but there is no definitive evidence for it.

South of the maguey field were tree crops, including a mature guayaba with

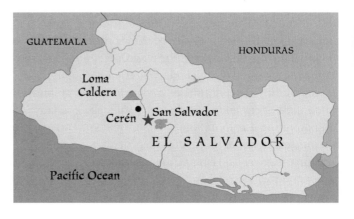

dozens of young fruit, as well as a cacao tree, the seeds of which were used to make a chocolate beverage laced with pepper, known to have been favored by Mesoamericans after the Spanish conquest and noted in numerous prehistoric archaeological contexts. It could also be used to make a spicy mole sauce like those served today. Southwest of the maguey was a zone of chili pepper bushes (see Plate 3) with stem diameters of about two inches, larger by far than the ones we grew in the backyard when I was a child in Arkansas.

Foodstuffs found in the various structures of the household complexes have been reported by Lentz and others (*Latin American Antiquity* 7:3 [1996]) and include examples of all the crops known from the gardens, including quantities of chili peppers, many of which had been hung from thatched roofs to dry, and pepper seeds in bowls, perhaps part of chili sauces for meals. Peppers are rarely found in archaeological contexts in Mesoamerica, and the ones at Cerén seem to be the first recorded outside of Mexico. The likely reason is that no other large habitation site sealed by volcanic ash has yet been excavated, a circumstance which surely accounts for the fact that, as the research team observed, more containers (mostly ceramic vessels) have been found with their original contents in situ at Cerén than at any other Mesoamerican site. Other foods found in the structures included at least two species of beans, various berries, maguey, calabash, cacao seeds (only in one structure), and maize in various forms. Lentz's hypothesis that a common method of preparing maize in the village was by steaming tamales made with ground squash seeds, corn, and bean paste intrigues me. My grandfather, Walter Lee Sullivan, operated a tamale business in North Little Rock, Arkansas, in the 1930s, and some of his descendants continued the business until the early 1990s. Usually made with beef or pork, Sullivan's tamales were a fairly frequent part of the family diet.

Cotton seeds and fibers were also found in a variety of contexts at Cerén, including some remains on a metate (grinding stone).

The latter suggests that cotton seeds may have been used to produce oil for cooking. Another possible function was suggested to me by Norman Hammond, an archaeologist and colleague at Boston University, who tells me that cottonseed oil might also have been used as an oral contraceptive. In China, according to a recent newspaper account, its use in cooking has been shown to reduce male fertility. Finally, there is also evidence at Cerén for the consumption of deer, ducks, dogs, and mollusks. The inhabitants of this sixth-century village appear to have had both an abundance of food, at least in the rainy season, and a highly varied cuisine. Sheets told me at one point in our discussion that he is thinking of writing a Cerén cookbook because the plants are indeed so varied, and so much has been learned from excavation and analysis about how they were grown and how they may have been used. ≜

PART II:

ARTS, RELIGION & CULTURE

9

MUSIC OF THE MAYA

A grave-site trove of flutes and figurine ocarinas in western Belize suggests a high order of musical sophistication among the ancient Maya.

by PAUL F. HEALY

MAYA CIVILIZATION—THIS EVOCATIVE PHRASE makes us think of many things: architecture, engineering, astronomy, mathematics, hieroglyphic writing, the fine arts and a host of intellectual endeavors. But in all likelihood we do not think about Maya music.

Yet the Maya were a musical people, as we know from Spanish chronicles, from frescoes and other sources. Drums, whistles, rattles, trumpets, flutes in varying shapes, pitched to different registers—all these instruments, and others, were characteristic of Maya music.

Now the archaeological record has increased our understanding of Maya musical practices. From a pair of elite tombs at the site of Pacbitun, in the Cayo District of Belize, come more than a dozen instruments from the Late Classic period (A.D 600–900). Included among the grave goods buried with two aristocratic women, these instruments are a valuable addition to the archaeological record, which is generally rather scanty in regard to Maya music. Remarkably enough, some of these instruments can still be played.

The instruments found at Pacbitun include a single drum, two composite flute-maracas, a group of five flutes, and eight impressively ornate "figurine ocarinas"—flutes that come in a variety of anthropomorphic and animal shapes.

The composite flute-maracas are the first such instruments ever discovered in a secure archaeological context. The finding of these instruments raises some very interesting questions about the nature of Maya music; and when we compare them with other instruments from Maya culture, we begin to see more clearly the social functions of Maya music.

One of those functions, clearly, was of a funerary nature. The instruments at Pacbitun, almost beyond question, played an important role in the burial ceremonies of the women in whose graves they were found. Professional musicians probably used these instruments to escort the funeral cortege to the tomb of the deceased, where some of the instruments may have been broken and left behind on purpose. The sound they produced must have been impressively solemn. Written accounts attest to the sad, doleful quality of Maya drum music, and the flutes and the maracas—a type of decorated rattle—would have added to the melancholy character of the procession.

But we also know from other sources that Maya music could be festive, and that pro-

fessional musicians played on other public occasions. A spectacular series of murals from Bonampak, Mexico, depicts musicians playing a variety of instruments during an occasion that may well have been historical in nature.

In one section of these murals, a group of musicians is depicted shaking maracas and beating both drums and tortoise carapaces during a procession; in another section, trumpet players seem to be playing some sort of fanfare.

The whole cycle of Bonampak murals apparently celebrates a battle with Maya adversaries. The figures are life-sized, and the depictions nearly floor-to-ceiling. In the murals of one room, scenes of Maya fighting are depicted; captives are being arraigned, and some are pleading with their captors.

In yet another room, Maya musicians are shown in the lower half of the wall space, while in the upper half, members of the elite who will play a prominent part in the ceremony are being appareled.

In every panel, the hierarchical rank of all the people depicted is perfectly evident; it would seem that musicians occupy a higher rank than that of the common people, but one that is somehow subordinate to the members of the elite.

Music may also have been important to the actual conduct of war, not just to the celebration of victories. The chronicles offer some suggestion that Maya warriors went into battle against the Spanish blowing whistles and beating drums and hollow tortoise shells. Whether such whistles would have been used to frighten opposing forces, to sound maneuvering signals, or to invoke the deities is not clear.

WE DO KNOW, HOWEVER, THAT WHISTLES were not an uncommon instrument among the Maya. They appear with some frequency in household contexts, where they may have served either ceremonial or non-ceremonial functions. Drums and other instruments, usually found in fragmentary condition, also occur in domestic contexts. But the record is slender enough that we do not really know yet what role music played in Maya everyday life.

But why are Maya musical instruments so scarce? The answer lies partly in the materials they were made of. In the tropical climate of Central America, perishable materials do not last long, and we know that a variety of drums and long Maya trumpets were constructed of wood. The chroniclers mention not only conch shell trumpets but also bone whistles and reed flutes. These materials, too, leave little archaeological trace. As it happens, the instruments from Pacbitun are all made of fired ceramic, and so yield evidence both of their use and their construction techniques.

The largest and artistically most interesting group of instruments are the figurine ocarinas, all of which come from the second Pacbitun grave we opened. Indeed, this burial also yielded the five flutes and one of the two unique composite flute-maracas.

There is considerable speculation about the function of Maya figurine ocarinas. Scholars have suggested that those instruments wrought in bird and animal forms may have been used in hunting as bird or animal calls. It has also been suggested that figurine ocarinas served as children's toys. But the association with elite activities and burials is reinforced by finds at other sites such as Lubaantun in Belize and Jaina in Mexico, where substantial collections of figurine ocarinas have been unearthed.

The figurine-ocarinas differ significantly in size as well as in design. The intact instruments range from 8.5 to 17.9 centimeters (roughly 2.5 to 6 inches) in height; each has two stops positioned on the backside of the figurine, and a protruding mouthpiece. Men, women, animals—all are represented in a wide variety of styles.

Of special interest is a beautifully crafted figure generally known as the Fat God. This portly male figure, who is seated in a Buddha-like posture, is dressed in a headpiece resembling a turban. He wears earspools, and is holding either a drum or, possibly, a circular fan. This deity is often associated with death in the Maya pantheon.

Another ocarina depicts a kneeling woman who wears elaborate Maya headgear and holds what appears to be a water lily. Mayanists have recently recognized the significance of the water lily in Maya iconography, and established its frequent connection with the afterlife.

Two other ocarinas depict male figures, modeled on quite different scales, wearing

> # The largest and most interesting group of instruments are the figurine ocarinas.

Royal Interments

Pacbitun is situated on a limestone promontory along the foothills of the Maya Mountains. Given the rampant looting of archaeological sites in the area, the site is in surprisingly good condition; it was first brought to the attention of the Belize government only in 1971. At that time a new road was being constructed near the site, which was covered with heavy vegetation. No research was carried out at the site until the team from Trent University began its work in 1980.

Although only a sampling of the total site area has been excavated, the entire site has been thoroughly mapped. The core zone—the heart of elite Maya activities—includes three main plazas, aligned east to west and covering an area of at least 0.5 square kilometers (roughly 0.3 square miles). More than forty mounds have been recorded. They range from two to sixteen meters high, and some are as much as 70 meters long. Hundreds of smaller, presumably residential mounds and associated agricultural terraces belonging to the Maya farming population have been identified on the periphery of Pacbitun, extending some three to five kilometers (two to three miles) from the center.

The core area is marked by a series of temple-pyramids, long, low range-type buildings commonly identified as palaces, two lengthy causeways, and a ceremonial ballcourt. Ten stelae (free-standing monuments) and seven altars, several with partially preserved carvings, have been located.

The two elite burials from which the musical instruments come were both discovered in Plaza A—the location of nearly all of the stone monuments, and clearly the central stage for ceremonial rites in the city. This plaza occupies the highest point on the Pacbitun acropolis, and is symmetrically surrounded by six major mounds. The graves of the elite women were opened in the two tallest pyramidal structures, which face each other across the plaza, and which contain many elite burials in addition to the ones that are being considered here.

The excavation of both structures has now been completed; the team hit sterile bedrock during the 1987 season, three-and-a-half meters below the plaza surface. The evidence indicates that each structure underwent a succession of construction phases starting in the Middle Preclassic period (ca. 500 B.C.).

Pacbitun ceased to function during the Terminal Classic period (A.D. 800–900) at the same time that many other lowland Maya centers abruptly collapsed. Why this occurred was one of the many questions which the team from Trent was pursuing, and the excavating of the major civic and ceremonial structures was a result of this interest.

Eleven axially placed burials were uncovered in these two structures. All of them contained the bedecked but badly decomposed bodies of Maya nobles, laid out with their heads positioned to the south. Bodies were extended in a supine position; and as best we could determine, granted the state of preservation, the legs were all crossed.

Virtually all of the burials contained impressive grave goods, and the two which yielded the musical instruments were no exception. The first woman was buried midway up and beneath the staircase of Structure 1, while the second woman was interred below the floor area of the final temple atop Structure 2. On the basis of the ceramics, both graves can be confidently assigned to the Late Classic period, and most likely to the terminal phase of the period. The burials may have taken place within one generation, or possibly two.

The first woman was twenty to forty years of age, and had been buried in a specially prepared cist—or stone-lined burial chamber—2.5 meters long and one meter wide. This woman's chest must have been totally covered by a remarkable shell necklace consisting of roughly 2,500 small, drilled shell beads that had been strung together. Two large manos—very smooth imported volcanic stone implements used to grind corn—had been placed at her side, and a jade bead had probably been placed in her mouth—a common Maya burial custom. A large orange-polychrome dish was positioned over her knees, and an unusual slate "wrench"—probably a ceremonial mace—was found near her feet at the north end of the grave. The two musical instruments recovered from this grave also lay at the woman's feet. They consisted of the drum and one of the unique composite flute-maracas.

The second grave was much richer in musical instruments as well as in other pottery furnishings. The cist was almost identical to the one in the first burial, but its sides were lined with limestone slabs and it was covered by a series of large, irregularly shaped slate slabs. The use of slate slabs for burial roofing was a common feature of the Pacbitun elite graves. Some twenty vessels included in this grave

> **It is not very likely that even a woman who loved music would have so many different instruments in her personal possession.**

fix the time of burial in the Tepeu 3, Terminal Classic period (A.D. 800–900). These vessels were concentrated near the feet and head of the deceased, and along the west side of the grave. A magnificently crafted brown flint bi-pointed dagger rested above the cranium along the edge of the cist. Also clustered near the head were three miniature vessels, a finely carved jade "portrait head" pendant, and a pair of small drilled jade beads. Again, an inverted large red dish covered the middle of the body, while the space near the feet was crowded with more than a dozen ceramic vessels, some of them stacked on top of each other. The fourteen musical instruments found in this grave were evenly divided between the head and the feet. It seems apparent from such a number that the instruments served a ceremonial function; it is not very likely that even a woman who loved music would have so many different instruments in her personal possession.

The archaeological work at Pacbitun has both confirmed and modified the existing record on Maya music. We now have first-hand knowledge of what particular instruments look and sound like, and we now know more certainly the role that music played in Maya funeral rites. A great deal remains to be learned about Maya music, and one can hope that future excavations at Pacbitun and other Maya sites will increase our knowledge.

elaborate Maya headdresses and displaying some of the elite clothing fashionable among the Maya a thousand years ago. One of these figures is kneeling and has his hands on his knees; he wears a combination rabbit/raptorial bird headdress. The other, smaller figurine represents a chubby man who is standing. This latter figure wears a long cloak and a headdress.

THE MOST EXQUISITE OF THE FIGURINE ocarinas is an elaborately dressed Maya woman wearing a *huipil*, or full-length dress. At one time, this figurine, like most of the others from the same grave, was painted a fugitive blue (so-called because the paint wore off easily). The woman is regally posed; she wears a strikingly brimmed and tasseled hat that is positioned stylishly atop her elongated head. Her skull appears, in fact, to have been artificially deformed, most likely during her infancy—a custom prevalent among many of the Maya of the Classic period. In any event, her hair is sharply cut in terraces and is coiffured to accentuate the square shape of her face. She also holds a pet bird perched on her left arm.

This last piece is a masterful representation, and offers us an intriguing glimpse of the Late Classic elite who lived at Pacbitun. Such figurine ocarinas have also been recorded at other lowland Maya centers, most notably at the island burial site of Jaina, off the Campeche coast of the Yucatan Peninsula. The effigy figures of the Late Classic in particular often display a striking degree of realism, elegance and sophistication. They are easily recognized as ceramic masterpieces that were never surpassed anywhere in ancient Mesoamerica.

Many of the ocarinas found at Pacbitun were badly fragmented—and may well have been deliberately shattered, in a ceremonial fashion, at the time of interment. Most of them were restorable to their original state, however, and the fact that they were broken gives us insight into their methods of manufacture. Several have remarkably detailed, mold-made heads and headdresses which were then tenoned into hollow, stylized torsos that were either hand-modeled or pressed into molds. Since no figurine molds have been recovered during excavations at Pacbitun, it is possible that these ocarinas were imported from elsewhere.

MUSICALLY, THE FIGURINE OCARINAS are interesting because recent studies suggest that frequently there is a difference between the musical registers of the male and female examples. Many of these instruments can still be played; they produce a piccolo-like sound. The male-figure ocarinas are generally pitched lower than the female ones—a difference in tone that was probably deliberate.

In the archaeological literature, these figurine instruments are often referred to as "whistles," but because they have more than one stop they are more properly called ocarinas.

The five flutes recovered from the second Pacbitun grave also had two stops. Like the ocarinas, they could play in multiple octaves, and hence could produce music of considerable complexity. Four of the flutes are similar in size; they average 18.5 centimeters (roughly 7 inches) in length and 1.9 centimeters (slightly less than an inch) in diameter. All of them have a circular mouthpiece, two finger-hole stops, and a small globular sounding chamber in the middle. In each one, the distal end—the end farthest from the mouthpiece—flares out slightly and is delicately modeled into the shape of an ornate flower. These ends all bear traces of the familiar blue paint. The fifth flute is shorter and, unlike the others, has traces of brilliant orange paint on its distal end.

The two unique instruments uncovered at Pacbitun, the composite flute-maracas, are of particular interest to us. Similar in size— roughly 16 centimeters (about 6 inches) long— these pieces combine a flute at one end with a rattle at the other. Each piece is evenly divided into the rattle ball and flute handle. The first one found in the grave containing the drum was painted red, whereas the second one was blue. The rattle end of both had originally contained from fifteen to twenty solid ceramic balls. The ends of both rattles are incised with side slits; feathers or some other kind of ornament may have been attached to these slits. The mouthpiece of the second instrument is a stubby, perpendicular projection from the handle. This instrument also has four stops, where the first one has two, so it can cover a wider range of the musical scale.

The drum found in the first grave, finally, is of the tall, tubular "pedestal vase" variety. Painted red like the maraca-flute found in the same grave, it has a bowl-like body with slightly outcurving sides, mounted on a somewhat narrower cylindrical or "pedestal" base. No drum cover survived, but either one or both of the ends would originally have been covered with some kind of membrane, probably animal or snake skin.

Ceramic hand drums have been found, though often in a fragmentary condition, at a half-dozen sites, particularly Late Classic centers in Belize—Barton Ramie, Benque Viejo, San Jose, and Altun Ha. The known pottery drums range in size from 15.6 to 30 centimeters (about 6 to 12 inches), which means that the drum from Pacbitun— which is 24 centimeters (about 9 inches) high—falls neatly in the center of the range. The wooden drums we know of were larger than the hand drums, and came in several types, two of which were the *tunkul* and the *pax*. These drums, however, were probably played with drumsticks, and are known from the written and artistic records.

Drums and rattles seem to have been commonly associated with one another by the ancient Maya. The Book of Chilam Balam of Chumayel is a Maya holy book that records widespread beliefs and practices from earlier Maya periods. In this book there is a passage which says, "the drum and the rattle of the Lord of 11 Ahau shall resound." The expression "11 Ahau" is a calendar date; so the phrase "Lord of 11 Ahau" refers to the ruler of this period. This book was composed in the Maya language during the early post-Conquest period;

> The sad, mournful sound of Maya drums brings us back to the funeral processions at Pacbitun.

though it was transcribed in Spanish letters, it is accepted by Mayanists as an important compendium of traditional Maya history and folklore.

The murals at Bonampak also depict a hand drum being played by a man who is also holding a rattle. The rattle is painted red, and bright yellow-green feathers decorate the instrument's end.

In addition, a beautiful ceramic figurine from Lubaantun in Belize depicts a Maya tapping a hand drum which is tucked underneath his right arm while he holds a rattle in his right hand. Like the Bonampak murals, this figurine dates from the Late Classic period.

The sad, mournful sound of Maya drums brings us back to the funeral processions at Pacbitun. When we consider the instruments interred with the two women, we begin to imagine the scene as it may have been a thousand years ago. It would have begun with all the elaborate preparations which preceded an elite burial: the tomb would be prepared; prized possessions and exotic offerings would be chosen for burial along with the deceased. Then there would be the full solemnity of a cortege-like procession to the exalted resting place. The spouse and children of the dead woman would be ornately dressed, as would other important persons and members of the family. Priests would intone special prayers while they burned copal (resinous-smelling) incense; and a dozen or more musicians would follow the litter to the graveside amid the mournful, hoarse sound of drums, rattles and flutes—a somber backdrop to a thousand-year-old rite of passage. ≜

10

IMAGING MAYA ART

Infrared video "prospecting" of Bonampak's famous murals yields critical details no longer visible to the naked eye.

by MARY MILLER

I N 1946 TWO LACANDÓN MAYA, ACASIO CHAN AND José Pepe Chambor, led photographer Giles Healey to the ancient ruins of a small city deep in the rain forest of eastern Chiapas, Mexico. On the site's tiny acropolis was a building with three doorways, each leading to a separate chamber. Within each room were brilliantly colored frescoes depicting hundreds of Maya dancers, musicians, warriors, and court officials at one-half to two-thirds life-size. Rumors of a "temple of paintings" had circulated in the archaeological community since the nineteenth century. Now one had been found. The only monumental Maya paintings to survive from the Late Classic period (ca. A.D. 600–850), the murals were an unparalleled discovery.

Sylvanus Morley, a Mayanist with the Carnegie Institution of Washington, christened the site "Bonampak," a rough Maya equivalent of "painted walls," and dispatched

Antonio Tejeda, the institution's best artist, to make watercolor renderings of the paintings for study and publication. Alfonso Caso, director of the National Institute of Anthropology and History (INAH) in Mexico City, sent Agustín Villagra to carry out the same task. Healey stayed on with Tejeda and the Carnegie team, photographing selected portions of the murals with color and infrared film. Images of charging warriors, bleeding captives, dancers, and musicians soon appeared in the *Illustrated London News* and *Life*.

Both Morley and J. Eric S. Thompson, the preeminent Maya scholar of the day, believed the ancient Maya were a peaceful people devoted to religious observance and contemplation. In his report on the murals published in 1955, Thompson focused on the festive scenes of dancers and musicians in room 1, playing down the scenes of war and sacrifice in rooms 2 and 3. He did, however, correctly date the paintings to the last decade of the eighth century. Caso saw the paintings as an historical document and posited that the glyphs in and around the figures might even be captions naming the people depicted.

A decade after the site's discovery, INAH embarked on a program to clear the acropolis and stabilize its structures. A roof was erected over the building containing the murals and its walls were consolidated. Little more work, however, was done to interpret the murals for nearly 30 years, by which time epigraphers had made advancements in the decipherment of Maya hieroglyphs, unlocking the histories of numerous sites, including Bonampak's neighbors Yaxchilán and Palenque.

In 1978 Peter Mathews, now at the University of Calgary, began studying Bonampak's stelae and other stone monuments. He was able to discern the names of several rulers, including Chan Muan (Sky Screech Owl), who reigned from A.D. 776 until the site's abandonment ca. 795. At about the same time I began studying the murals in what had come to be known as Structure 1. I saw them as a dynastic work, a three-part narrative of the life and deeds of Chan Muan, who is named as the building's owner in room 1. I interpreted a scene on the room's central panel showing a small child offered to the king by a group of nobles as the presentation of Chan Muan's heir; an adjacent dance scene as a celebration of his inauguration; the scenes of battle and sacrifice in room 2 as the king's military triumphs; and his genital self-mutilation while dancing atop a pyramid in room 3 as a ceremonial bloodletting. Through this ritual, Maya lords renewed the world and paid back the "blood debt" they owed powerful gods. I also assumed that unclear texts would name Chan Muan as the principal performer of the dance rituals depicted in rooms 1 and 3.

By this time, however, efforts to save the paintings had made them nearly impossible to see. Once the walls were kept dry by the protective roof, the salts that had accumulated on the surface dried into an opaque crust. With the original paintings obscured, I based my interpretations on Healey's photographs and the renderings of Villagra and Tejeda, the latter preserved in Harvard's Peabody Museum. Looking at the photographs, especially those taken with infrared film, I soon realized that the renderings lacked much detail.

In the mid-1980s specialists from INAH's Churubusco Center for Conservation cleaned the paintings, scraping off the accumulated crust and carefully filling holes, ancient defacements, and recent losses. After the restoration was completed, National Geographic Society photographers took pictures of some of the paintings with infrared film. Ancient Maya painters used black, carbon-based pigments to write texts and outline figures, which are far easier to discern with infrared film, which eliminates most of the color spectrum, than with color film. The results of the National Geographic Society project were astonishing. Hitherto unknown details of faces and hands suddenly became visible.

Was there still more to see? To answer this question, Stephen Houston of Brigham Young University, Karl Taube of the University of California, Riverside, Beatríz de la Fuente of the Universidad Nacional Autónoma de Mexico, and I launched the Bonampak Documentation Project at the beginning of 1996, funded initially by the National Geographic Society, the Getty

High-Tech Videography

The infrared video technique we used at Bonampak is ideal for resurrecting faded images no longer visible to the naked eye. For those interested in learning how the murals at Bonampak were recorded using infrared, here are the technical specifications: We videotaped the Bonampak murals with a Hamamatsu C2741-05ER infrared Vidicon camera connected to a C2400 controller. The camera's spectral response extended to a wavelength of 2.2 µ in the mid-infrared. The images were stored using a Panasonic AG-DS550 S-VHS recorder. When the camera was operated in the black-and-white mode the specified signal-to-noise ratio was greater than 50 dB. The combined resolution of camera and recorder was approximately 400 lines.

The camera could record an area about five inches high by six inches wide. Two floodlights were used to illuminate each segment. During the January 1996 expedition the camera was equipped with a 700 nm long-pass infrared filter yielding a wavelength response from 0.7 to 2.2 µ. During the May 1996 expedition we improved image contrast by equipping the camera with a 1.0 µ long-pass filter yielding a pass band of 1.0 to 2.2 µ.

All images from the first expedition were obtained by scanning the murals left-to-right and top-to-bottom with the camera mounted on a tripod. This covered about a 48-inch-square segment at each tripod setting. During the second expedition, we used a rail system to bring the camera lens closer to the mural surface, eliminating angular distortions at the periphery of each image.

Determining how each frame will fit into a final composite photograph is a multistep process. A grid is placed over each digitized image. Four to 20 specific features that appear in pairs of overlapping images are then marked. Their coordinates are plugged into a program that computes how the images must be manipulated to match up the features in the image pairs. To increase the accuracy of the mesh, the computer compares tiny regions around each feature and adjusts the coordinates.

This program gives researchers more flexibility in the field. It allows them to take pictures as best they can on-site and "warp" them later to fit together. In contrast, manual image composition requires that pictures be taken under controlled conditions, from vantage points that may be inaccessible.

—GENE WARE, chief technical specialist, College of Engineering and Technology, Brigham Young University, and KIRK DUFFIN, Computer Vision Laboratory, Brigham Young University

Grant Program, and the Foundation for Ancient Religion and Mormon Studies, and conducted under an INAH permit.

The goals of the project included complete photographic documentation of the murals using color and infrared film. At Houston's suggestion, we decided to experiment with infrared video to overcome one of the drawbacks of using a still camera fitted with an infrared filter—the inability of the photographer to see what the camera will record. Using a videocamera, we can see on a television monitor what is being recorded. So far, this process of video "prospecting" has revealed fascinating details invisible to the naked eye. Although the resolution of large-format film can surpass that of videotape, the latter has alerted us to areas we will want to study further.

Shortly after we began videotaping one of the side panels in room 1 in January 1996, Houston called me in to look at a text that had never been recorded. On the television screen was the hieroglyphic notation for five "*pi kakaw*", inscribed on one of the huge white bundles piled under and beside a throne where a royal family presides. Just in front of the throne a servant holds out a young child, while an assembly of lords dressed in white capes observes. These lords, some of whom reappear on the walls of room 3, may well be paying costly cacao to attend a celebration or to guarantee the child's presentation at court. They could even be demonstrating what good taxpayers they are. We may never know the identity of the recipients of these gifts, however, because the caption space above the royal family is blank, presumably left to be filled in later.

On the central panel of room 3, servants drag a dead captive down the steps of a pyramid. They are partly hidden by dancers holding some sort of sticks. Between the dancers are a few dark marks on painted steps. As we studied the area with infrared video, these smudges came to life. Tiny figures dance atop a sketch of the head of a Maya hunting god. We zoomed in on a brief hieroglyphic text above them, and recognized name glyphs for Shield Jaguar II, a late eighth-century king of nearby Yaxchilán and possibly one of Chan Muan's brothers-in-law.

We now believe that the two dancers are holding up the ends of a ceremonial banner. At the time of the Spanish conquest, such banners or paintings on cloth, called *lienzos*, were used to record histories, genealogies, and tribute lists. But the antiquity of this practice was unknown. Bonampak shows that *lienzos* could be of Classic Maya origin.

When I published a study of the paintings more than a decade ago, many of the texts, particularly those in room 3, had never been properly recorded. Now that we can read many more of these inscriptions, my interpretation of the murals is in need of serious revision. Chan Muan, whom I have long considered the subject of the murals, might not be among the elite receiving tribute in room 1 even though he is named in that chamber as the building's owner. And the dancers of room 1 do not include Chan Muan, as I had originally thought. They are identified by the glyph for *chok*, or young lord, and reappear identically captioned in room 3, where they stand atop a pyramid. With feathered fans extending from their waists, the figures bleed from their genitals as they engage in a whirling dance.

Such new details are revolutionizing the

study of the Bonampak paintings, not only making it possible to see the complexity of the events depicted on the building's walls, but also raising questions about how and why the paintings were executed. Insignia and regalia distinguish one group of Maya nobles from another in the paintings. Different groups bear different glyphic titles, identifying them as regional governors, court attendants, or feather dancers. We may never know who commissioned these paintings, but they were costly to execute—the blue, for example, was made with azurite, one of the most precious minerals of the Precolumbian world. Perhaps, like special groups among the modern Maya responsible for raising funds, venerating a patron saint, or providing hospitality during celebrations, the groups depicted in the Bonampak murals paid for rituals and celebrations, and maybe even to have their portraits painted.

And what of the building itself? Painted with precious pigments and decorated with scenes picturing elite Maya, Structure 1 celebrates wealth and conspicuous consumption. Such a building may have served as a repository for jewels, costumes, and cacao. We have also discovered traces of a red-and-white paint scheme on the exterior of the building—large alternating vertical bands topped by a row of painted glyphs.

Having recently completed the photo documentation of the murals, we have begun to stitch the digitized images together into a seamless web of paintings, which we will eventually use to create a "virtual" Structure 1. Because of the irregularity of the building's plastered walls and the fact that some of the images, especially those frames shot near the corbel vaults, were taken at odd angles, piecing the photographs together poses a particular challenge. Many of the frames need to be stretched and manipulated before they fit properly into the puzzle. The next stage will be to restore the paintings digitally. Using data gathered from the infrared film, which enhances outlines of figures and texts, artists will correct the scanned images to approximate the paintings as they appeared in the eighth century A.D. By 2001, our odyssey will be complete, and Bonampak will be available as a CD-ROM or a site on the worldwide web. Specialists, students, and amateurs alike will be able to study the murals and the architectural and cultural context in which they were made. ▲

11

THE SEARCH FOR SITE Q

For years scholars have been looking
for the source of an array of
unprovenienced Maya sculptures
in collections here and abroad.

by ANGELA M.H. SCHUSTER

IN THE SPRING OF 1965, THE ART INSTITUTE OF
Chicago acquired a magnificent Late Classic Maya
carved panel depicting two ballplayers. An inscription
identifies one as Chak Kutz (Great or Red Turkey) and tells
of his witnessing a calendar ritual at *Oxte'tun* (Three Stone
Place) in A.D. 690. Bought from New York antiquities dealer
Walter Randall for $12,500, the limestone panel is one of
more than two dozen sculptures that have entered this
country since 1960, sawn off monuments at a place known
to archaeologists only as Site Q.

The search for Site Q (the letter stands for "*¿qué?*", Spanish for "which?") began in the late 1970s when Peter Mathews, then a Yale graduate student, noticed that the
inscriptions on a number of unprovenienced monuments in
American and European collections, many of which were

text panels, shared several epigraphic features, most notably an enigmatic emblem glyph bearing a snake head, possibly the name of the site from which the sculptures had been taken. Furthermore, the texts on some panels continued on others, proving that the monuments had been broken apart to ease their export and facilitate their sale.

With the help of Ian Graham of Harvard's Peabody Museum and William Ringle of Davidson College, Mathews compiled a catalog of the sculptures—30 to 35 in all—detailing their whereabouts, measurements, and discernible glyphs. To it he attached drawings of the sculptures contributed by colleagues. Circulated in photocopied form, the manuscript remains the most comprehensive work on the monuments to date.

Based on the sculptures' extraordinary workmanship and the fine, marble-like quality of the limestone in which they were carved, Yale University's Michael Coe suggested that the plundered site probably lay along the Usumacinta River, the border between Guatemala and Mexico, a region well known for its superb sculptures. An important ancient trade route, the river cuts through the heart of the Lowland Maya world. When Graham began investigating the heavily looted Late Classic site of El Perú , which he had discovered in 1972 near the Río San Pedro in the Petén region of Guatemala, he speculated that the monuments might have come from there. Within a few years, however, Stephen Houston of Brigham Young University identified El Perú's emblem glyph, a series of symbols that we now know to read phonetically, *?-nal-wak*. Though several inscriptions found at the site contained the snake-head emblem glyph, it was clear from the syntax that it was the name of a foreign place. El Perú was dismissed as a candidate for Site Q. Nonetheless, two of Mathews' monuments, which he had labeled stelae 1 and 2 and which are now in the collections of the Kimbell Art Museum in Fort Worth and the Cleveland Museum of Art, had in fact come from El Perú, as their shattered bases, found at the site, proved.

Meanwhile, Calakmul, in southern Campeche, Mexico, was gaining recognition as a candidate for the mysterious snake-head state, an idea put forth some years earlier by Joyce Marcus of the University of Michigan at Ann Arbor. With more than 6,000 visible structures, Calakmul ranks among the largest sites in the Maya Lowlands. In 1989 Houston and David Stuart, then a graduate student at Vanderbilt University, identified two place names that appeared in several Calakmul inscriptions, *Oxte'tun* (Three Stone Place) and *Nab Tunich*, the meaning of which is still unclear, and suggested that these were the names of places controlled by the snake-head state. In 1994, British epigrapher Simon Martin revised the reading of Nab Tunich to Chik Nab (one of numerous possible translations being Waterlily Tree), and confirmed the association of both place names with Calakmul in inscriptions on fragments of monuments newly unearthed at the site. For Martin and others, Calakmul's identity as the snake-head state is secure. But to assign the Site Q sculptures to Calakmul is another matter. For example, the stone of the Site Q monuments, particularly of the six ballplayer panels, is far superior to the stone used to carve sculptures at Calakmul, which is quite porous and crumbly. According to Martin, those at Calakmul are in such poor condition that they are hardly worth removing. Looters took a few pieces from the site in the decade following its discovery, but fortunately they were photographed prior to their theft, and, in all but one case, their current whereabouts are known.

If Calakmul is the snake-head state, why does its glyph figure so prominently in texts on monuments that clearly did not come from that site? The snake-head emblem glyph has been found in inscriptions at sites in Belize, Guatemala, Honduras, and Mexico, attesting the site's once preeminent position in the Classic Maya world (see page 28, *Maya Superstates*). Unlike the majority of these inscriptions, however, references to the snake-head state on Site Q monuments refer to it not as a foreign polity, but rather as a sovereign, suggesting that the sculptures came from a site, or even sites, under Calakmul's dominion too weak to possess an emblem glyph.

While Martin, Stuart, and others believe that Calakmul is the snake-head state and that the monuments assigned to Site Q belong to at least one of Calakmul's subordinate polities, scholars such as Richard Hansen of the University of California, Los Angeles, contend that Site Q and the snake-head site are one and the same city, whose ruins have yet to be found. "Based on the epigraphic evidence, Calakmul is the strongest candidate for the snake-head site put forth to date," says Hansen, "but there are a lot of really big sites out there in the Petén, such as Nadz Can and Naachtún, southeast of Calakmul, where little or no work has been done. Until we have examined these sites, I think it's just too early to pass judgment on whether Calakmul is the snake-head site. We may find far better epigraphic evidence at the site from which the sculptures in Mathews' catalog were taken."

Careful examination of the Site Q monuments suggests that they may in fact be from more than one site. "Site Q is a sort of grab-bag category," says Stuart. "A lot of these monuments probably do not come from the same site, but rather from 'Sites Q.'" Like Stuart, Martin and Mathews believe that all monuments originally attributed to Site Q are not from one site but from two or three and can be broken into three categories:

1. Those belonging to El Perú, which include the Kimbell and Cleveland stelae (now known as El Perú stelae 33 and 34), a side panel from stela 33 (sold as a separate artifact), and possibly an altar now in the Dallas Museum of Art. The two stelae have

carved dates corresponding to the early 690s.

2. Two square stone blocks, one in the Denver Art Museum, the other in the San Bernardino County Museum, together bearing eight glyphs recording a long-count date of 9.15.1.6.15, or December 29, A.D. 732, some 40 years after the dates carved on most of the other sculptures on Mathews' list. Most scholars agree that these two blocks belong together, but how they fit with the other monuments is still unclear.

3. The remaining 23 sculptures are broken into two stylistic groups: The first includes four text blocks with 12 glyphs each (Mathews' panels A–D) and two large slabs with hieroglyphic inscriptions, each of which was split in half (Mathews' panels 1, 2, and 3, and

a fragment, which was recently identified in a private collection, designated panel 4). The second group includes six ballplayer sculptures and a series of nine text blocks, five of which have inverted L-shaped inscriptions. In nearly all cases the sculptures were sawn off their blocks and are only one to two inches thick. "While the first group came from at least three monuments," says Stuart, "Coe suggested some time ago that the second group of [15] sculptures may have come from a single structure, possibly serving as risers for a ballplayer staircase much like the one adorning Yaxchilán structure 33, built sometime around A.D. 761."

But where did the Site Q staircase come from? A possible breakthrough came with

New Maya Site Stirs Excitement

The ruins of a Maya city have been discovered near a tributary of the Río San Pedro in northern Guatemala. The site came to the attention of scholars in February 1996, when a local guide took environmentalist Santiago Billy there on a survey of nesting scarlet macaws.

Ian Graham and David Stuart, of Harvard University's Peabody Museum of Archaeology and Ethnology, went there this past May to map the site and photograph and draw any surviving inscriptions. "The ruins are not extensive," says Graham, "but everywhere there are vast looters' excavations." Because five small temples standing in a row reminded the guide of a crown, Graham and Stuart named the site La Corona.

"On the first day," says Stuart, "we found two clear references to Great or Red Turkey, a ballplayer mentioned by name on a carved panel now in the Art Institute of Chicago." The source of this panel is unknown, but it seems to belong with a number of other unprovenienced monuments in American and European collections: the inscriptions on many

of these panels include a snake-head emblem glyph, and texts begun on several of them continue on others in the set. The epigrapher Peter Mathews, now of the University of Calgary, called the undiscovered city from which the panels came Site Q.

Stuart also says that the "inscriptions at La Corona also include numerous references to political events involving the snake-head site." This emblem glyph appears in texts at sites throughout the Maya Lowlands, including Calakmul, a large site 40 miles north of La Corona, in southern Campeche, Mexico. Most epigraphers think that Calakmul is the snake-head state because inscriptions there refer to it as a sovereign polity, while elsewhere it appears as a foreign state. But Calakmul has been well excavated (see page 28, Maya Superstates), and archaeologists have not found a building, staircase, or monument missing tablets the size and shape of the Site Q panels. That La Corona might be the source of some of the Site Q monuments is causing a great deal of excitement among Mayanists, but so far there is no conclusive evidence.

the discovery of La Corona, a site in the northern drainage area of the San Pedro, 40 miles south of Calakmul (see page 78, *Mission to la Corona*). "The new site in the Petén is very interesting in lots of ways," says Stuart, who with Graham, traveled there in May. "On the first day we found two clear references to Great or Red Turkey, one of the ballplayers mentioned by name on the Art Institute of Chicago panel. The site has been heavily looted, monuments have been broken apart, and there are tunnels and trenches all over the place. Scattered on the jungle floor we found several blanks [dressed stone blocks that were not inscribed] that are similar in size and shape to the L-shaped panel group—perhaps risers for the staircase from which the ballplayer panels came. The inscriptions at La Corona also include numerous references to political events involving the snake-head site. While the evidence is intriguing, it is likely to be some time before we know for sure just how many of the Site Q monuments might have come from this ancient city." If Stuart and Graham determine that the 15 panels in the ballplayer group come from La Corona, only ten unprovenienced sculptures will remain on Mathews' list. Where they come from, only time will tell.

Documenting how these sculptures came to be in collections here and abroad has been the recent work of Hansen, who, like Graham and Boston University's Clemency Chase Coggins, has spent decades tracking looted artifacts from their origins at undocumented sites to their arrival in museums and private collections. "None of these sculptures entered this country legally," says Hansen. "There have been patrimony laws on the books in both Mexico and Guatemala since the middle part of this century." According to Hansen, sculpture continues to be stripped from sites at an alarming rate, but ceramics are now the most commonly looted artifacts, in particular so-called codex-style ceramics, black-line-on-cream wares that depict mythological and historical scenes. While many of these bear the snake-head emblem glyph, according to Martin, like the monuments on Mathews' list they do not appear to come from Calakmul, a site that has produced few such ceramics. "One codex-style vase was recovered during the excavation of a tomb within the site's temple 2," says Martin, "however, the pottery was clearly of a different clay, made by potters in Nakbé."

Prices for Maya artifacts have skyrocketed in the three decades since the ballplayer panels sold for between $10,000 and $15,000 each and the panels with L-shaped texts for $1,500, says Hansen. The money offered for artifacts, compounded by a steep decline in the market for chicle (the primary ingredient in chewing gum), is a big incentive for chicleros to participate in the looting business. Local dealers will pay a looter as much as $1,000 for a single polychrome plate, for which a gallery in New York or Brussels will

Local dealers will pay a looter as much as $1,000 for a single plate.

pay $20,000 to $30,000. Museums and private collectors will often pay more than twice that, as attested by the recent sale of a Late Classic Maya plate with the painted image of a scribe at Sotheby's for $112,000. The price would have been far higher if the plate had not been broken and repaired in a number of places.

According to Hansen, many of the dealers and the looters they hire operate out of Carmelita, in the heart of the Petén. Artifacts are loaded on trucks and driven across the border to Belize, and from there shipped on to Belgium. They are then brought into the United States with few restrictions given their European point of origin. "Looting is big business in this part of Central America, especially in the Mirador Basin [in the far north-central Petén region], which is rich in undocumented archaeological sites," says Hansen.

This past April, Guatemala embarked on a twofold campaign to recover its lost heritage. The country will document its own collections and seek restitution of all artifacts exported from the country illegally. It has also entered into negotiations with one American museum for the return of a monument taken from El Perú. ≜

12

MISSION TO LA CORONA

A new Maya site may fail to qualify as Site Q.

by IAN GRAHAM

THE EXISTENCE OF AN UNKNOWN MAYA SITE HAS long been suspected on the basis of 25 relief sculptures, in various museums and private collections, which appear to have come from the same site. But the site's location has remained an enigma—hence its name, Site Q, for the Spanish "¿qué?" for "which?". References in their texts to rulers from Calakmul suggest that the sculptures may have come from northwestern Petén. In February 1996, guided by Carlos Catalán, an erstwhile jaguar hunter and looter who had seen the error of his ways and become an apostle of eco-tourism, a friend of mine named Santiago Billy found a site in this area while engaged in a Conservation International campaign to protect the few remaining scarlet macaws. At his request, Tom Sever, a NASA archaeologist, studied satellite images of the area and saw what looked like causeways. Sever visited the site in July 1996, with Billy, Jim Nations of Conservation International, and remote-sensing specialist Dan Lee, and found the causeway-like features; determining whether they are manmade will require excavation.

In mid-May, David Stuart, who assists me in running the Maya Corpus Program (see page 112, *Maverick Mayanist*), and I went to Guatemala to investigate the site. We drove 40 miles from the town of Flores to Carmelita, a settlement founded by chicleros, who gather sap for chewing gum. From there, we set off down a narrow track with a local guide. More than five hours later, we made camp, and the next morning walked for three hours to a chiclero campsite called Lo Veremos.

The ruins are nearby. The main plaza is about half the size of a football field, and flanked by two tall structures and an impressive acropolis, but there is little else, save scattered mounds toward the southeast. These structures end in a north-south row of five small temple-mounds, shoulder-to-shoulder. Since their appearance reminded our guide of a crown, we adopted La Corona as the name of the site. Everywhere are vast looters' trenches. Usually, broken pots rejected as unsalable lie nearby, but here, oddly, there is nothing.

The west side of the plaza is bounded by a long, low mound. At the foot of its stairway, looters left a number of carved tablets, much smaller than the Site Q tablets and badly eroded. In front of the stairway lie two fragments of an altar; most of the other fragments are nearby, and David was able to reassemble much of the altar. It carries a partly legible inscription, one of the longest on any Maya altar, which may document a political alliance between La Corona and another site. A second altar celebrates the twentieth anniversary of a Calakmul king's accession on May 1, A.D. 636. A third one shows ballplayers, though there is no ballcourt at La Corona. An incomplete stela quite far from the plaza caused the greatest excitement. As David studied the inscription, he uttered a cry of delight on finding a name that can tentatively be read as Great or Red Turkey—a name found in only one other inscription, on a Site Q panel in the Art Institute of Chicago. For the first time, a Site Q personage can be linked to a known site.

In the course of our 12-day visit, David drew all the inscriptions, while I took many pictures of them and mapped the site with compass and tape. Our expedition was highly rewarding, although I doubt that La Corona is the source of the Site Q panels, since the sculpture remaining there does not match the style of those panels.

I once hoped that we would be able to determine the source of the Site Q panels by finding the carcasses (as we call them) from which the sculptures had been sawn, but now I believe they were taken intact to a place like Carmelita before being cut up: When I inspected the backs of several Site Q panels, I saw the marks of a power tool, and looters do not bring generators with them to a ruin.

One day we may find the eroded brethren of some of the pristine Site Q tablets, which probably owe their preservation to rubble that fell over them. There is a good chance that others in the set were unprotected and spurned by looters as too weathered or fragmentary. We are getting closer to Site Q. The search will go on. ▴

13

WRITTEN IN THE STARS

The celestial origin of the Maya Creation Myth

by RICHARD A. WERTIME and ANGELA M.H. SCHUSTER

O VER THE COURSE OF COUNTLESS NIGHTS ancient Maya astronomers considered long and hard the movement of the stars and planets. Living in a world without light pollution, these gifted observers beheld a sky that was as limpid as a mountain stream. The nearness and the brightness of the celestial bodies led them to read in their movements significant elements of human history, including the miracle of creation itself.

Scholars have had only a fragmentary understanding of these matters in the past. Now, for the first time, they are beginning to comprehend the intricate connection between Maya creation myth and the movements of the stars. It is a remarkable story being pieced together by a cluster of scholars who have patiently decoded a complex legacy of Maya writings and artworks.

The interconnections between the observable sky and Maya creation myth find expression in surviving Maya codices, in important sacred texts such as the *Popol Vuh,* in hieroglyphic inscriptions, and in a vast range of artworks—carved bone, ceramics, murals, and sculpture. Says epigrapher Linda Schele, "We used to view Maya iconography as a collection of discrete units. Now there's a whole pattern to it; all of the parts are related to phenomena that can be observed in the sky by anybody who lives away from the light of the modern world."

What makes these interconnections particularly exciting is that they are supported by ritual practices and religious beliefs of the modern Maya. There is compelling evidence for strong cultural continuity between the Maya and their modern descendants. Maya artisans, like their ancient counterparts, express their cosmic vision through almost every conceivable medium: in the patterns of fabrics, in the hearthstones of the traditional household, in the temporary shrines built to invoke the rain gods—shrines whose form mimics the cosmos.

Some of the early pioneers in Maya studies had intimations of what is now being forcefully argued. Herbert Spinden and Sylvanus G. Morley—early students of Maya art, writing, and calendrics—suggested that the Maya creation myth was linked in deep ways to Maya astronomy. In time, however, there was a reaction against such cosmological interpretations. "Astronomy was banned," recalls Dennis Tedlock, an ethnologist and translator of the *Popol Vuh*. By the 1950s and 1960s ethnology was also discounted as a reliable source of data. But all this began to change in the 1980s when archaeoastronomy emerged as a new subfield in archaeological studies. "In the New World," says Anthony Aveni, an archaeoastronomer at Colgate University, "we seem to

be developing an anthropology of astronomy rather than a history of astronomy. It deals with the complex relationship between astronomy and politics, economics, and cultural history."

This past decade has seen major breakthroughs in the drawing together of Maya creation myth and astronomy, and in the linking of the work done by epigraphers, art historians, ethnologists, archaeologists, and archaeoastronomers. At the annual Maya Meetings at the University of Texas, Schele proposed a major new synthesis, one that links critical passages from the creation myth of the *Popol Vuh* to artistic, hieroglyphic, and ethnographic information contributed by a host of colleagues in the field. She argues that the story of Maya creation was mapped in the night sky, that acts critical to the world's creation in Maya mythology were all elaborately played out in the movements of the Milky Way and a host of constellations including the Big Dipper, Scorpius, Orion, and Gemini.

The Maya story of creation, as written on a stela at the site of Quirigua in highland Guatemala, begins, "On the night of 4 Ahaw 8 Kumk'u [August 13]...they, the paddler gods, made the image of the three [hearth]stones appear...." According to this account, as interpreted by Schele, with the lighting of the hearth First Father comes into the world, reborn from the shell of a tortoise. Exactly 542 days later [February 5] he raises the sky and creates the World Tree, which takes the form of a vast crocodile at the center of the cosmos. With this act First Father divides earth and sky into eight partitions, sets time in motion by turning the heavens about a central point, and links the earth to

Mediators in a Universal Discourse

Ancient Maya notions about the cosmos were quite different from those to which we subscribe today. They rested on a broader kind of faith; that the everyday human world was intimately related to the natural world and that these two worlds functioned in harmony. The universe was a distinct whole, with all parts intricately laced together, each aspect influencing the others. Nature and culture were one. Sky myths explained the unfolding of history, politics, social relations, and ideas about creation and life after death. The Maya forged links between the sky and just about every phase and component of human activity—what we call astrology. And they celebrated this knowledge not only in texts but also in art, architecture, and sculpture. Their universe was animate—breathing, teeming, vibrant, and interactive. The Maya talked to the stars, listened to the planets. They commanded and evoked, restrained and constrained, made incantations, pressed their ears to the oracle. They saw themselves as mediators in a great universal discourse. At stake was the battle between fate and free will, between body and soul.

The Maya were motivated not by a desire to express the workings of nature in terms of inert mathematical equations, but rather by the need to know how to mediate an alliance between the inherent power within the universe and their own direct physical well-being, between knowledge and human action. Today we might attribute a planet's change of color to an atmospheric effect, a shift in position to a dynamic effect, an alteration in brightness to a distance effect. The Maya would carefully watch the color, brightness, position, and movement of the planets because they believed all of these properties considered together were indices of the power of the gods, whom they hoped to influence through dialogue. Maya cosmic myths like the Popol Vuh may strike us as amusing stories, but behind the planetary, solar, and lunar alliances lie real people asking the kinds of questions we no longer ask of the sky: What is the origin of gender and sex? Where does fertility—or for that matter any power—come from? Where do we go when we die? How can we know the future? Answers to many of their inquiries were framed in the metaphor of visible planetary characteristics and changes: descent and resurrection (particularly for Mercury and Venus), dyadic and triadic bonds (sun, moon, and Venus). No wonder all these concepts were so prevalent in the early sky mythologies that grew up in both Old and New World civilizations, for the planets look the same the world over.

Which came first, the myth or the sky observation? No one can really say, but I think watching the movement of lights in the sky surely must have served as a very early practical time-keeping device, at least for those cultures like the Maya who invested a great deal of effort in looking upward. Naming the phases of the moon for human activities that accompanied them, or associating the course of the sun across the zodiac or the orientation of the Milky Way with seasonal activities—these habits date back into history farther than any document can reach. Marrying the act of telling stories about everyday affairs to witnessing changes in the world of nature would be a logical way both to embellish life and to lend a meaningful structure to time. With the process of story-telling came the expansion into more fundamental and speculative questions: Where did we come from? What will happen to us in the future? In some instances, especially in highly structured societies like the Maya, the relationship between people and the sky became formalized through the ruling class. Cosmic myths expanded to extraordinary proportions and so did the temporal cycles that framed them. Scholars may debate where myth and history intersect in the writing they decipher on the Maya stelae, but we can be sure the rhyme and meter of these texts have their origin in the cosmos.

—ANTHONY F. AVENI

both the heavens and the underworld (Xibalba) with the World Tree, whose roots lay deep in the southern sky. The World Tree, according to Schele and others, takes its form as the Milky Way. As a canoe bearing the paddler gods, it transports First Father to his birthplace. As the road to Xibalba, it conveys the dead to the underworld.

The night of creation begins with the Milky Way/canoe stretching from east to west across the night sky. By dawn on this night, explains Schele, the three hearthstones are at zenith within the constellation Orion and are represented by the stars Alnitak (the southernmost in Orion's belt), Rigel, and Saiph. At the center of the triangle formed by these three celestial bodies is the Orion nebula, alight with the glow of newborn stars—the hearth fire. The hearthstones are once again at zenith at dusk on February 5. During this night, the hearthstones sink toward the west, preceded by the Pleiades, a star cluster in the constellation Taurus that represented to the Maya a handful of maize seeds to be planted in the earth. Around midnight, the seeds bear fruit and the World Tree—the Milky Way—rises in the night sky.

Themes in Maya art no doubt originated from celestial observations of this sort. Scholars like Schele note that the ecliptic— the path of the sun, moon, planets, and the constellations of the zodiac—is represented in Maya vase paintings by a double-headed serpent that crosses the World Tree at right angles on the night of creation. When the Milky Way lies in a north-south orientation on creation night, the ecliptic intersects it at similarly precise right angles. The double-headed serpent probably reflects the Maya observation that certain constellations like the zodiac undulate throughout the year, imitating the movement of a serpent.

"It's like being able to read Genesis in the heavens," says Schele, "Astronomers use mathematical formulas to describe the movement of the cosmos...the Maya used mythology. The texts carved on Maya vases are not just quaint stories told by an ancient people but rather precise descriptions of how the heavens changed throughout the year." Some advocates of the new thinking like Barbara and Dennis Tedlock caution against excessive enthusiasm. Says Dennis Tedlock, "When the smoke clears, we're going to find that some of the astronomy got pushed a bit too far." He thinks Schele's interpretation of the Milky Way as the World Tree is very much on target, as is her suggestion that the double-headed serpent depicted in Maya art represents the celestial path of the sun, moon, Venus, and the constellations of the zodiac. But Tedlock remains unconvinced that the Milky Way so clearly doubles as a celestial crocodile (a configuration for which, according to Schele, there are ample Aztec sources) and the canoe that carries the Maize God to the place of cre-

> 'The Maya understanding of how the world works has millennia behind it.'

ation. Schele's arguments do confirm what Barbara Tedlock has been suggesting for some time: that the Maya weren't limited to "horizon-based astronomy"—calculations of celestial motions dependent on the horizon—but had fully mastered star-to-star astronomy, or "relational astronomy" as it is technically known.

Schele and others are also beginning to pay more attention to ethnography. "I think there is a tremendous amount of this ancient heritage that still survives," she says. "The way in which the modern Maya organize their world is not some hybrid overview inherited from the Spanish; it comes from a very ancient stratum of indigenous thought. The Maya understanding of how the world works has millennia behind it. That may not seem a miracle to us, but for people who have had their history appropriated by others, who have been told that they exist only as a by-product of what the Spanish made them after the Conquest, that's a bloody miracle!"

One thing is certain. Maya calculations were extremely accurate. In their fables they plotted the stations of Venus over periods of 104 years or longer. Their almanacs indicated planetary cycles, lunar phases and eclipses, solstices and equinoxes, and a host of celestial motions by which they regulated their lives. Unfortunately, the burning of quantities of Maya literature in 1562 by the Spanish missionary Fray Diego de Landa leaves many questions about the nature and practice of Maya astronomy unanswered—like how many and which gods were associated with the stars and constellations and how the

various planets such as Jupiter, Saturn, and Mars were tracked.

Perhaps even more important than the recent discoveries is the larger frame of reference that archaeoastronomy is beginning to unfold. Says Schele, "It seems that the interaction of astronomy and mythology was common in other cultures as well. Scholars working in South America have found similar kinds of systems in the Amazon. There may be something like it in Pawnee lore, and perhaps the Hopi have something resembling it. The Maya may have been using a way of thinking about the sky and using it in their mythology that was very ancient indeed. I'm even prepared to accept that much of the cosmology/mythology came straight across the Bering Strait, and that it may be 10,000 or 15,000 years old; it may be 20,000 years old. I think it may be possible that we have tapped into a very ancient stratum of human thought. If it did come across with the first Americans, then we may be in touch with one of the two or three great human intellectual traditions that we as a species have ever evolved, part of the fundamental 'software' that all of the peoples of the Americas and Asia have utilized." Schele cautions that proving such a hypothesis will be difficult, maybe impossible. Nonetheless, studies are under way.

The new thinking will no doubt spawn heated debate among archaeologists for years to come. For Mayanist Peter Mathews, the connections now being made between Maya myth and cosmology "open up a whole new world of discovery. We stand on the threshold of something truly new." ≜

14

LIVING CONSTELLATIONS

A Maya reading of the story of the stars

by DENNIS and BARBARA TEDLOCK

BEFORE EYEGLASSES OR TELESCOPES EVER CAME to the highlands of Guatemala, the Quiché Maya already had objects they called ilb'al, or "instruments for seeing." They used crystals to divine the outcome of future events and bowls of liquid to observe the reflections of solar eclipses. But their most important instrument was the Popol Vuh, an allegorical text consulted by kings and their councils of lords. The ancient Popol Vuh no doubt resembled the Dresden Codex, a Maya hieroglyphic text from the Yucatan, but the only version that has come down to us was written, just after the Spanish conquest of Guatemala, in Quiché using the Roman alphabet.

The Dresden Codex and Popol Vuh chronicle the movement of the cosmos as it is measured by the 260-day Maya divinatory calendar. The Popol Vuh opens by positing a world that is nothing more than a calm sea under an empty sky, where time is measured by the same 260-day cycle that appears at the beginning of the Dresden Codex. In both books this calendar is followed by sections on the cycles of Venus, the timing of lunar and solar eclipses, and the dawning of the solar year. They concur on the rising of Venus, noting its first morning appearance on a day named Junajpu in Quiché, and Ahaw in Yucatec, and its first evening appearance on the day named Kame or Kimi in the same two languages.

The books differ in that the Dresden Codex is principally a tabulation of calendrical and astronomical data, while the Popol Vuh tells the story of the hero twins Junajpu and Xbalanque and their triumph over the flamboyant and egocentric Seven Macaw, his two sons, and the Lords of the Underworld (Xibalba), which made the world safe for the coming of humanity. The adventures of the hero twins coincide with the movement of Venus as it progresses along the ecliptic (the celestial path of the sun, moon, and planets).

Recently there has been major progress in reconstructing the roles played by fixed stars and the Milky Way in ancient Maya astronomy, progress that would not have been possible without research among contemporary speakers of Mayan languages. In our own fieldwork with the Quiché, we learned just how closely events mentioned in the Popul Vuh followed the movements of the night sky. For example, we found out from a calendar keeper that the dense whitish half of the Milky Way is called Saq B'e or "White Road," while the half that has a dark cleft running through it has a pair of names: Q'eka B'e, "Black Road," and Ub'e Xib'alb'a, "Road of the Underworld." In the Popol Vuh, the hero twins come to a road with the same pair of names, which intersects the

ecliptic at the edge of the earth. Choosing to follow the Road of the Underworld, the twins vanish. The arrival of the twins at the intersection represents Venus' last appearance in the east before it falls below the horizon, having followed the ecliptic to where it crosses the rifted half of the Milky Way. Prior to its arrival at the intersection, which lies in the constellation Sagittarius, Venus passes through Scorpius, a constellation the Maya saw as a scorpion, as we do. In the Popol Vuh, the twins encounter scorpions just before they come to the intersection. These events take place in late December, when Sagittarius is on the eastern horizon at dawn.

Near the point where the ecliptic crosses the White Road half of the Milky Way are the Pleiades, a star cluster whose Quiché name is *motz*, meaning "fistful," as in a fistful of seeds, or the number 400. For the modern Maya, the western setting of these stars in March is a signal that planting time has come. In the Popol Vuh, their setting marks the death of 400 boys, who were flattened when Zipacna, one of the sons of Seven Macaw, brought their house down on top of them. The most notable feature of the house is its main crossbeam, an enormous tree trunk. In Classic Maya sources, as interpreted by Linda Schele, the Milky Way (or portions of it) was sometimes viewed as a tree or tree trunk. Following this lead, Matthew Looper, a graduate student at the University of Texas, noticed that when the Pleiades set in the west they precede the Milky Way, whose movement resembles a falling tree or crossbeam.

There are still further connections between the Popol Vuh and the movements of the stars. In the story, the north is ruled by

Seven Macaw, or Wuqub' Kaqix, represented in the night sky by the seven stars of the Big Dipper. Seven Macaw appears early on in the story, just after creation but before the appearance of the sun and the moon. With his bejewelled teeth, shimmering metal eyes, and reflective white beak, he claims to be both the sun and the moon—that is until he is exposed as a fraud by the hero twins. In the text, Junajpu shoots Seven Macaw with a blowgun while he is feeding high in a nance tree. In December, when the Big Dipper is at its highest point in the sky just before sunrise, the constellation Scorpius appears on the eastern horizon. This explains the otherwise enigmatic presence of a scorpion in a scene on a Classic Maya vase that shows Junajpu shooting a treetop macaw with a blowgun. Both Junajpu and the scorpion are at ground level, which is to say that Venus and Scorpius are on the horizon at the same time. Schele has suggested this part of the story takes place on a July evening, but that would put Seven Macaw lower in the sky and make the identification of the blowgunner with Venus as the morning star impossible. His jaw broken by the blowgun shot, Seven Macaw spends the beginning of the rainy season falling from his tree. Each night the Big Dipper appears lower in the sky.

By July, when the hurricane season arrives, three hearthstones appear on the eastern horizon. These stones, as the contemporary Quiché see them, are in the constellation Orion and consist of Alnitak (the southernmost star in Orion's belt), Saiph, and Rigel, and form a triangle around the great Orion nebula (M42), which to the Quiché is a smoky hearth fire. Seven Macaw (the Big Dipper) drops completely below the horizon when the three stones appear. The Popol Vuh accounts for the correspondence between the descent of the Big Dipper and the arrival of the hurricane season

Comet Gazers

Did the ancient Maya take note of Halley's comet? According to Williams College professors Samuel Y. Edgerton and Jay M. Pasachoff, a figure of the Maya "God L" smoking a cigar carved on a panel at Palenque's Temple of the Cross is a personification of Halley's comet. An inscription associated with the figure bears the date January 17, A.D. 684 (Julian calendar), six months before a known visit by Halley's comet, which passes earth about every 76 years.

The Temple of the Cross and its inscribed panels were commissioned by Chan Bahlum ("Snake-Heaven-Jaguar"), twelfth ruler of Palenque and the eldest son of Pakal, who reigned from A.D. 684 to 702. According to Edgerton and Pasachoff, Chan Bahlum knew of the comet's 76-year average cycle and used it to recalculate the births of gods important to Palenque and his own lineage group. Indeed, the birth dates of "First Father" (the maize god), First Mother ("Lady Beastie") and "God K" (the god of royal accession), recorded on the Temple of the Cross panel, are separated by multiples of 76 years.

Although archaeoastronomer Anthony Aveni of Colgate University agrees that the smoking god figure could be interpreted as announcing a comet, he remains unconvinced that the Maya could distinguish Halley's comet from any number of other comets that pass near Earth. "The fact that several of the dates recorded on the Temple of the Cross panel are divisible by 76 is coincidental," says Aveni.

—ANGELA M.H. SCHUSTER

by saying that the primordial god Juracan (from whom the word hurricane comes) ordered the hero twins to rid the world of the imposter Seven Macaw.

In Schele's reading of the Classic Maya evidence, another set of gods, the canoe paddlers (who transport First Father, the maize god, to the place of creation) make the hearthstones appear at a time when the sky lies flat on the surface of the earth, having fallen there after an earlier attempt at creation. We prefer to keep the point of contact between sky and earth at the horizon, and we suspect that the celestial "falling" Schele finds in her texts is not a collapse of the sky onto the earth but the descent of stars toward the western horizon. Indeed, the standard Quiché term for sidereal movement in general is *qajib'al ch'umil*, "star descent."

In the Popol Vuh Seven Macaw next appears at his house, still pained by his broken jaw. The hero twins devise a plan to finish him off. Junajpu and Xbalanque convince their grandparents, an elderly peccary (a pig-like mammal) and a coati (a relative of the raccoon), to pose as doctors and go to the aid of Seven Macaw. Instead of mending his broken jaw, however, the eld-

erly couple pull out Seven Macaw's bejeweled teeth and metal eyes, thereby stripping him of his brilliance. In Classic Maya art the grandparents are both elderly peccaries and correspond to a Maya constellation. According to Victoria and Harvey Bricker of Tulane University, who have been studying the zodiacal almanac in the Maya hieroglyphic book known as the Paris Codex, the peccaries are located in the eastern part of Leo. This is precisely where the ecliptic comes closest to the Big Dipper. Moreover, when the eastern portion of Leo appears on the eastern horizon, the Big Dipper rises at the same time.

The Big Dipper and the eastern part of Leo begin their joint ascent just before sunrise in September, when Venus is about to disappear from the eastern sky. Seven Macaw receives his first blow from the morning star when it rises in the company of a scorpion, and his second blow 260 days later when Venus comes much closer to him in the company of the elderly peccary and coati. With Seven Macaw neutralized and unable to be anything more than the seven stars of the Big Dipper, the path is cleared for the hero twins, who become the true sun and full moon. ▲

15

RITUALS OF THE MODERN MAYA

A strong undercurrent of Precolumbian belief pervades much of today's religious practice.

by ANGELA M.H. SCHUSTER

THE MURMUR OF CHANTING FILLED THE CHURCH of San Juan Chamula; the fragrance of pine needles crushed underfoot mingled with the scent of candles and burning copal incense. Pilgrims moved slowly from station to station, beseeching saints for health, wealth, and luck in love. An elderly woman had come with a shaman bearing fresh eggs and a chicken. Egg in hand, the shaman traced the woman's body several times, praying aloud as he worked. He then broke the egg into a bowl, the pattern of its yolk revealing the affliction. With further incantations and offerings, the shaman "transferred" the illness to the chicken, which he then sacrificed by breaking its neck. A three-foot-tall Colonial period polychrome figure of John the Baptist stood near the altar, dressed in layers of embroidered garments—tokens of gratitude from those whom he had helped. Patron saint of this Tzotzil Maya church in highland Chiapas, Mexico, the Baptist was responsible for bringing rain and ensuring the fertility of crops and animals. Had he assumed the mantle of Chak, the Classic period water god?

Despite Catholic trappings, the rites I witnessed in 1996 were rooted deep in antiquity. In recent years, archaeologists and anthropologists have opened a dialog with those who practice the old ways, and are coming to realize just how much Precolumbian ritual has survived. "Considering that 500 years have elapsed since the Spanish Conquest," says Harvard University ethnologist Evon Z. Vogt, "I am impressed with the enduring nature of Classic Maya religious concepts and beliefs."

In the Chol town of Tila, in highland Chiapas, Nicholas Hopkins and Kathryn Josserand of Florida State University have documented the cult of a "Black Christ" known as the Señor de Tila, an amalgam of Christ and Ik'al, a Precolumbian cave-dwelling earth deity. Each January and June, tens of thousands of pilgrims come to the town to seek the support of the Señor de Tila, who is venerated both in the local church and in a nearby rock-shelter, which contains a large soot-blackened stalagmite believed by townspeople to be a representation of Christ. According to local tradition, Ik'al is a manifestation of "Earth Owner," the master of souls who holds the key to health and wealth and must be petitioned and rewarded through prayers and sacrifice. "For the people of Tila," says Hopkins, "the Precolumbian idea of making sacrifices to ensure the well-being of one's family and

loved ones echoes Christ's giving of his life to pay for the sins of the world."

"Modern Maya see little conflict in merging the two faiths," says Robert M. Laughlin, an anthropologist with the Smithsonian Institution who has lived among the Tzotzil of Zinacantan for more than 30 years. "It is common on feast days for a procession to begin at the Church of San Lorenzo with a mass for Christ the Sun God and his mother the Moon Goddess, and then proceed to a nearby hill for the veneration of ancestors and Maya gods, including Chauk, an earth and water deity."

Dark, secretive, and full of exotic geological formations, caves have played a key role in Mesoamerican religion for more than 3,000 years, serving as portals to the Otherworld—the realm of deities, demons, and ancestors. There are more than 25 known painted caves in the Maya world, the earliest being Loltún in Yucatán, whose paintings have been dated to the Late Preclassic, ca. 300 B.C. James Brady of George Washington University has documented the continued veneration of Naj Tunich, a two-mile-long painted cave in the southeastern Petén region of Guatemala. Naj Tunich began attracting pilgrims early in the first century B.C., when stone platforms were erected just inside the cave's entrance. Offerings such as ceramics and jadeite pendants were deposited atop platforms adjacent to several large stalagmite columns. The majority of the cave's painted inscriptions, some 40 in all, were executed during the seventh and eighth centuries.

Three verbs associated with pilgrimage—*hul* (to arrive), *pak* (to return), and *il* (to see or witness events at a foreign place)—pervade the Naj Tunich texts, according to Andrea Stone of the University of Wisconsin, Milwaukee, who has studied the inscriptions. The presence of emblem glyphs from a number of cities suggests that the cave was used by people living throughout the region. One inscription notes that lords from the Lowland Maya city of Caracol, 30 miles to the north, performed a *k'ak' kuch*, or "burning" ritual in the cave in A.D. 744. Burning incense may have served to appease local gods and guarantee safe passage for dignitaries traveling through foreign territory. Brady and his team have recovered potsherds encrusted with the charred resin of the copal palm spanning the entire Classic period (ca. A.D. 250–900), attesting the prolonged practice of such rites.

Today's pilgrims, mostly from the Kekchi villages of Tanjoc and Alta Verapaz, ten to 15 miles away, come to the cave before the rainy season, which begins in late May and early June, to burn incense and light candles to ensure a good harvest. "Though some ritual aspects have certainly changed," adds Brady, noting the singing of Christian hymns and the participation of women, "cave worship continues to figure prominently in Maya religion."

According to Vogt, there are five classes of sacred topography among the Tzotzil of Zinacantan—*vits* (mountains), *ch'en* (holes in the ground such as caves), *hap 'osil* (mountain passes), *ton* (rocks), and *te'* (trees)—geographic features rife with spirit activity. "For Zinacantecos," says Vogt, "mountains are the most important features on the landscape, being places of contact between heaven and earth." The veneration of mountains, he believes, stretches deep into the Precolumbian past, serving as the impetus behind the building of pyramids. "Pyramids are artificial mountains," says Harvard University epigrapher David Stuart, "both represented by the glyph *wits*" (the Classic period form of the Tzotzil word *vits*). According to Stuart, there are numerous references to buildings as mountains in the epigraphic record, perhaps the best example being temple 22 on the Copán acropolis. "The building is actually labeled 'mountain,' its doorway, the gaping maw of the earth monster, a metaphor for a cave," he says. "One would have entered the 'cave' of temple 22 to converse with the ancestral spirits, surely in association with all sorts of ritual activities, including incense burning and bloodletting."

As caves and mountains occur together in the landscape, both serve as doorways to the Otherworld. To journey through them and return alive, however, requires the special talent of a shaman. In antiquity, Maya kings interceded with the gods and ancestors on behalf of their cities. Today, in many Maya communities, mayors and healers are one and the same, responsible for their people's physical and spiritual health. "Shamans are specialists in ecstasy, a state of mind that allows them to move freely beyond the ordinary world—beyond death itself—to deal directly with the gods, demons, ancestors, and other unseen but potent things that control the world of the living," says David Freidel of Southern Methodist University in Dallas, who has participated in shamanic rites at a *ch'a-chak* or "bring rain" ceremony in Yucatán. "When we began our summer field season at Yaxuná in 1989," recalls Freidel, "the nearby community was in the midst of a crisis. A severe drought had destroyed two plantings and measures were needed to ensure the success of a third." With the help of the villagers, Don Pablo, the local shaman, built an altar of young saplings, baby corn plants, and hanging gourds—a portal between this world and the next through which he could summon *chakob*, or rain gods. For three days, he chanted and prepared offerings of corn bread, incense, stewed meats, and honey wine. "At the climax of the ceremony," says Freidel, "Don Pablo, aided by copious amounts of aguardiente, a sugarcane brandy, entered a trance state in which he remained for more than ten hours. It is in sleep, whether a trance or dream state, that Maya spirits communicate with shamans. Shortly after the ceremony, we heard the deep rumble of thunder. Had the *chakob* heard the shaman's prayers?"

> As caves and mountains occur together in the landscape, both serve as doorways to the Otherworld.

According to Freidel, such an altar, known as a *ka'an te'* or "wooden sky," represents the cosmos. The leafy green saplings, tied together several feet above the table's center, symbolize the arching of the Milky Way across the night sky. Thirteen gourds suspended from the saplings represent the constellations of the Maya zodiac. The building of the *ka'an te'* can be traced back as early as the Classic period, from which there are depictions on several stone vases, including one from Escuintla in southwestern Guatemala.

Shamans are also traditional healers—bone setters, midwives, and herbalists. The most skilled are the *h'men*, doctor-priests who treat the minds, bodies, and souls of villagers. For the Maya, physical and spiritual health are one and the same. According to the late Mopán Maya *h'men* Don Elijio Panti, ailments could be brought on by a restless soul or profaned gods and ancestors. To cure an illness took not only prescribed remedies but spiritual reconciliation.

Among the Quiché of highland Guatemala, says Barbara Tedlock, a State University of New York, Buffalo, anthropologist and trained shaman-priest, "some illnesses can even be a call to serve gods and ancestors." There are six such illnesses—snake, horse, twisted stomach, dislocated bone, inebriation, and money loss—all of which incapacitate a patient. To cure them requires becoming a daykeeper, one who burns incense and offers prayers at shrines on designated days of the *tzolkin*, the 260-day sacred calendar.

The Quiché believe that when great shamans die, their souls congregate at lineage shrines where they worshiped during their lives. As the shamans' souls accumulate, the shrines—known as *warab'alja*, literally "sleeping places"—are endowed with increasing power. Each lineage group has four such shrines built in the form of small stone boxes where prayers are offered on specific calendar days and to commemorate births, deaths, marriages, plantings, and harvests.

"These shrines are also used to demarcate lands owned by a lineage group," says Dennis Tedlock, also a trained Quiché shaman-priest. "When a property is sold in the Quiché region, new landowners remember previous landowners in prayers at recently acquired shrines. The location of each shrine is dictated by the landscape, there being a distinct preference for mountains, caves, lakes, and springs."

Linda Schele of the University of Texas at Austin believed that *warab'alja* is a derivation of the Classic Maya phrase *waybil*, which also means "sleeping house." *Waybilob* are well known from Classic period sites. In 1989 Juan Pedro Laporte of Guatemala's Instituto de Antropología e Historia was excavating a large compound of houses and temples at Tikal in the Petén when he came across just such a shrine embedded in a later altar platform. An open-sided stone box, the structure was filled with burnt offerings. Two particularly fine miniature stone shrines, labeled *waybil* in hieroglyphs, were found in a cache behind structure 33 at the Classic Maya city of Copán in Honduras.

By studying modern Maya religious practices, archaeologists and anthropologists are beginning to gain critical insight into rites often depicted in ancient Maya art. "We still have much to learn about Classic Maya religious practices," says Vogt, "but the progress made so far is astounding. The next decade promises to bring even more discoveries as scholars continue their cooperative work on Maya culture." ≜

16

SEEING THROUGH MAYA EYES

A vernal-equinox appearance of the feathered serpent highlights a 7-day cruise to the Yucatán.

by ANDREW L. SLAYMAN

SOME 45,000 PEOPLE STOOD BEFORE THE GREAT temple at the heart of the vast site of Chichén Itzá in northern Yucatán. Families had gathered here from across Mexico, and foreign tourists had come by bus, plane, and ship. Roving hippies bearing bongo drums and beat-up guitars tried to slip through the gate, but the police turned them back, fearing their music would compete with the narration of the long-awaited celestial event over the public-address system. On the grassy plaza beside the temple, known in Spanish as the Castillo, a bare-chested man with long, flowing black hair crouched at the center of a dozen sun worshippers, flat on their backs like the spokes of a wheel, forming an image of the sun. It was March 21, and the crowd had gathered to witness the appearance of

Kukulcán, the feathered serpent of the ancient Maya. Beginning about 4:30 P.M. the rays of the setting sun shone across the temple's stepped northwestern corner, casting a zigzag shadow along the balustrade of the northern staircase. Within an hour alternating triangles of light and shadow stretched from top to bottom, much like a diamondback rattlesnake in profile. As the seventh and final triangle of light touched the carved stone snake's head at the foot of the balustrade, onlookers gasped, then burst into cheers.

I had prepared for this extraordinary event during a two-day voyage from Galveston, Texas, aboard Sun Line's *Stella Solaris*, a 700-passenger ship that cruises in the Caribbean and elsewhere. A superb program of lectures and videos schooled us not only in the equinox experience but also in the greater cosmic consciousness of the Maya. Headed by Anthony F. Aveni, the Russell B. Colgate Professor of Astronomy and Anthropology at Colgate University in Hamilton, New York, the *Stella Solaris'* team of lecturers included Edwin C. Krupp, director of Los Angeles' Griffith Observatory; George T. Keene, an amateur astronomer, photographer, and retired Eastman Kodak engineer; and physical anthropologist Rebecca Storey and archaeologist Randolph J. Widmer, both of the University of Houston.

On the morning of March 20 we docked at Playa del Carmen, a small resort town on the eastern coast of the Yucatán Peninsula. From there convoys of buses made day trips to Tulum, a small Postclassic (ca. A.D. 1200–1521) trading post perched atop a cliff overlooking a sandy beach, and Cobá, a 26-square-mile site best known for its miles of

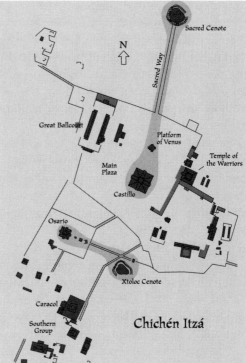

Chichén Itzá

sacbeob, or causeways. Tulum and Cobá were a warm-up for our excursion to the much grander Chichén Itzá, occupied at least from the seventh through the early thirteenth centuries. Unlike many other Maya sites largely forgotten until their rediscovery in the nineteenth and twentieth centuries, Chichén Itzá has been known to Europeans since the Spanish Conquest. Diego de Landa, a sixteenth-century bishop of Yucatán, mentioned the ruins in his *Relación de las Cosas de Yucatán*. He wrote of the Castillo and a great sinkhole, the Sacred Cenote, into which the Maya "were and still are accustomed to throw men alive as a sacrifice to the gods in times of drought." Nearly three centuries later the American explorer John Lloyd Stephens described Chichén Itzá at length in his *Incidents of Travel in Yucatan*, which was illustrated with 21 engravings of the site's monuments by the artist Frederick Catherwood. In 1894 the site was purchased for $500 by Edward H. Thompson, the American consul in Mérida, the capital of Yucatán. Thompson dug there from 1904 until 1922. The following year the Carnegie Institution of Washington began a 20-year project under the direction of Sylvanus G. Morley to excavate and restore many of the principal structures, including the Temple of the Warriors on the eastern edge of the Main Plaza.

The Castillo's "serpent of light" was first noted in 1948 by the photographer Laura Gilpin, who titled an image of it "Sunlight and Shadow on the Balustrade of the North Stairway." She did not mention its calendrical or mythological significance. That the Maya might have seen the event as a manifestation of Kukulcán was first suggested by Jean-Jacques Rivard in a 1969 article in *Katunob*, a Mesoamerican anthropology newsletter. Once the god reached the foot of the stairs, noted Rivard, he might have kept going. With serpent heads at the base of the stairway and the grand doorway at the top giving entry to the sacred precinct, the northern side of the Castillo is clearly the most important. North of this monument is a stone platform marked with four-pointed stars symbolizing the planet Venus, and beyond this a *sacbe*, known today as the Sacred Way, leads past a natural rock outcropping to a small temple on the brink of the Sacred Cenote. It was here, argued Rivard, that Kukulcán was heading when he began his equinoctial descent.

The keen interest of the ancient Maya in the yearly progress of the sun is evident in a number of structures here and elsewhere in Mesoamerica. About 1,000 feet south of the Castillo is a round tower known as the Caracol, several of whose windows point toward the equinox sunset and the southernmost and northernmost points on the horizon where Venus rises. At the site of Uaxactún in northern Guatemala, an observer atop one of the site's temples can look out past a row of three other shrines to the points on the horizon where the sun rises on the equinoxes and solstices. Two structures at Yaxchilán, in Mexico's Usumacinta Valley, face the summer solstice sunrise, and at nearby Palenque a person standing atop a four-story tower (part of a complex of buildings known as the Palace) on the winter solstice sees the sun set into the temple-tomb of the great king Pacal. Writings on stone stelae, ceramic vessels, and codices indicate widespread interest in many other astronomical phenomena, including eclipses and the cycles of Venus.

Various features of the Castillo occur in numbers that mirror the ancient Maya fascination with calendrical cycles. Landa reported that each of the four staircases had 91 steps; together with the step around the top they totaled 365, one for each day in the Maya year. Similarly 52 recessed panels on each side of the Castillo may refer to the 52 years in the Maya calendrical cycle known as the calendar round; the pyramid's nine stories may have to do with the nine Lords of Xibalba, the Maya underworld.

Though the specific myths on which Kukulcán's appearance is based are long lost, much of what the feathered serpent stood for appears to relate to Maya solar and calendrical cycles. Because they shed and regrow their skins, snakes are symbols of renewal. The life cycle of the diamondback rattlesnake, which Chichén Itzá's serpent of light seems to resemble, is also related to the changing seasons. In the dry spring of northern Yucatán the rattlesnake sleeps all day and comes out only at dusk, but once the summer rains begin it becomes active during the day. Kukulcán's appearance on the Castillo may have heralded the coming of summer and the period of renewed activity for the snake.

Did the Castillo's architects have Kukulcán's annual appearance in mind when they built it? "We really can't know," says Anthony Aveni, "but the more I watch it the more I think the Maya must have seen what was going on." Edwin Krupp believes the recent restoration of a temple southwest of Chichén Itzá's Main Plaza, which appears to be a smaller version of the Castillo, may be relevant. Known as the Osario, or High Priest's Grave, the structure was excavated between 1992 and 1994 by Peter J. Schmidt of the Museo Regional de Antropología y Historia in Mérida. In a line stretching east from the Osario stand three stone platforms, of which the westernmost resembles the Venus platform north of the Castillo. Beyond these a *sacbe* leads past a natural rock outcropping to a temple on the edge of a second cenote, the Xtoloc. This sequence of structures is similar to that joining the Castillo and the Sacred Cenote, but it leads east instead of north, so a serpent could not have slithered down the Osario's balustrade to the Xtoloc Cenote—or not, at any rate, on the equinoxes. Whether any shadows are cast on its balustrades, and if so when, remain unanswered, but as Krupp points out, a date of June 20, A.D. 842, inscribed on a stela found atop the Osario suggests that "someone ought to take a look at this mini-Castillo at the summer solstice."

Absorbed by visions of Maya cosmology, we reboarded the *Stella Solaris* for our return to Galveston, experiencing during the voyage a heavenly spectacle of a different kind. As the Big Dipper rose above the dark horizon we saw, off the end of its handle, a fuzzy light the size of the moon trailing a diffuse tail. Comet Hyakutake, the brightest since Comet West in 1976, was nearing its closest approach to earth on its first visit to the inner solar system in 8,000 years. On its previous fly-by the forebears of the Maya had not yet settled down or begun to record their thoughts on bark paper or stone, but they cannot have missed the great light in the sky. Their descendants would have called it by one of several names, according to Tulane University graduate student Weldon Lamb, including *budz ek*, "smoking star," and *ikomne*, "windy tail." Lamb recounts one Postconquest legend about a comet sent by an angry god that struck the earth and made a giant crater, the cenote at the site of Dzibilchaltún north of Mérida. This year on the vernal equinox the feathered serpent appeared at Chichén Itzá, and a smoking star blazed across the night sky. What would the Maya have made of that? ◢

17

EXTREME SPORTS

Once the game of Maya kings and Aztec warriors, *ulama* lives on in the dusty playing fields of western Mexico.

by COLLEEN POPSON

EVERY SUNDAY AFTERNOON AROUND THIS TIME OF year, while millions of Americans crowd around their television sets to watch 250-pound men in helmets and pads pound each other over pigskin in huge stadiums, another Sunday sports tradition is honored in a tiny Mexican village 800 miles south of the border, between the Sierra Madre Mountains and the Pacific coast. There, two five-man teams of farmers wearing nothing but headbands and deerskin loincloths ricochet a heavy rubber ball off their hips across a packed-dirt playing field. Each explosive *thwap* of the ball is an echo of similar games played throughout Mesoamerica for over three millennia.

I've come to the village of Los Llanitos, population 151, with a motley group of academics, tourists, philanthropists, and bureaucrats from the nearby coastal city of Mazatlán, where we've been attending the First International Congress for the Mesoamerican Ballgame. The version of the game played here is hip *ulama* (from *ullamaliztli,* the Náhuatl, or Aztec, word for *ballgame*), and from what scholars can tell, it is the game that most closely resembles what was played in the large Prehispanic stone courts from this part of Mexico to the Maya lowlands of Yucatán, Guatemala, Belize, Honduras, and El Salvador.

Excavations in western Mexico have turned up ceramic ballplayer figurines and ballcourts as old as the fourth century A.D., and rubber balls have been found near the Gulf Coast that date to 1500 B.C. Yet today it is an endangered sport. "Hip *ulama* survives in only a few communities," says Manuel Aguilar, an art historian at California State University, Los Angeles (CSULA). He and CSULA archaeologist James Brady have brought a small group of graduate students here as part of a project on *ulama.* Awaiting the start of a game, Aguilar tells me there are only about two hundred players in the whole state of Sinaloa, and the number of younger ones is declining. "The game is at risk of dying," he says.

Modern *ulama's* deep roots attract scholars eager to understand how Precolumbian ballgames were played and the rituals associated with them. That ballcourts occupy a central position adjacent to temples in nearly every Mesoamerican city—hundreds have been identified—is a testament to the game's Prehispanic importance. Depictions of the ballgame in Mesoamerican art are ceremonial in nature: a figurine of a ballplayer molded onto the handle of a 3,000-year-old ceramic bloodletting knife indicates the game's early association with ritualized bloodshed; Maya friezes and figurines depict noble players bedecked with deer-head headdresses, jaguar skins, and jade jewelry; fifteenth-century Mixtec codices from south-central Mexico show ball players with knives through their hearts; and Aztec ballcourts studded with carved stone skull racks suggest decapitation was a common outcome to matches.

As a group of us assemble, small clusters of players prepare for a day of games; a boy helps a younger one knot his loincloth; men mark the sides of the long, narrow court with chalk; and others practice knocking the ball back and forth with their hips. Ears of corn, soft drinks, beer, and mangoes on sticks are sold out of coolers to a growing crowd of spectators.

Of the villages with *ulama* teams, Los Llanitos is one of few with its own court or taste. Roughly one-fifth of the town plays, and children are introduced to the sport at age four or five. There are players in other towns, but they must come to villages like this one to actually participate in a game. Today's simple dirt courts are a far cry from the massive stone constructions of the past, whose vertical or banked walls framed an I-shaped field (players who have participated in ball-game demonstrations at ancient sites have noted that the walls add extra excitement to the game, because the ball is kept in play longer). These monuments were also a source of pride for their communities and often were embellished with intricately carved stone altars and panels in part to impress or outdo rival cities.

The early source scholars turn to most often for the ritual meaning of the ballgame is the Quiché Maya creation myth from the

Popol Vuh, or "council book." In it, hero twins, playing ball too loudly, disturb the Lords of Death and are summoned into Xibalba, the underworld. They outwit the Lords of Death, become like gods themselves, and resurrect their father and uncle whom the Lords had killed and buried in a ballcourt. The twins then rise to take new form as the sun and the moon, and their father and uncle together become the maize god. Much of Mesoamerican ball-game art depicts themes of this story: sacrifice and bloodletting link the ballcourt with the underworld, while plants and the maize god imply the court was also a place of rebirth and fertility. Blood spilled during sacrifice was thought to feed the maize god, mimicking the watering of the earth in maize cultivation.

> ...sacrifice and bloodletting link the ballcourt with the underworld...

As the ball is hipped back and forth in long, high volleys between the Los Llanitos and Escuinapa teams, the crowd hollers and applauds. The players leap high in the air, seeming to defy gravity as they sail hip-first toward each oncoming ball. "Don't take your eyes off the ball," CSULA student Maria Ramos warns me, as we watch from the sidelines. "You don't want it to hit you." She's right. The fast-moving, nine-pound, solid rubber ball often careens out of bounds, and has seriously injured spectators. Over their lifetimes, the players develop permanent black bruises, or calluses on their hips, and children are introduced to the game early so they won't be afraid of the ball.

It's this aspect of the game that often keeps girls and women, many of whom enjoy playing, from competing at the level of the men. Mothers fear they might get hurt or that play could compromise their ability to bear children. Still, one of *ulama's* rising young stars is Dulce Villa, a thirteen-year-old girl. Villa plays *ulama de antebrazo* (a version of the game where players hit a much smaller ball with only their forearms) with fierce intensity, regularly beating boys her age and older. She comes from a long tradition of female players. "For as long as people can remember, there were women playing," says Brady. Ceramic figurines of women in ball-game attire have been found all over Mesoamerica and date as far back as 1200 B.C.

The balls used in *ulama* may be the clearest link with the Precolumbian past. Spanish chroniclers marveled at the properties of the rubber balls they saw used by Aztecs. Dominican missionary Diego Durán wrote in 1570 that "jumping and bouncing are its qualities, upward and downward, to and from. It can exhaust the pursuer running after it before he can catch up with it."

According to records in the Aztec Codex Mendoza, written circa 1545, the southern province of Tochtepec was required to produce 16,000 rubber balls a year for the Aztec capital of Tenochtitlan. Since a rubber tree will produce less than half of what is needed for a single ball, the people of Tochtepec would have needed to collect sap from some

50,000 trees. This would have required armies of workers. Considering each ball takes about fifteen hours to make, additional labor equivalent to more than 16,000 work days would have been needed. Once produced, those 16,000 balls, weighing more than 100,000 pounds, had to be carried some two hundred miles to Tenochtitlan by human porters. "There had to have been organized production in these communities," says Brady, "and it would have had major implications for land use and social organization all down the line."

About an hour into the match, the players' hips have begun to glow red, and their hands are black with dirt from bracing themselves for low returns. A quarrel between the two teams over a rule of the game has suspended play. After much name calling and challenging of manhood, it appears there will be no resolution. So we break for a dinner of locally butchered beef and fresh salsa and tortillas.

The fascination of *ulama* hasn't gone unnoticed. A 1980s documentary about *ulama* by Mexican filmmaker Roberto Rochín inspired great interest in the game for a time. Many players from western Mexico have traveled all over Mesoamerica, donning Maya headdresses when they play the courts at Copán or Cancún. "But they were being exploited," says Aguilar. "Tourists were paying thirty dollars for a ticket to these spectacles, and the players were getting crumbs." Many have returned to their farms in Sinaloa where they want to promote the game their way.

Meanwhile, government and academic advocates of the game will continue to urge the Ministry of Education to have it recognized by UNESCO. Alida Zurita, president of the Mexican Federation of Indigenous and Traditional Games and Sports, is working to have *ulama* taught in schools. If the players of Los Llanitos and other *ulama* supporters get their way, they will one day watch their children compete professionally in televised games in great regional arenas before cheering crowds of thousands, all of whom know the rules and the game's fascinating history. Sunday afternoons will never be the same. ≜

PART III:

READING THE MAYA PAST

18

THE GREAT CHRONICLER OF MAYA ART

Merle Greene Robertson has spent a lifetime documenting Mesoamerican sculpture, carvings, and paintings.

by TOM GIDWITZ

IN THE SUMMER OF 1962, A SMALL PLANE TOUCHED down on the jungle airstrip at Tikal, Guatemala. On board were dozens of cases of expensive Scotch and two women, who had wedged themselves amid the plane's cargo. Summer art students from the University of Guanajuato's San Miguel de Allende Art Institute, they had come to spend the weekend and see Tikal's ruins. Stepping off the plane, one spotted a snake, hopped right back on, and went home without seeing a single temple. The other woman was Merle Greene Robertson. "A little old snake wasn't going to send me away," she says. Robertson had a special interest in Precolumbian art. When she reached the ruins, she found herself in wonderland.

University of Pennsylvania archaeologists working at Tikal were nearly halfway through their 15-year excavation of decorated vessels, mysterious carvings, and buried kings. They needed an artist to record their findings and invited Robertson to stay. Within a few days, she was climbing a scaffold each morning to draw the friezes on the palace in the Central Acropolis.

This was one of the century's landmark digs, staffed by some of the field's most famous veterans and a new generation of passionate young scholars. By day they would make discoveries and record magnificent art—wondrous sculpture and beguiling glyphs, relics of a people then thought to be peaceful worshippers of the stars, gods, and time. At night they would revel in what seemed a dreamscape, dancing atop pyramids in the light of the moon to orchestral music played over loudspeakers. Robertson's weekend visit lasted the entire summer, and her love of Maya art became an obsession. "Once I became a Mayanist," she says with an emphatic motion of her hand, "that was it—all the time."

In the four decades since, Robertson has ventured deep into the jungle, spending weeks in dank tombs and recording thousands of Maya masterpieces before their destruction by looters and time. She has authored five books and scores of scholarly articles, edited a dozen studies of Maya art and history, and helped bring about one of the twentieth century's great accomplishments: the decipherment of the Maya script.

It's not hard to find Merle Greene Robertson. Just go to the street named in her honor, Calle Merle Greene, in the modern town of Palenque, Mexico. Here stands her modest house she named Na Chan-Bahlum—Chol Maya for House of Serpent Jaguar—in honor of the brilliant king responsible for much of Palenque's most astonishing temples and art. Na Chan-Bahlum draws a constant stream of visitors. Built 30 years ago by Robertson and her late husband, it is at once dorm and research lab, the site of breakthrough discoveries and years of collegial studies. At the research season's height, from January through May, as many as 18 sit down to share dinner every day.

At the center of this whirlwind is Robertson herself. Funny and feisty, with wide, round eyes and snow-white hair, she's been plagued by falls and broken bones, but her verve never flags. The day before my visit, despite recent surgery to repair a torn tendon in her leg, she had climbed Palenque's 50-foot-high temple XX to inspect her team's preparations for opening a tomb. In the coming weeks she planned to rub carvings at Chichén Itzá, return to her second home in San Francisco to work on her next book, meet in New Orleans with her archivists, and confer with curators at Mexico City's Museum of Anthropology about an exhibition of her rubbings.

Maya relief sculptures are a maze of subtle details that resist reproduction. For photographs, the lighting must cast the stone carvings in sharp contrasts with shadows that accentuate yet don't obscure. Pencil drawings can fall prey to an artist's individual style or to lapses of the eye. Many carvings are in damp, cramped tombs inhospitable to both cameras and sketch pads.

In 1962 at Tikal, Robertson watched archaeologists uncover Altar 5, a pristine, ornate, five-foot-diameter stone monument with carving worthy of more than a mere pencil sketch. She had an idea—she stretched a bed sheet across the altar, secured it with stones and rope, and, gently pressing on the cloth with oil paint on her thumb, created a startling black-on-white rubbing of two figures and a death's head, encircled by 31 glyphs.

At a stroke, Robertson had brought a new tool to Maya studies. Life-sized rubbings reveal details that escape even the most experienced observers. "If you're looking at the clothing that the elite might have worn, you can see every little line, every little pattern in the fabric," she says. The following year, when Alfred Kidder of the Carnegie Institution visited the site and saw her work, he was so impressed he asked her to make rubbings of all the carvings at Tikal.

Robertson returned the next summer with more sophisticated materials: six-foot sheets of handmade Japanese rice paper, and dense, black sumi ink used in Japanese brush painting. She taped large sheets of the paper to each sculpted stone, wet them down with a brush, then pressed the paper tightly into every cut and crevice. Applying the ink with small cotton balls covered with fine silk or with a small silk square wrapped around her thumb, she gently dabbed inch by inch, coaxing the image into being. Sometimes it took thousands of applications before the result was sufficiently dark. Once the ink and paper dried, she'd peel the rubbing off the stone.

"The first ones I did I didn't like, so I tore them up and burned them," says Robertson, but by the end of that second summer at Tikal she had completed dozens. Kidder encouraged her once again. "He said 'Merle,

go up into the jungles and do everything at all these sites up and down the [Usumacinta] river.' And I did. And that was really, really great." She traveled by mule, foot, and dugout canoe, searching out ruins known only to jungle residents or to Mayanists familiar with the forest. Side by side with a small team of workers who cut trails and set up camp, she struggled with heat, snakes, dirty water, and voracious insects. With her enormous sheets of paper, stored in Bakelite cases, she could pack little more than a change of clothes, Halzone pills to treat muddy swamp water, and a few cans of freeze-dried food. She enjoyed eating from the jungle's menu: stewed monkey, roast boar, armadillo, fish, and frog.

Robertson loved the jungle and its endless spectacle of birds and flowers, and its hidden trove of art. Many of the carvings, overgrown or face down in the mud, had not been touched for centuries. With a thin, green stick, its end feathered with a knife, she would gently scrape off moss and roots that shrouded a carving, then repeatedly rinse it with water from nearby waterholes or streams. "Finally you get it clean, and then you have to wait, sometimes days for it to dry before you can even start doing the rubbing," she says.

Many rubbings became endurance tests. Robertson spent three weeks deep inside Palenque's Temple of the Inscriptions, recording the elaborate sarcophagus that shows King Pakal (K'inich Janahb' Pakal) at the moment of his death, sliding down the world tree into Xibalba, the underworld. Each day she climbed the seven-story pyramid and descended the interior vaulted staircase into the dank crypt to work by lantern, often up to her ankles in water. "I would come out of the tomb completely soaked and covered from head to toe with wet, white, lime plaster," she says. She made 220 square feet of rubbings there and lost ten pounds.

Born in Miles City, Montana, as a child she loved watching her neighbor and hero, the famous western artist Charles Russell, paint his evocative canvases of cowboys, Native Americans, and the open plains. Robertson went on to become an artist herself; she has worked in 23 countries and has had major exhibitions of her paintings in six. After studying art at the University of Washington, San Francisco State College, and the University of California, she received her M.F.A. from the University of Guanajuato, in 1963— her thesis topic was Maya art—and in 1987, she received an honorary doctorate from Tulane University, where she currently serves as research associate at the Middle American Research Institute.

In 1965, Robertson began teaching art at Robert Louis Stevenson School for Boys in Monterey, California. Her husband Bob, the school's dean, often accompanied her each summer when she took her students into the jungle to conduct fieldwork. "She was like a den mother squiring us all around," recalls Arlen Chase, one of five students who went with the Robertsons to Ixtutz in the Petén, Guatemala, in 1971. Robertson had learned about the site from her crew of local work-ers; it was unknown to Guatemalan authorities and not on any map. The group slashed its way through deep jungle at the foot of the Maya Mountains, through vines so dense that they had to be cut away before the team could put down their packs. There they discovered stelae, plazas, and a terraced acropolis. "It was just a fabulous experience," says Chase. "We got in there, we made a preliminary map, we found new inscriptions, and she did rubbings of the inscriptions as well as the stelae. It was quite exciting."

Robertson inspired Chase to become an archaeologist himself. "She baited the hook," he says, and for that he dedicated his doctoral dissertation to her. With his wife Diane, Chase now heads the excavation of Caracol, a powerful Maya city in western Belize that was once home to an estimated 140,000 people and covered more than 120 square miles.

> Robertson's ambition was to record the art of the Maya world before it disappeared.

Robertson's ambition was to record the art of the Maya world before it disappeared. From her first days at Tikal, she had witnessed newly excavated monuments, long shrouded in dirt or tree roots, begin to crumble when exposed to the sun and deteriorate in the region's acid rain. Algae growing on the monuments softens the stone, allowing small insects to bore into the carvings. Tikal's Altar 5, for example, was in perfect condition when she made her first rubbing. Now the carving has eroded away. "Have you seen it today?" Robertson asks.

PLATE 2: *Plaster cast of a maguey plant exca-vated at Cerén. A double strand of two-ply braided twine made of maguey fiber, lower right, was also replicated by casting.*

PLATE 1: *An aerial view of the sixth-century site of Cerén, a rural village on the periphery of the ancient Maya world.*

PLATE 3: *Cast of a mature chili pepper bush from Cerén, one of three in the garden of a sin-gle household.*

PLATE 4: *A photograph taken by a looter show the facade being removed for shipment. Remains of the temple from which the sculptured panel was taken, as well as the airstrip used for its transport, have been found at the site of Placeres, 35 miles south-east of Calakmul.*

PLATE 5: *The facade as it currently appears in the National Museum of Anthropology in Mexico City.*

PLATE 6: *Another photo taken by a looter shows the facade in situ.*

PLATE 7: *The facade as it appeared before being stolen and offered for sale in New York.*

PLATE 8: *Temple 216 at the abandoned city of Yaxhá.*

PLATE 9 & 10: *An infrared satellite image of Temple 216 at Yaxhá (left). Researchers (right) use such imagery to locate hidden sites in the* bajos.

"It's terrible. You look at it now, and you can't even see it."

Discoveries brought another threat. Wealthy collectors developed a taste for Maya art, prompting waves of theft that continue to this day. Robertson sometimes arrived at sites a step behind the thieves, finding stelae cut in pieces, their carvings sliced away. In 1970, she and her students were returning to their jeep from a muddy jungle trail in Guatemala. "I had just taken my boots off, ready to get in, when these guys came out of the jungle with sawed-off shotguns and pointed them right at our stomachs." Robertson showed them her permit, and they waved the group on. When she reported the incident, the police deduced they were looters from her description of their soft, city hands. They captured the men, threw them in jail for two days, then advised Robertson to flee—if the thieves wanted revenge, Robertson would be easy to track since "there was no one up and down the river with blonde hair except for

Prize Palenque Finds

Recent excavations on the jungle-cloaked South Acropolis at the Late Classic (ca. A.D. 379–799) Maya city of Palenque in Chiapas, Mexico, have yielded a tomb decorated with the first painted murals ever found at the site, a 12-foot-tall sculptured support pier bearing the portrait of a king, and a limestone throne inscribed with more than 200 glyphs.

Project codirector Alfonso Morales and field director Christopher Powell of Mexico's Instituto Nacional de Antropología e Historia found the tomb while investigating anomalies detected using ground-penetrating radar atop an unexcavated pyramid known as temple XX. "Our first clue that this was a tomb," says project codirector Merle Greene Robertson of the San Francisco-based Pre-Columbian Art Research Institute (PARI), "came when we found the capstone shortly after we began digging a test trench. We removed the capstone and peered inside. With the aid of a flashlight, we could see that the walls were decorated with murals, which include an image of God K, the celestial lightning god. Eleven intact pottery vessels and numerous pieces of jade were scattered about the chamber floor." Excavation and stabilization of the tomb is likely to take several months.

Work undertaken in a nearby mound, known as temple XIX, yielded a 12-foot-tall sculptured support pier with portraits of a ruler and his subjects, and a rectangular bench or platform, possibly a throne, which is in pristine condition save for a break in the center of one side. Carved on the sides of the platform, which measures five by nine feet, are 12 figures and more than 200 glyphs. The figure depicted on the front is Kinich Ahkal Mo' Nab, ruler of Palenque from ca. A.D. 721 to 764. The inscription tells us that the king was an incarnation of an important primordial Maya god, whom scholars call GI and who, according to the newfound inscription, began his mythical reign on March 10, 3309 B.C.

"We have found what is perhaps the most important Maya inscription to come along in years," says project epigrapher David Stuart. "It records mythological history before the birth of the site's three patron gods, known as the Palenque Triad. Moreover, it underscores the importance of a king's relationship to the site's founding deities."

On the floor of temple XIX, archaeologists found part of what may be a second pier with the head of an important person, perhaps a ruler, beautifully carved in limestone. For more information on recent work on the South Acropolis, visit PARI's web page: www.mesoweb.com.

—ANGELA M.H. SCHUSTER

me." At midnight, they packed their bags, hopped into a truck the police had provided, and fled to Naranjo, a site near the Belize border.

In time, Robertson's rubbings will be the only evidence that many of these masterpieces ever existed. Two thousand of them are archived at Tulane University's Latin American Library in New Orleans, where, protected in polyethylene and climate-controlled storage, they are available for study. These rubbings are "a corpus of data which is crucial and still will be 100 years from now," says Chase. "They would be almost impossible for anybody else to duplicate."

In her book *The Sculpture of Palenque*, Robertson writes, "If one city can be spoken of as the most exquisite, the 'jewel of the Maya realm,' it is Palenque. Approaching the city early on a misty morning, with the sun just beginning to penetrate the mist hanging over the delicate Palenque roofcombs, one is forced to stop and take in this overpowering beauty for a moment lest it escape forever. The Maya are known for having picked many beautifully situated places for their cities, but at Palenque they seem to have found everything."

Robertson first visited Palenque in 1960, when a single jeep was the town's taxi, and the road to the ruins was a muddy rut. She returned so often that in 1970, the Robertsons built Na Chan-Bahlum at the edge of the modern village, five miles from the ruins. "Every place is really special for one thing," says Robertson. "Yaxchilán is noted for its beautiful lintels, Tikal for its stelae, and Copán for the sculpture all over its buildings and its stelae. But Palenque is the place that has the finest portraiture of any place and the finest stucco sculpture."

Between jungle trips, Robertson documented Palenque's fragile sculpture, carvings, and paintings. She took photographs from tall scaffolding, and studied and sketched for hours. The result, *The Sculpture of Palenque*, is a multivolume work that minutely examines Palenque's most important structures. The first volume was published in 1983, and Robertson is now preparing the series' fifth, which will include finds from recently discovered temples, sculptures in foreign museums and collections, and the multitude of figurines found at the site. Archaeological investigation at Palenque continues to thrive with support from the Precolumbian Art Research Institute (PARI), a nonprofit corporation operated under the direction of Robertson, who started it with her husband in 1971. Alfonso Morales, chief archaeologist of PARI's Palenque Project, grew up a few houses away from Robertson on Calle Merle Greene; his father was Palenque's head guide.

Na Chan-Bahlum quickly became what archaeologist Michael Coe calls "a Mecca for Palencophiles," its doors open to both professionals and amateurs under the Maya spell. Robertson's husband Bob was a laid-back yin to her energetic yang. He would gently screen each visitor, guarding Robertson from unnecessary interruptions. One enthralled amateur was Linda Schele, who returned again and again, eventually becoming Robertson's assistant, best friend, and one of the leading Mayanists of her time (see page 126, *The Glyph Decoder*).

Maya dates deciphered decades ago revealed that Palenque flourished between

A.D. 440 and 790, but almost all other Maya inscriptions resisted translation. By the late 1960s, four Palenque rulers had been identified, yet were known only as A, B, C, and D. Progress had stalled. Epigraphy was "in the doldrums," recalls Chase. Then along came Robertson, whose interest in art history, he says, "actually brought epigraphy back to life."

One evening in August 1973, says Robertson, "a bunch of us were sitting on the porch here having a beer. We thought, 'wouldn't it be fun to have a group interested in Palenque come down and meet?'" Maya studies was still a small field: they could think of only about three dozen people to invite.

The response was quick. Back in California that September, "I hadn't gotten my jacket off and the phone was ringing," Robertson recalls. La Primera Mesa Redonda de Palenque—the First Palenque Round Table—convened at Na Chan-Bahlum that Christmas vacation. It was an unprecedented gathering of art historians, epigraphers, and archaeologists, as much a reunion of friends as a scholarly conference. Word spread. Students from Mexican universities began to arrive, and local townspeople showed up.

One afternoon epigraphers Floyd Lounsbury, Peter Mathews, and Schele sat down at Robertson's kitchen table, hoping to expand on the list of known Palenque rulers. In less than four hours, studying drawings of the inscriptions, the work of their predecessors, and their own research, they deciphered the names, accession dates, and deaths of the last 200 years of Palenque's royal family. That night, the trio presented their timeline to the round table, and Lady Sak K'uk' who ruled for nearly 30 years, her son Pakal, and his son Chan Bahlum were reintroduced to the world. The anonymous carved faces and the bodies in the tombs suddenly "had become real people, real kings who lived and ruled the city where we had come to study," Robertson wrote in her introduction to the proceedings of the Sixth Palenque Round Table Conference, held in 1986. A cascade of discoveries followed, unveiling five centuries of Palenque's history and a new picture of the Maya, a civilization immersed in war, human sacrifice, and mystical rituals.

Robertson has never pursued publicity; her contributions to the field speak for themselves. In 1994, the Mexican government awarded her its highest honor for a noncitizen, the Order of the Aztec Eagle, for her efforts to preserve and document fragile Mesoamerican art. "I was so overwhelmed by the fact that Mexico was honoring me this way that I was almost in tears," she remembers. "But I was extremely happy and grateful to all of Mexico, a country I had come to love so much." ▲

19

THE MAVERICK MAYANIST

Ian Graham's crusade to record every known Maya monument has earned him a place in the constellation of great Mesoamerican explorers.

by JOHN DORFMAN and ANDREW L. SLAYMAN

ON JUNE 28, 1959, A 35-YEAR-OLD SCOTSMAN stood drinking a Coke at a snack bar in Sayaxché, a frontier settlement in the Petén jungle of northern Guatemala. An amateur photographer, he was hoping to scare up material for a coffee-table book on the ancient Maya, and the shopkeeper offered to show him some ruins he had seen while hunting monkeys. The next morning, in a driving rain, the two of them climbed into a small motorized canoe and headed ten miles up the Río Petexbatún, then across a lake and a short distance up a stream. What happened next is still fresh in Ian Graham's mind:

We got out of the boat and climbed up a steep escarpment on the top of which there was a great ravine with little bridges across it, and there were some ruins. I'd read enough to know the site was unknown. There stood a small stela draped in philodendron and shaded with palms, the most amazing sight to me. That was the first Maya monument that I ever, as it were, discovered.

On the stela, a Maya priest-king posed in a feathered headdress, a buck-toothed skull staring out from the center of his breastplate. Above the figure were rectangles packed with tiny shapes coiled tightly against each other; some resembled gesturing hands or grotesque humanoid heads, while others appeared quite abstract.

A little further on, there were these fallen monoliths, some of them with sculpture on the upper surface still more or less preserved. Some had uncarved surfaces on top, but when I put my fingers underneath I could feel the sharp grooves of sculpture. That was really the crucial moment; I mean, this was just simply a boy's romance of discovery. Here was a great monument presumably carved in curious figures and writings which nobody had seen for a thousand years. It was irresistible.

Since that day, Graham has done more than any other person to save the fragile written record of the ancient Maya from destruction by looters, harsh weather, and acid rain. He has been painstakingly recording monuments in the jungles of Mexico, Guatemala, and Belize, and since 1975 publishing them in an ongoing series of folio volumes titled the *Corpus of Maya Hieroglyphic Inscriptions.* Paperbound in crimson covers, these volumes contain black-and-white photographs and line drawings of the carvings, and a map and brief description of

each site. The ultimate goal of the *Corpus,* based at Harvard University's Peabody Museum of Archaeology and Ethnology, is the documentation of all Maya inscriptions. Although Graham is far too modest to put it this way, he is very much like the scribes of the Middle Ages: As they preserved the writings of the classical world with quill and parchment, he is saving, with camera and drafting pen, the only historical record of the Precolumbian world. In recognition of his efforts "preserving and cataloguing Maya relics," Graham won a prestigious MacArthur Foundation "genius" award in 1981, the first year they were given out.

Graham still divides his time between the Peabody, the house in England where he was born, and the field. He spent this past spring wrapping up work at several sites in Yucatán and the Petén. His Central American base is a bungalow he built in the 1970s in San Andrés, Guatemala. Nearby, in the middle of Lake Petén Itzá, is the island town of Flores, which was the last bastion of the last independent Maya kingdom, the Itzá, until its defeat by the Spaniards in 1697. Although gracious from the outside, Graham's house is barely furnished, a single room divided by wooden partitions, with a porch overlooking the sapphire lake. A tough, spare figure with bright blue eyes and a full head of gray hair, Graham moves about with ease, carrying water from the well and firing up the gasoline-powered generator that is the only source of electricity. Each evening, he observes a genteel cocktail hour on the verandah with a drink he concocts from local rum, lime juice, and tonic water.

It is a warm, clear day in mid-March, and Graham has only one week to get to the site of El Perú (35 miles away as the crow flies) for his fifth and final visit, finish his work there, and get back in time to meet a friend in Cancún. Up at 5:00 A.M., we set out for the neighboring town of San Benito in a 25-year-old Land Rover to pick up Graham's longtime assistant, Anatolio López Pérez, a former guard at Río Azul and other sites in the Petén. The first stage of the journey is a 40-mile drive (about an hour) over dirt roads to the rustic outpost of Centro Campesino. It is the dry season, and the tires of passing cars kick up choking clouds of dust. From Centro Campesino, we must bounce for nine miles along a rutted track cut through scrubby brush to a landing on the bank of a nameless tributary of the Río San Pedro, normally a one-and-a-half-hour drive. But the Land Rover's four-wheel drive is not working, and the vehicle gets stuck in a nasty hole. Graham wrestles with the gearshift—but it breaks off in his hand. Calmly he reaches behind the seat for his tool bag, pulls up the floorboards and gearbox cowling, and soon has a vise grip on the broken stump to serve as a shift lever. Within an hour we are creeping back to San Andrés, and the day is lost.

At the house, Graham cannibalizes a gearshift from another Land Rover, but he lacks the parts to repair the aged vehicle's four-wheel drive. The next morning we rent a Toyota pickup with a functioning four-wheel drive, and by midday we are back at the scene of the previous day's debacle. The pickup easily negotiates the pitfall, passing beneath a hanging branch that Graham dubs a "triumphal arch." When we get to the landing, the motor launch he ordered is nowhere to be seen; there is only a heavy old red and yellow rowboat tethered to a tree, with a single paddle. Graham is unfazed, and we follow him into the boat. Anatolio starts rowing; soon Graham, preternaturally fit for a 73-year-old, takes over. Before long we hear a motor in the distance; it is the launch, which takes us on board, turning what would have been a three-hour ordeal into a half-hour spin on the tributary and then the San Pedro itself.

From the dock to the ruins of El Perú is an hour and a half's walk on a trail through the dense forest of rubber trees, hanging lianas, and giant ceiba trees. Spider monkeys rustle the branches overhead, and the quiet is broken now and then by the squawking of a scarlet macaw or the unearthly roar of howler monkeys. Little seems to have changed in the land of the Maya since 1840, when John Lloyd Stephens, a New York lawyer, was sent by President Van Buren to find out whether the Central American Federation (an abortive attempt to unify the region) still existed. In his immensely popular *Incidents of Travel in Central America, Chiapas, and Yucatan* (1841), Stephens wrote, "The country through which we were now travelling was as wild as before the Spanish con-

> ## Graham was trained as a physicist, not an archaeologist, and this knowledge has come in handy.

quest…a forest so overgrown with brush and underwood as to be impenetrable." Shortly before sunset, we reach our camp, in a clearing halfway from the river to El Perú. Graham starts taking his gear from antique packing cases made of sturdy varnished cardboard trimmed with brass, a legacy of earlier Peabody expeditions. We hang our hammocks and mosquito nets under a champa, a thatched roof on poles. Unlike warier gringos, Graham quenches his thirst directly from a nearby stream; he also regards mosquito repellent as a nostrum for the weak. Later we cook Spam, black beans, and maize tortillas over an open fire in the site guards' makeshift wooden house. Graham chats in Spanish with the guards until the gas lamp burns out, and by 9:00 P.M. we are all asleep.

Ian Graham corrects a field drawing of hieroglyphs at El Perú, Guatemala.

The next morning we hike 45 minutes to the site itself, an important Maya city-state from A.D. 300 to 700. The only traces of its once-formidable architecture are hundreds of low mounds scattered across the rain-forest floor, many barely visible to the untutored eye. No palaces, no pyramids remain to be seen. A few round altars survive intact, but everywhere shattered stelae litter the ground, the detritus left by looters. Like many Maya sites, El Perú was plundered in the 1960s. The thieves were usually woodsmen who had started out as chicleros, collectors of tree sap for chewing-gum companies. Known locally as *huecheros* after the Maya word for the armadillo, which scrapes the ground with its front claws when foraging for food, they would butcher the monuments with hand saws or smash them with sledgehammers, then slice off the carved surfaces. Dismembered, the stones were more easily hauled out of the jungle and smuggled abroad. Two stelae from El Perú are now in the Cleveland Museum of Art and the Kimbell Art Museum in Fort Worth.

Graham sends Anatolio and Manuel, one of the guards, to cut stout branches for levers. The three men then insert them under stela fragments and heave them into a standing position. Graham was trained as a physicist, not as an archaeologist, and from time to time this education comes in handy. By using various configurations of levers, ropes, and winches, he has been able to raise whole stelae weighing a ton or more by himself. The next job is cleaning off the moss and dirt. Graham and his assistants wash the newly raised stones with water, pouring it over the surfaces and cleaning them with paintbrushes. Then they use stiff palm stalks to scrape out the grooves in the carvings. "That's coming up really nicely," says Graham in his crisp Oxbridge accent. "This reads nine *baktuns* [400-year calendrical periods]. This is the number of katuns [20-year periods]; they can't be higher than five because of space." Pointing to another specimen, Anatolio exclaims, "*Puros glifos— Que finos, que lindos!*" ("Pure glyphs—How fine, how beautiful.")

Now Graham photographs the stones using his Hasselblad, with a separate flash unit set atop a tripod positioned to one side, so that its light rakes across the monument's face at a low angle, increasing the contrast and improving the legibility of the low-relief carvings. When photographing large sculptures at other sites, he must make sure that the film is parallel to the stone's face to eliminate even the slightest foreshortening. With his usual mechanical ingenuity, Graham has devised a simple technique: He hangs a small mirror on the surface of the monument, then positions the camera to get the reflection of the lens centered precisely in the viewfinder.

Often the subtleties of a glyph or figurative design do not show up well on film but can be read only by studying the actual monument, feeling its surfaces with one's fingers. Only field drawings can capture these features, and Graham executes them with great care. He has brought preliminary drawings of many of the carvings to El Perú, and, with a looseleaf notebook on his lap, he fills in missing details and makes corrections.

Glyphs drawn swiftly in ballpoint on paper contrast oddly with their ancient counterparts, carved laboriously in limestone with obsidian or basalt chisels. Often Graham examines inscriptions at night by artificial light, which can bring out details hard to see in the diffuse daylight that filters through the forest canopy.

After three days of work at El Perú, we pack up. Graham has not fully recorded the site, but he knows he never can. Many of its monuments have been broken into fragments too small and too widely scattered ever to be reassembled. Graham does, however, have one pet project in mind: In a European museum is the looted top portion of El Perú stela 39. This monument was sawn into blocks, its carvings sliced off and most of them carried away. Some of the carved pieces, along with uncarved blocks from the core of the stone, were left at the site. The pattern of cuts and natural irregularities in the stone gave Graham clues about how they might fit together. He took photographs of the broken blocks and, on paper, pieced as much of the stela together as he could. Using this as a guide, he hopes eventually to reassemble the stones at the site into a standing mockup of the gutted stela, to be called the Monument to the Unknown Looter.

Back in Cambridge, Graham will develop and print his photographs, do the final drawings and maps, and write the descriptive text. His base there is a fifth-floor aerie at the Peabody Museum, overlooking a leafy cul-de-sac well away from the bustle of Harvard Square. On the wall above his desk hangs a large, nineteenth-century lithograph of a brightly colored quetzal bird, sacred to the Maya. A locked metal cabinet houses his collection of rare books and manuscripts, including letters and memorabilia of Alfred P. Maudslay, a Victorian scholar and explorer who was the first to try to document Maya inscriptions systematically. On a drafting table is a work in progress: a drawing of a stela at Piedras Negras, in Guatemala, executed in ink on a two-by-three-foot sheet of Mylar.

Not all of the photographs in the *Corpus* are the product of Graham's own fieldwork. Sometimes he has to use photos of plaster casts, or images that he has managed to obtain of monuments in private collections. (Once he even used a photocopy when nothing else was available.) Pictures taken by Graham's two past assistants, Eric von Euw (who worked on the *Corpus* in the 1970s) and Peter Mathews (early 1980s), are included. Also scattered throughout the volumes are photographs from the Peabody's vast collections, perhaps 50,000 images that constitute a near monopoly of archival-quality negatives of Maya sculpture. Among these are many nineteenth- and early twentieth-century photographs that preserve now-vanished inscriptions, including more than a hundred by the photographic pioneer Teobert Maler, who at the turn of the century traveled through Central America taking pictures of ruins (see ARCHAEOLOGY, September/October 1990). Graham would like some day to make these photos more readily available via the Internet or on CD-ROM.

Graham has had to be a cartographer as well. Though by his own estimate only about 20 of the more than 240 known Maya sites with inscriptions have been adequately mapped, he does not insist on the same exacting standard in mapmaking that he adheres to in transcribing hieroglyphs. The site plans in the *Corpus* serve mainly to show the monuments' locations rather than to depict precisely the size and shape of every building; making a better map he regards as the duty of archaeologists who may work there later. Surveying ceremonial centers several square miles in size entails trudging through the bush with a transit on a tripod slung over one's shoulder. At Uxmal, to save six months, Graham made a composite map based partly on the efforts of earlier surveyors and partly on his own work; at other sites he has had to content himself with compass-and-tape surveys. Despite their flaws, his maps are often the best available. They also have the same meticulous look as his drawings of glyphs, and his chief worry is that this appearance of accuracy might deter future mapmakers from improving upon them. As a reminder to his successors, Graham is careful always to include what he calls, laughingly, an *"apologia pro charta sua."*

When drawing hieroglyphs, Graham usually goes through four drafts before arriving at the finished product. Linda Schele of the University of Texas at Austin, an epigrapher who got her start as an artist, says, "Ian has set the standard for what good drawing is. All of us follow his standard." If a photograph of a monument already exists, Graham traces it quickly in soft pencil on paper. This drawing goes with him into the field, where he corrects it in hard pencil by looking at the monument itself. Then he erases the soft pencil marks, leaving those made by the hard pencil behind. In his office, he will enlarge the best available photograph of the monument to twice publication size. He will trace this photograph with a drafting pen on a transparent sheet of acetate, which allows easy correction by scraping off the dried ink with a razor blade. He will refine the ink drawing, referring to his field drawings and other photographs. Then he will affix a sheet of translucent Mylar to the acetate and trace the entire drawing in ink one last time. Finally he will add stippling to help the reader's eye distinguish between the foreground and background of a relief. This is tedious work. "You need to have something of a totally bovine nature like me," he says with a smile, "to go all the time, dot dot dot dot *dot*. I sometimes find myself stippling insanely in time with the oom pah pah on the radio."

When monuments are badly weathered, Graham uses dotted lines to show where he is less sure of his reading. "My job is to show what can't be read as well as what can," he explains. In a 1980 review in the journal *American Antiquity*, James A. Fox of Stanford University criticized the *Corpus* for its generally conservative readings, asserting that the drawings showed no more detail than the photographs alongside them. But Graham believes it is important to record eroded hieroglyphs as impartially as possible to avoid reading into an inscription something that is not there. Epigraphers in search of what Fox called more "daring" readings may take advantage of Graham's invitation, in the introduction to the *Corpus*, to visit the Peabody and examine the original materials.

When drawing hieroglyphs, Graham usually goes through four drafts.

In the same conservative spirit, Graham decided to omit translations of hieroglyphic texts from the *Corpus*. "Anything that one could translate now, in three years, five years, ten years would be hopelessly out of date," he says. "Interpretations have no place in the *Corpus*." David Stuart, a master epigrapher who is Graham's current collaborator, agrees, but he envisions the *Corpus* growing beyond the "big red books." More interpretive works, perhaps including a dictionary of Classic Mayan, which Stuart is compiling, might be published under the umbrella of the *Corpus* but outside the current series of volumes. Jeremy A. Sabloff, the director of the University of Pennsylvania Museum of Archaeology and Anthropology, voices a sentiment common among Mayanists: "Ian has a deep and rich understanding of ancient Maya civilization. I would like to see him write down more of his interpretations. The *Corpus* is not the place for that, but it would be unfortunate for the field if he did not utilize the vast empirical knowledge he has accumulated."

All Mayanists agree on the importance of Graham's work. In the years since the *Corpus* was conceived, scholars have gone from being able to read about ten percent of the hieroglyphs to as much as 70 percent. "The *Corpus* project was driving the decipherment," says Stuart. "In epigraphy, the more examples you have, the faster it goes. Only by the mid-seventies did scholars have hundreds of texts to work with, due primarily to

Ian." Schele agrees, noting the "kind of democratic access to the material" that the *Corpus* provides. "This access is one of two major factors that have opened up epigraphy," she says. "The other is copy machines." So far, 16 volumes of the *Corpus* have appeared, covering 17 sites, and there are about 220 sites to go. Of these, Graham has the raw materials for about 30; most of the rest have hardly any inscriptions. After Graham retires, Stuart will take over. "I have a feeling the *Corpus* will last far beyond my days," says Stuart. "It's one of those projects that will take decades to complete."

IAN GRAHAM WAS BORN IN 1923 IN THE tiny village of Campsey Ash, in Suffolk, England, where his father, a younger son of a Scottish duke, was a farmer. He can claim descent from both King Charles I and his executioner, Oliver Cromwell, whose shrivelled, embalmed head he was shown as a child. (After the restoration of the monarchy, Cromwell's body was exhumed and hanged from the gallows at Tyburn, in London, then taken down and decapitated. His head was impaled on a spike and exhibited for a while at Westminster Hall, and eventually found its way into the hands of a village parson near Graham's home.) Although Graham calls himself a country boy, technology has always been his ruling passion. He learned about mechanics and workshop practice from a handyman, radio electronics from the parson, and photography from his nanny. By the time he was 11, he was a published photographer, a picture of his church's nativity play having appeared in a local newspaper. At 13, he was sent to Winchester, a boarding school established in the fourteenth century, where

he found the routine stifling and, by his own admission, did little good. He did, however, build himself a radio—an activity forbidden to students—which he traded to the captain of the cricket team in exchange for absolution from the hated game. Like many boys he was fascinated by fireworks and explosives, but instead of just buying them he made his own; at one point he even built a functioning .22 pistol using a length of copper pipe for the barrel.

In 1942 he went on to Trinity College, Cambridge, where he took courses in physics, but the war interrupted his studies. He joined the Royal Navy in 1943 and was assigned to a secret installation called the Telecommunications Research Establishment. There he helped develop a radar navigation system for aircraft and even "lent a hand soldering" the famous Colossus, an electronic protocomputer used to crack the Geheimschreiber, Hitler's most sophisticated cipher. After the war, Graham resumed his studies at Trinity College, Dublin, and earned his bachelor's degree in 1951. The same year, he accepted a fellowship from the Nuffield Foundation to study techniques of art restoration at the National Gallery.

THE KEY TO HIS FUTURE AS A MAYANIST turned out to be, of all things, a car. "One day in 1955, walking in London not far from Piccadilly," he recalls, "I saw looking at me out of a commercial garage the most extraordinarily beautiful, lean, sporting Rolls-Royce with bodywork coming to a point at the tail and flared fenders, which I just fell in love with." The car was a 1927 Phantom I, and it was for sale. Seduced by this "beguiling creature," Graham devised a plan: He would somehow scrape together the cash, buy the car, keep it in London as long as he could afford to, then ship it to New York, drive it to Hollywood, and sell it to an American millionaire at a handsome profit. He put his plan into action. In 1958, after spending a few months in New York (where the car lived better in a Park Avenue garage than he did in the 23rd Street YMCA), he set out for California. But distractions soon presented themselves: "I thought, 'Oh yes, that invitation to the hunt ball in Maryland does sound rather nice.' So that was my first straying from the true path." A couple of weeks later he was in Texas, where he saw a gas station sign saying, "Last gas before Mexico." So he thought to himself, "Ah, Mexico, that's an idea."

In Mexico City, he drifted into the National Museum, where in one gallery he saw Aztec art, which was familiar to him but not particularly appealing.

"Then I went to the next gallery," he says, where there was totally different stuff by these guys called the Maya. I knew absolutely zero, zilch, nothing about the Maya. I mean those four letters M-A-Y-A were completely unknown to me. So I went to a bookstore to see what there was in the way of well-illustrated books and found that there didn't seem to be any that covered the whole Maya area. Since I was at a loose end, being unemployed, and this was the heyday of the coffee-table book, I thought, "Why don't I have a crack at it myself?"

The seed was planted, but Graham still had to unload the Rolls. He pressed on, spent a night in the Nogales, Arizona, jail on a vagrancy charge (he had only $24 in his pocket), eventually reached California, and sold the car for a profit, albeit a small one.

Graham went back to England. He read up on his quarry in the British Museum, then set off once more for Mayaland "with a couple of cameras and lots of film and one spare shirt." At the end of his trip, after wandering around for nine months or so, he found himself drinking that Coke in Sayaxché and going to some ruins that came to be known as Aguateca. He could spend only one day there, but he was back the next year, long enough to produce a three-page report for the *Illustrated London News*. He never did publish a coffee-table book on the Maya; instead, he compiled his drawings, photos, and findings from Aguateca and five other sites into his first scholarly work, *Archaeological Explorations in El Peten, Guatemala*, which appeared in 1967.

In the meantime he eked out a living as an odd-job photographer. The pay was not good, and once he even had to sell a valuable antique camera to make ends meet. In New York, he worked briefly as an assistant to the photographer Irving Penn, relegated to shooting lemon meringue pies instead of gorgeous models. He also took the pictures for two sumptuous if not very substantive volumes: *Great Houses of the Western World* (1968), an "architectural anthology...of sophisticated housing" in Europe and the United States, by Nigel Nicolson; and *Splendours of the East* (1965), a tour of Asian temples, tombs, and palaces, edited by the archaeologist Mortimer Wheeler. The latter project gave Graham the opportunity to play a prank on the eminent Sir Mortimer. Turning in a portfolio of photographs of Asian monuments, he included a picture he had once taken on the Jungle River Cruise at

Disneyland, showing what looked like a Bodhisattva statue in front of a Khmer temple. Picking this one out of the bunch, Wheeler exclaimed, "Oh splendid, this, splendid! Yes, we might consider this for the cover." But in the end it was not used.

During the 1960s, Graham spent as much time as he could roaming Mesoamerica, photographing and drawing monuments at a number of Maya sites. In May 1962, he set off from Poptún, in the southern Petén, to a site that he named Machaquilá after a nearby river, not long after Hurricane Hattie had clogged the route through the forest with fallen trees. It took 27 days to hack 50 miles through the jungle—a three-day walk under the best of circumstances—fending off mutiny from mules and guides all the way. By day 13 he was reduced to passing spare time trying, as he wrote in his journal, "to decipher Chinese hieroglyphics, using Quaker Oats tin as Rosetta Stone. (It has instructions in 6 languages.)" In these early days, before the invention of global positioning systems, which read latitude and longitude from radio signals broadcast from satellites, Graham was often forced to calculate the locations of sites by dead reckoning. On the trail back, he would try to walk at a constant speed, reading his compass once every minute and marking his direction in a pocket notebook. Later he would use those figures to try to reconstruct where he had been.

To some extent, Graham still suffers from a syndrome he criticizes in his Winchester classmates: wanting never to seem to try. Though his tales can give the impression of a life lived by graceful accident, in fact Graham has faced great hardships. Not only were there physical obstacles to surmount,

but many university-trained archaeologists were suspicious of his early efforts. On one occasion, he dragged tubs of latex into the bush to make molds of sculptures at Aguateca, which he later showed to a prominent American archaeologist. "I did not get a good reception," Graham recalls.

He said, "You don't seem to understand that here you've been messing around with these ruins and what we archaeologists are always trying to find are virgin ruins." I said "Well, you know, ruins are rather like young ladies: You have to look for them." They never had, you see.

In England, Graham wrote out of the blue to J. Eric S. Thompson, then considered the dean of Maya studies, describing what he was doing. Instead of suspicion or dismissal, Graham got a positive response, and he and Thompson became good friends. Gordon R. Willey of the Peabody Museum, who was directing excavations at the site of Altar de Sacrificios in the southwestern Petén, also offered encouragement, and gave Graham his first opportunity to work with archaeologists. The two men met in Sayaxché in 1960 and saw each other occasionally until 1964, when Willey invited Graham to act as surveyor for a new project at Seibal, near Altar de Sacrificios. "To my astonishment," says Graham,

Willey asked if I would do the job, so I said, "Well, I'll give it a try." I went and bought the bible of surveyors, by two authors called Breed and Hosmer, the sort of book you would buy if you were going to survey Manhattan real estate at $10,000 a square meter. It had pictures of transits and all the multifarious knobs and crystals and so *on, but I didn't really absorb it. Then the time came and I presented myself at Altar de Sacrificios, and at some point Gordon said, "Well, Ian, here's the transit you'll be using," and produced this nice mahogany box which had seen service in Panama '09 and Uaxactún '26. So I opened it up rather apprehensively and said, "Aha, it's got one of these, good." Then we all set off the next day in a big canoe. But halfway to Seibal—Gasp—Left the transit behind! That was definitely a Freudian slip.*

Luckily, Graham was able to have the transit sent along with the next boatload of supplies, and inexperience notwithstanding, he and two graduate students managed to produce a map of the site. "My picture of Ian is of a dedicated explorer-scholar," says Willey. "I have always been amazed at his rugged and fearless conquest of the Maya bush, so much of it accomplished virtually single-handed, especially in his early days."

Graham was not, however, working in a vacuum. Between 1952 and 1960, scholars had made three crucial breakthroughs in reading Maya hieroglyphs. In 1952 the Soviet epigrapher Yuri Knorosov had claimed that some elements of the glyphs were phonetic, though it was a number of years before his findings were taken seriously in the capitalist West (see page 137, *Triumph of Spirit*). In 1958 Heinrich Berlin, a retired German wholesale grocer with a keen interest in the Maya, suggested that certain glyphs, which he called emblem glyphs, stood for the names of individual cities or their ruling families. And in 1960 the Harvard Mayanist Tatiana Proskouriakoff published a paper in which she argued that the inscriptions recorded largely historical data rather than abstruse speculations about the stars.

Not long after these three discoveries launched modern scholarship on the inscriptions, the inscriptions themselves were imperiled by a big jump in the systematic looting of archaeological sites. Dealers raced to satisfy the appetites of private collectors and museums, mainly in the United States and Europe. All told, perhaps 100 large pieces were smuggled out of Central America in the 1960s.

The timing was therefore especially good when in 1968 Edgar H. Brenner, a Washington lawyer who had become fascinated by the Maya, conceived the idea of a systematic publication of the whole body of Maya inscriptions—along the lines of the *Corpus Inscriptionum Graecarum* (1828–present). Such a series would immensely aid scholars whose ability to read the hieroglyphs was getting better and better, and serve as a permanent record of monuments that might any day be destroyed or carried off. Brenner, a trustee of the Stella and Charles Guttman Foundation, offered to organize funding of a pilot study for such a publication. The Center for Inter-American Relations in New York formed a committee to plan the project, and perhaps through Thompson's good graces, Graham's name came to its attention. He was offered six months' salary. After preparing a spring-bound volume of sample pages with photographs and drawings, he turned in his study in September 1969. In 1970 the Peabody Museum offered the project a home, and the National Endowment for the Humanities pledged grants for the next two years. Graham took on von Euw as an assistant and went to work on what would become the *Corpus of Maya Hieroglyphic Inscriptions*.

At the same time, Graham was fighting the looters with more than just his pen and camera. In several instances, he helped police track them down, and his testimony led to two convictions. In 1971, Graham heard that a stela stolen from Machaquilá was for sale for $300,000 through a California dealer named Clive Hollinshead. With a colleague's help, he managed to inform the Department of Justice. Hollinshead's shop was raided, and he and a conspirator were convicted in federal court on charges of interstate transportation of stolen property. The judge imposed fines and probation, but neither man went to prison; the stela was turned over to the Guatemalans.

On a different occasion, working with a Canadian television station and posing as a reporter, Graham interviewed another major dealer in looted Maya art. Since Graham's picture had recently appeared on the front page of the *New York Times* in a story about looting, he decided to wear a disguise. "I went to three different places," he recalls, "trying to buy a sort of drippy hippie wig. Eventually I found the right place, where some of the rock musicians would buy their hairy appendages." At $300 apiece, though, the appendages in question were prohibitively expensive, so he had to settle for a simpler costume: "I laid hands on a pair of very large tortoise-shell spectacles, rubbed a lot of Pond's cold cream into my hair, parted it in the middle, and stuck on this false moustache. I tell you I

Not all of Graham's encounters with looters make for amusing stories.

looked like a perfect fright." Soon Graham was chatting with the dealer, when his wife remarked in passing, "Oh, of the archaeologists the worst of them is that Ian Graham." It got hotter and hotter under the television lamps, causing him to sweat. "I think you'd better excuse yourself and go to the bathroom," prompted one of the assistants. "There I saw that half of my moustache was falling off," says Graham, "and I had forgotten to bring spirit gum. Oh God, it was awful." Graham spent the rest of the interview with his hand posed contemplatively on his chin, holding up the drooping moustache with his index finger. He learned only later that the dealer and his wife had known who he was all along.

Not all of Graham's encounters with looters and their agents make for amusing stories. One afternoon in March 1971, as Robert Reinhold reported in the *Times* story, Graham and three guides were setting up camp at the site of La Naya in the eastern Petén, when they were ambushed by looters. One of the guides, Pedro Arturo Sierra del Valle, was shot, and died minutes later in Graham's arms. Graham and the other guides fled into the forest, where they spent a terrifying night lost without gear or provisions. Several months later, the police arrested a local deputy who admitted to the killing but denied being a looter; he was convicted of murder and sentenced to 20 years in prison.

Nowadays, although ceramics and other

small objects continue to come out of Central America, the looting of big sculpture is not as much of a problem. "There's not much point in my mounting my gleaming white charger and crashing about anymore," says Graham. "I'm a retired warrior from this fray." He explains that there is little left to take and that sites are better guarded than they used to be. Jeremy Sabloff attributes the progress made against looting over the past 20 years largely to Graham's efforts. "He was one of the very few voices in the seventies, but the cause has been picked up much more broadly," says Sabloff. "He was instrumental in educating the field and also government officials."

ALTHOUGH AN ENDEAVOR LIKE THE *Corpus of Maya Hieroglyphic Inscriptions* could easily consume every waking hour, Graham still finds time for a few serious avocations. Currently he is at work on two side projects: a book on the nineteenth-century Maltese painter Amedeo Preziosi and a biography of Alfred Maudslay. Several years ago, Graham came across a notebook of Preziosi's watercolors in the collection of a relative living in Australia. He was captivated by the intricate technique of these picturesque images of everyday life in Ottoman Turkey, Romania, and western Europe. Preziosi was never famous, but Graham thinks he should be. The book will consist of photographs of the artist's best work accompanied by several essays, including one by Donald Preziosi, a UCLA art historian who is a direct descendant of Amedeo. "I can't be too ambitious," says Graham, "because I'm stepping well outside my field." That he takes to Preziosi should surprise no one: The artist's work

bears striking similarities to that of another of Graham's heroes, Frederick Catherwood, an architect who perfected his own watercolor technique painting Near Eastern scenes and went on to illustrate John Lloyd Stephens' *Incidents of Travel*.

As for his other project, "Maudslay is a natural thing for me to do," says Graham, "in fact a slightly delicate thing, because it's very easy to identify oneself with one's biographee, especially if one is engaged in precisely the same kind of work." Born in 1850, the scion of a prominent English engineering and manufacturing family, Maudslay traveled widely in the colonial service. From 1881 to 1894 he amassed a huge collection of photographs and drawings of Maya ruins. Many of these superb images were published between 1889 and 1902 as part of a series titled *Biologia Centrali-Americana*, where they constituted the first attempt at a corpus of Maya inscriptions. Like Graham, Maudslay fell into Mayanism more or less by chance, and, also like Graham, he was strongly attracted to rough living among people far from his native milieu. Of his service in Fiji, Maudslay wrote, "I have myself had personal friends ...who had been notorious cannibals whom I found in other respects to be courtly gentlemen." Graham takes similar pleasure from the quiet straightforwardness and late-night tale-telling of Petenero frontiersmen, with whom he enjoys an easy friendship.

When asked what it is that keeps him going in the meticulous labor of the *Corpus*, Graham hints at a sense of historical mission: "It is stirred by the reflection that nobody has bothered to do this since Maudslay gave up in 1894." Graham seems to have a strong desire to be of service: He speaks of wanting to "do something useful," of the *Corpus* as "something which needed to be done." He seems also to have a need to subordinate himself to his work. In the introduction to the *Corpus*, he expressed a wish for anonymity worthy of a medieval scribe. "Here it is opportune to suggest," he wrote, "that in all references to the *Corpus*, the compilers' names be omitted and the abbreviation CMHI be used."

Graham is uncomfortable with broad questions like "What do Maya studies mean to you?" "For me it was just a game," he says. "It's a kind of stamp collecting, a matter of all the squares in the page." In general he distances himself from anything too abstract or philosophical, even if it means minimizing his own achievements. On occasion he will go so far as to disavow all lofty sentiments about preserving the past and claim that he started to record Maya glyphs only because he perceived an "empty niche" in the field. Graham's offhand manner is partly an aristocratic conceit, but partly a reflection of something genuine. "I'm glad I never went

to graduate school," he says. "If I had, I wouldn't be doing what I'm doing today." He explains that what he does, the impartial gathering of raw data, ceased to have a place in archaeology when it began to see itself as an experimental social science with testable hypotheses. "But fortunately I was ignorant of that, and went ahead and did it anyway," he says cheerfully.

Graham is in good company, for Mayanism has always attracted more than its fair share of talented amateurs. Berlin, Proskouriakoff, Maler, Stephens, Maudslay, and today Linda Schele—all were self-taught, all came to the work from other fields. Maya studies have profited immensely from the contributions of individualists and mavericks, and such people tend to defy classification. So the question poses itself: What is Ian Graham? Is he an archaeologist? A collector? A mere technician? More than anything else, he is what the writer Victor von Hagen called John Lloyd Stephens—a "Maya explorer," perhaps the last one there is, or ever can be. ≜

20

THE GLYPH DECODER

Pioneering epigrapher and scholar Linda Schele has helped shape a whole new vision of the humanity of the Maya.

by GILLETT GRIFFIN

THIRTY YEARS AGO, IT LOOKED AS IF THE DECIpherment of Maya hieroglyphs—one of the world's most intricate and difficult writing systems—was at an impasse. The ancient Maya were called "mysterious"; scholars disagreed on how to read Maya texts, and the foremost student of the field, J. Eric S. Thompson, painted a glowing picture of a peaceful people. The Maya, according to Thompson, were governed by astronomer-priests who were devoted to contemplating the stars and the endless flow of time.

Linda Schele blundered into this ostensibly idyllic world in 1970 with a vanful of students from the University of South Alabama at Mobile. A fledgling instructor of painting and drawing, she and her husband David had opted to spend their Christmas vacation touring Maya sites in Mexico with some of her students. It was entirely new territory for the Scheles, and the trip was filled with mishaps: no one in the group spoke Spanish, they got lost, had trouble with their van, and various members of the party fell ill. One day in Villahermosa a Guatemalan they met told them, "There's a place called Palenque about 30 kilometers [18 miles] off the highway. You've got to go there. And ask for a man named Moises. He's a special man." A flip of the coin persuaded them to follow this advice; they would go to Palenque and spend an hour or so at the site. Instead, they stayed for more than 12 days.

That coin toss changed the course of Linda Schele's life—and with it the course of modern Maya epigraphy, the science of deciphering ancient texts. Today she ranks among the most important pioneering Maya epigraphers, and has emerged as perhaps the most prominent spokesperson for the Maya world view. The author of several highly influential books, and a famous leader of glyph-reading workshops, particularly at Austin, where she teaches at the University of Texas, Schele has helped to shape a whole new vision of Maya civilization.

Schele could not have known, that first day at Palenque, how the next 28 years of her life would unfold. On her very first visit she met Moises Morales, that very special man who had shared the magic of Palenque with thousands of pilgrims over the years. Moises took the Scheles and their party for a walk deep into the jungle. He showed them the beautiful cascades that splash down into stone basins under the dense jungle canopy, and revealed to them the presence of ruined walls and buildings everywhere. They met Robert Rands, who knows more than any-

one about the ceramic history of Palenque, and they also met Merle Greene Robertson, who was making rubbings of the carved stone tablets that are unique to the site. Robertson led them down the 68 steps into the extraordinary tomb in the Temple of Inscriptions where the greatest king of Palenque, Pacal, was buried. Every day they planned to leave, but the magic of the ancient city held them in its grip.

Within several years, the Scheles had bought a house in the nearby town. Possessed of an insatiable curiosity and driven by a hunger to understand the ancient Maya, Linda Schele devoted all of her free time to the study of Palenque. What or who drove these people to build one of the great cities in the world of its time on an unstable and precariously narrow bench on a mountain slope, deep in a rain forest? Questions like this became her abiding preoccupation for years.

The Palenque whose ruins we see today was built in a little over a hundred years, from the mid-seventh to the mid-eighth centuries. Someone or something of great power must have galvanized the people to raise such a city in such a place, but everything that Schele read about the site she found wanting. None of the writings addressed even the simplest and most obvious of questions, such as what purpose or social functions the buildings had served. She discovered, moreover, that even though Palenque had been visited and mapped a number of times since the late eighteenth century, only that portion of the site near the center—the area open to the modern visitor—had been adequately mapped. Guided by her own need for thoroughness and using local children as assistants, she spent many months walking daily out into the muddy, snake- and tick-infested jungle with compass and tape measure to make a sketch map of as much of the site as she was able. It remains, thus far, the most complete map of the city of Palenque.

My own first encounter with Linda Schele in August of 1971 was pure happenstance. I had been asked by Hugh and Suzanne Johnston, film makers from Princeton, New Jersey, to be an advisor for a television documentary on the Maya. They insisted that I determine a leitmotif for the film, and I suggested that we attempt to rediscover an important Maya building that had been lost for 60 years. The building in question was Temple B at Rio Bec, a small but impressive site hundreds of miles to the northeast

Linda Schele

of Palenque. This building, constructed in an unusual regional style, was discovered on Easter Sunday in 1912 by Raymond Merwin, a Harvard anthropology student, and Clarence Hay, the son of Nicholas Hay, Abraham Lincoln's secretary and biographer. The two young men were thrilled by the architecture and preservation of Temple B, and made maps, drew plans, and took photographs of the structure. They walked out of the region in May of 1912 and, as far as anyone knew, no one had seen the building since. The Carnegie Foundation sent in two

extensive expeditions in 1934 and 1935 to relocate the building, whose form archaeologists used to define the architectural style known as Rio Bec. They located other buildings and structures that Merwin had discovered, but not Temple B.

Finally, in 1936, convinced that Temple B would remain a captive of the forest, Clarence Hay had a Japanese sculptor make a plaster model of the building, to be distributed to museums around the world so that the structure's beauty would not be forgotten, and posted a $2,000 reward for its rediscovery. A number of Mayanists had made a hobby of trying to find Temple B, to no avail.

So in August of 1971 I arrived with the film makers at Palenque; it was to be the Johnstons' first extensive look at an ancient Maya site. We were hot and tired from a wrenching six-hour drive and were sitting at a restaurant having a beer, when a voice behind me, thick with a Southern drawl, said, "Yesterday we went to Rio Bec...."

We jumped all over the owner of the voice. It was Linda Schele. "You were in Rio Bec?"

"Yes," she said. "The forest is awfully dry."

"How did you get there?" we asked.

She said that they had driven. "It's a pretty rough drive," she said, and added, "We broke an axle."

And that is how I met Linda Schele. It

turned out, very fortuitously, that she had visited a building similar to Temple B at Rio Bec that had just been discovered by Juan Briceno, the guardian of the ruins. A year-and-a-half later Briceno led us to Temple B.

Linda was at Palenque most of the times I visited the site over the next several years, and we delighted in becoming closer friends with each visit. On one visit I found her seriously ill; she was bedridden with an amoebic infection that had nearly destroyed her liver and taken her life. As hardy as Linda seems, she gets so caught up in the rush of her interests that she often ignores her own health.

A visit with Linda in June of 1973 proved pivotal to the development of her interest in epigraphy. I was then at Palenque with David Joralemon, a graduate student of Michael Coe's at Yale. The previous year, Michael had conducted a special seminar on the Late Classic Maya gods depicted on carvings, wall panels, stelae and architecture at the sites of Copán and Palenque. Who were these gods, what function did they serve, and how and why were they important to the ancient Maya of these two cities? Joralemon's head was swimming with the enigmatic depictions of these gods and their apparent roles in Mayan kingship. I asked Linda to go to the site with us because she knew every carved stone in the city.

Linda, at last, found herself talking with someone fresh from discussions of Classic Maya iconography and the current state of glyphic decipherment. David pointed out a curious depiction of a god with a smoking cigar sticking out of his forehead and observed, "That's God K." Pointing to a very similar god, Linda said, "We call this one the

Jester God, because of the jester's cap he's wearing. We've had to come up with some of our own names."

By the time we had dragged ourselves back to the veranda of Merle Greene Robertson's house, Linda was exploding with excitement. She had never talked with anyone so steeped in the latest interpretations of Maya iconography. Gesturing with a planter's punch in one hand and peanuts in the other, she excitedly suggested that if one could only get all of the greatest experts on the Maya together for a conference—Eric Thompson from England, Tatiana Proskouriakoff from Harvard, Michael Coe from Yale, Yuri Knorosov from the Soviet Union, and David Kelley from Canada—there could be an interchange and discussion, and if there were any questions, everybody could go out to the site and actually examine the monuments *in situ*.

I chimed in, "Let's have a roundtable." David Joralemon said, "A *mesa redonda*" And Merle said, "We'll have it!" And Merle Greene Robertson organized the first Palenque roundtable to be held at the site and longest (seven days) ever held on one topic in Mexico. She invited by mail all Mexican archaeologists, especially those working in the Maya area, as well as Mayanists everywhere. She scheduled it for December 1973, less than six months away, and some 40 people showed up for the Primera Mesa Redonda de Palenque.

Another young person was going to help make the conference a success. He was Peter Mathews, an Australian who was a junior at the University of Calgary in Alberta where he was a student of David Kelley's. Peter had spent most of his savings to make his first pilgrimage to a Maya site. Quiet and shy, he wore a hand-painted T-shirt and sported a moustache and long hair. It gradually became apparent to those most interested in Maya glyphs that Peter knew more about them than anyone else present; he had brought with him four notebooks in which he had copied every glyph ever recorded from Palenque since the late eighteenth century.

As a morning session ended several days into the conference, Michael Coe stood up and said, "Linda knows every stone in Palenque and Peter knows every glyph— why don't the two of you see if you can put together a dynastic history of Palenque? No one has attempted that yet." That evening the two stood up and Linda said, "We have six rulers and the man in the tomb is named Shield."

With that pronouncement Moises Morales stood up and angrily asked, "Why is it that when a name is given to such a king it is put into *English* or *Spanish*?: 'Shield,' '*Escudo*'? Why? These rulers were Maya, and what's more the people who built Palenque were *Chol*. The Chols still live and speak Chol in the mountains behind Palenque. We have a Chol in the audience and we have a Chol dictionary."

People were uncomfortable, but Moises was right. After a rapid check it turned out that there was no word in modern Chol for "shield," but two other Maya languages contained two words for "shield"—*chimal* and *pacal*. Chimal is Nahauatl, or Mexican, and so pacal was chosen. (David Kelley has deciphered a similar name at Chichén Itzá as Kakupacal. Since both names had the same shield sign in them, "shield" became pacal, the original Chol Maya word for "shield.")

Someone later recalled that David Kelley had phonetically transcribed the glyph for this ruler five years earlier as *Pa-ca-la*, or Pacal. Floyd Lounsbury, himself one of the major epigraphers at the conference, then translated the title *Ma-kin-ah*, or "great lord." Makinah Pacal. Out of 1,300 years of dark silence and ignorance, the sound of the name of a great man who had created a great city where there had been little before came to us as if it were a gift from the ancients.

Suddenly we had the name of Pacal's mother, Lady Sak K'uk, who had given her son the city of Palenque when he was 12 years old; Lady Ah-Po-Hel, his wife; and their oldest son, Chan Bahlum, who had built the four buildings known as the Cross Group to legitimize and glorify himself. In other words, for the first time in our era we had history as the dynasty of Pacal had recorded it. We had Maya personalities and their portraits. The floodgates of glyphic decipherment were opened.

For Linda Schele, the first Mesa Redonda was an especially pivotal moment. She had earlier decided that Maya glyphs were beyond her, and reading J. Eric Thompson's *Maya Glyphs Without Tears* had corroborated that decision. Thompson was one of several major scholars who had declined the invitation Merle Greene Robertson sent out. Stunned by the success of the team at Palenque, Linda was determined to teach herself to read Maya glyphs. New friends sent her copies of drawings and lists of dates, for neither was available to her in Mobile. And thus she began a great adventure.

The next pivotal moment grew out of the first. One of the participants at the first Mesa Redonda was Elizabeth Benson of

Dumbarton Oaks in Washington, D.C., long an important center for Maya studies. Eager to sustain the impetus of the first Mesa Redonda, Benson decided to hold a mini-conference in Washington that would carry the work, as well as the energy and enthusiasm, forward. She invited all of the most important Maya glyphicists in the world to a restricted session.

Yuri Knorosov again was unable to leave the Soviet Union, and Eric Thompson was too ill to come from England, but most of the greats in the field did come.

The conference got off to a poor start. Differences in temperament and methodological assumptions kept the participants from interacting freely, and after a politely cold standoff many of them left. Those who remained formed a hard core of glyph enthusiasts. Linda was among them.

But even this group found interactions difficult, so great were the disparities between backgrounds and assumptions, not to mention ages. It turned out, interestingly, that some of the older participants were more daring in their approach, while some of the younger people proved to be more conservative. Still, they worked together with Maya dictionaries, natural histories, codices, and cups and cups of coffee.

It was the first of seven mini-conferences held by that pioneer group at Dumbarton Oaks. The participants agreed that *everyone* present had to accept a decipherment for each glyph, or the glyph would be shelved until there was a consensus. Prior to the first Mesa Redonda, the meanings of roughly 30 percent of the glyphs at Palenque could be guessed at, mostly glyphs for dates. Within a decade more than 95 percent of them could be read. Now some texts can be read, using modern Maya intonations, as poetry!

A decoder of Maya glyphs must have an extraordinary mind. He or she must be an exacting linguist; be able to manage mathematics, astronomy, and anthropology, and have a working interest in natural history; and, above all, be able to think or conceive the world like a Maya. Linda exemplifies such abilities. Having been a painter as well as an art historian, she draws glyphs with both precision and elegance. She can walk up to a blackboard and write in Maya glyphs as easily as she might write in English. She is possessed of an unbelievable visual memory, and she sees Maya images through Maya eyes. She is also at home with a computer, and used one to set her doctoral thesis as a book. That book, *Maya Glyphs: The Verbs*, won recognition as the best technical work published in America in 1982.

Schele not only sets her own books, she designs and prints the illustrations for them as well. For *The Blood of Kings: Dynasty and Ritual in Maya Art*, which she coauthored in 1986 with Mary Ellen Miller, she drew some 70 line illustrations; and for her most recent work, *A Forest of Kings. The Untold Story of the Ancient Maya* (1990), coauthored with David Freidel, she provided nearly 100 elegant drawings.

> ## She can write in Maya glyphs as easily as in English.

The Blood of Kings constitutes a turning point in Maya studies in this part of our century. It tells as never before the story of Maya blood sacrifice, which constituted one of the central rituals of Maya kingship, and unveils for the reader the complex, sophisticated story of court life during the Classic Maya period, which lasted from roughly A.D. 200 to 800.

A Forest of Kings extends the same story by looking for the first time at the histories of eight ancient Maya cities—Palenque, Copán, Tikal, and Chichén Itzá among them—over a period of 1,500 years. This recent work treats questions of Maya politics, warfare, and dynastic succession in unprecedented detail, thanks in large measure to the gains in epigraphy that Schele and David Freidel have helped to make.

But Linda's importance in the field of Maya studies rests on much more than her scholarly attainments. Her collegiality is exemplary; indeed, she has become an institution. Utterly committed to the open exchange of information, she works closely with a wide range of experts in other fields, and regularly visits such sites as Copán, Palenque, Yaxchilán, and Tikal to keep abreast of the archaeological work going on there and to consult with other epigraphers. David Stuart, probably the foremost glyphicist in the world today according to Linda, was one of her proteges. From the time David was 12, when he began reading glyphs with the encouragement of his Mayanist father George Stuart, Linda insisted that he observe the highest standards. Schele teaches by insisting that her students discover and work out for themselves how glyphs and texts must be approached. She does not hand out the rules, but gives hints and lets each person find out through trial and error, one might say despair, how the Maya put sentences or ideas together in their special system of writing. Her approach has made famous her annual workshops on glyphic writing at the University of Texas at Austin, which are now in their fifteenth year. She has also conducted workshops in Mexico, Guatemala, and throughout the United States. Recently, at a workshop in Antigua, Guatemala, she taught modern Maya how to read and write their language in its ancient, elegantly expressive form.

Schele, of course, has her critics, and her ideas have met with sharp opposition— mostly from those who are illiterate in Maya glyphs. Others argue that the "history" that she reads in glyphic inscriptions is merely the propaganda of the Maya elite and must be treated with caution. Linda grants the point freely; yet she also insists that it remains a true, if slanted, voice from the ancient past.

Schele combines an array of talents, energy, mental brilliance, and depth—any one of which virtues would make her a remarkable person. Her dedication to the field and to good scholarship is profound.

She shuns taking too much credit for herself, preferring to emphasize a collaborative approach. "We attempt to bring many minds with different agendas and experiences together in an atmosphere of generous and unrestricted sharing," she says. "No one person can know everything or even enough different things to command the field. I have spent my life collaborating with many different people—and our work together is my great strength." ▲

21

HONORING LINDA SCHELE

Students and colleagues gather to pay homage to a magnificent Mayanist.

by ANGELA M.H. SCHUSTER

IT WAS A COLD FRIDAY NIGHT BY AUSTIN STAN-dards, barely above freezing, as Maya scholars from the United States, Europe, Mexico, and Central America met around a massive stone fireplace in a dimly lighted gourmet Tex-Mex restaurant. Sipping frozen margaritas and munching nachos, they swapped stories of recent excavations, new decipherments, and adventures in the Mesoamerican wild. This was no ordinary gathering of the world's top Mayanists, but the beginning of a three-day tribute to Linda Schele, whose work has broadened our understanding of the ancient Maya. In the summer of 1997, the 56-year-old University of Texas epigrapher, whose coauthored books include *Blood of Kings, Forest of Kings, Maya Cosmos*, and *Code of Kings,* was diagnosed with inoperable cancer and given little more than a year to live.

"Some of us," reflected David Kelley, professor emeritus at the University of Calgary, "go back to the very beginning, back when we all used to smoke, drink, and eat lots of red meat." Other luminaries at the meeting, many of whom have worked with Schele during the past 30 years, included Elizabeth Benson, formerly of Dumbarton Oaks; Gillett Griffin of Princeton University; Olmec scholar Kent Reilly of Southwest Texas State University; David Freidel of Southern Methodist University; and young scholars like British epigrapher Simon Martin and David Stuart of Harvard's Peabody Museum. The dean of the group was legendary Yale linguist Floyd Lounsbury, 92, whose pioneering work on the native languages of the Americas set the stage for much of Maya hieroglyphic decipherment.

For many the gathering was a last chance to savor the spirit of this extraordinary Mayanist, who, with Merle Greene Robertson of the Pre-Columbian Art Research Institute, organized the first Palenque Round Table, a conference held every three years at the Late Classic site in Chiapas, Mexico. Schele also established the Maya Meetings at Texas, an annual ten-day colloquium now in its twenty-second year. For others the meeting was a final opportunity to engage in a test of intellect with a preeminent authority—a "force to be reckoned with," according to Andrea Stone of the University of Wisconsin, Milwaukee.

Schele reveled in the spotlight and seemed pleased, if a bit puzzled, by the attention. "I don't know why you all are celebrating me when it's because of you that I've been able to do what I've done."

Encomiums, nonetheless, were forthcoming from a succession of speakers. Addressing the assembled scholars from a podium at the University of Texas auditorium, Gillette Griffin, curator of the Precolumbian collec-

tion at Princeton's art museum, recounted the time he first met Schele, in a pub in San Cristobal de las Casas in Chiapas. "I had gone down to Mexico with a film crew in an attempt to rediscover Temple B at Río Bec, which had been discovered in 1912 but then quickly lost. At the next table was this woman with this heavy southern drawl going on about how she had just been to Río Bec and had come across this wonderful little temple deep in the jungle."

Many of Schele's graduate students expressed their gratitude for her shepherding them through the "tangled web of epigraphy," as one put it. "Linda has this way of making you come to your own conclusions through a process of discovery," said Andrea Stone, Schele's first graduate student. "I think what has made her so special has been her ability to communicate. She has her own way of describing things, phrases like 'spaghetti syndrome,' that overwhelming tangle one senses when trying to understand a Maya relief for the very first time."

"Linda could always tell when one of us was looking a bit thin," recalled Kent Reilly, another former graduate student. "She would find odd jobs for us around campus and make personal loans to help [make] ends meet. When I finally became self sufficient and tried to pay Linda back she wouldn't hear of it. Instead she said 'Kent, one day one of your kids will be in need. The best way to pay me back is to help them.'"

The gathering was not without academic papers. Simon Martin presented new ideas on the dynastic succession at Tikal during the Middle Classic, which he and Nikolai Grube of the University of Bonn had worked out based on texts carved on two newfound stelae at the site. "We just have so many references to a ruler named Jaguar Paw that until now have been hard to sort out," said Martin. "We know that there were at least two rulers by that name during the fifth century, but exactly where they fit in the dynastic succession has been unclear. With the recent discovery of stelae 39 and 40 we have a much better fix on their regnal dates." "You know," Schele responded, "you kids are onto something."

Honduran archaeologist David Sedat—wearing paper goggles, imitating those worn by Tlaloc, the central Mexican rain god—offered an interesting, albeit controversial, interpretation of Hunal, the earliest known building beneath Structure 16 on the Copán acropolis, which some believe contains the skeletal remains of K'inich Yax K'uk Mo (Sun-Faced Blue-Green Macaw), the city's founder. Sedat suggested that the bones in the tiny fifth-century temple, found in 1996, may actually be those of the man Yax K'uk Mo defeated. While unproven, the theory may help explain why the temple was not reverentially buried like subsequent ones built on the spot. "For someone so highly regarded according to later inscriptions," said Sedat, "we would have expected Hunal to have been carefully preserved before the next building layer was added." Sedat was accompanied by a colleague, clad in goggles and a jaguar-print loincloth, and carrying a cardboard cut-out of a manikin scepter, a quintessential Maya symbol of kingship, which he gave to Schele at the end of the talk.

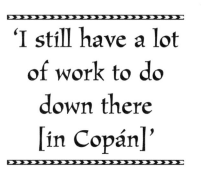

'I still have a lot of work to do down there [in Copán]'

David Freidel and Kent Reilly presented results of their recent work on the use of wooden scaffolds in royal accession rites, a tradition they trace back to Olmec times. They even proposed that giant stone Olmec heads were actually recarved altars. Altars, they suggested, were carved as accession monuments and then reworked into heads upon a ruler's death.

Schele may be best known among scholars for her work on Maya cosmology, joining archaeological and epigraphical evidence with studies of modern Maya beliefs (see page 80, *Written in the Stars*) "What Linda has discovered about the Maya," said Reilly, "applies to cultures throughout the Americas." This point was underscored by David Kelley's recent research on the modern-day Kogi people of the Tairona region of Colombia, whose cosmology closely resembles that of the ancient Maya. "They, too, regard the Milky Way as a world tree and run on a calendar of 20-day months," explained Kelley. "Moreover, the Kogi make many of their observations with the aid of a concave obsidian mirror, much like those found in Maya burials and dedicatory caches. While flat obsidian disks are great for observation, concave mirrors essentially constitute telescopes. Intriguing, isn't it?" What could account for these similarities? "According to Kogi myth," said Kelley, "the ancestors, traveling in nine canoes, came to the Tairona region from the north many generations ago. Whether there is any truth in this only time will tell." "Kelley," said

Schele, "every time you have a hunch it turns out to be right—too often in my book."

A poignant moment came on the second morning when Quiché-trained daykeeper (shaman-priest) Duncan Earle built a shaman's altar with pine boughs, woven textiles, and lighted candles on the auditorium stage. As billowing clouds of burning copal filled the room, blanketing prominent "no smoking" signs, Earle summoned the gods of heaven, earth, and the four directions, creating a portal to the otherworld. He offered an ancestral prayer for Schele, ending "Wise Woman of the Stars, Reader of the Book, Speaker of Truths." Addressing the audience, he noted that, thanks to Schele, "five centuries of silence have ended, [and] the ancient Maya now speak for themselves."

Exuberant, Schele finally took the stage herself. "I want to thank you for encouraging this redneck from Nashville. I can't tell you how much it meant to me that you,

who held positions at prominent universities, took the time to listen to me, encourage me, and guide me. As for my students, you are my children. Your job is to take what you have learned and teach others."

The meeting ended with a Texas barbeque at a noisy Western-style restaurant on the outskirts of town. Schele was frank about her condition, but optimistic nonetheless. "I was at the hospital on Tuesday and things have changed little in the past few months. David [her husband] and I decided to try a bit more of this experimental chemo. If all goes well I will be at Copán in May. I still have a lot of work to do down there." ≜

Linda Schele died in April of 1998. After her death, friends and colleagues established the Linda and David Schele Chair in the Art and Writing of Mesoamerica at the University of Texas at Austin.

22

A TRIUMPH OF SPIRIT

How Yuri Knorosov cracked the
Maya hieroglyphic code from
far-off Leningrad.

by MICHAEL D. COE

THE STORY OF THE RUSSIAN SCHOLAR YURI
Valentinovich Knorosov is a study in the triumph of
spirit and intellect over almost insuperable odds.
This great epigrapher, who until recently had never been
permitted to leave the Soviet Union to visit a Mesoamerican site, who had never seen first-hand any of the great
Maya inscriptions, cracked the phonetic code of Maya
hieroglyphic writing in the confines of his Leningrad study.

I first visited Knorosov with my Russian-speaking wife
Sophie in 1969, during the grim, gray "years of stagnation"
under Brezhnev. It was January, and it was bitterly cold in
Leningrad. Knorosov's office was, and still is, located in the
blue-and-white Kunstkammer, the baroque building on the
Neva built to house Peter the Great's "cabinet of curiosi-
ties" (including the skeleton of his giant manservant). Here,
Knorosov shared his modest office with four colleagues at
the Ethnographic Institute—privacy of any kind is in short

supply in the Soviet Union. In this crowded scene, our friend occupied a desk in the corner near a window, while the ever-present samovar bubbled away, the source of the tea without which Russian intellectual life would be unthinkable. I gazed in awe at the view from the window: beyond the frozen river, the feeble rays of the low-lying winter sun were picking out the golden Admiralty spire celebrated in Pushkin's poetry. It was a

An Epigraphic Coup

Knorosov's epigraphic breakthrough resulted from his use of four types of evidence to piece together the phonetic value of puzzling glyphs. The first consisted of glyphic texts and illustrations that occur in close proximity in the Dresden Codex and Madrid Codex, two of the four surviving bark-paper books of the Maya. Second, he drew on dictionaries of Yucatec Maya, one of 28 surviving Mayan languages; some of these dictionaries were compiled early in the Spanish Colonial era. Maya scholars are in agreement that the language of the codices, which were written late in the pre-conquest era, was reasonably close to that of sixteenth-century Yucatán, although there may have been some differences due to the use of archaic speech in these books. The third type of evidence Knorosov drew on has been crucial to the efforts of every recent epigrapher. It consists of a syllabary—a list of how syllables were written—mistakenly identified as an alphabet by the Spanish prelate Diego de Landa in his massively influential sixteenth-century text, Relación de las cosas de Yucatán. *The accuracy of this syllabary, whose real nature Knorosov helped to establish, has been verified by much recent work; in many ways it is the Rosetta Stone of modern Maya decipherment. The final type of information that Knorosov drew on was the known values of certain hieroglyphs, values securely established by earlier scholars. Beginning with known values, and by matching glyphs in the codices with their relevant illustrations, Knorosov was able to extrapolate both the sounds and the meanings of a series of hitherto bewildering symbols. Listed here are the nine steps he followed in revolutionizing Maya epigraphy and establishing his phonetic approach.*

1. The sign for "west" has been known to scholars since the last century. This is read in Maya as chikin, *and consists of a sign like a grasping hand (phonetic* chi), *followed by the morphemic sign for "sun,"* kin.

2. ku *(given by Landa) plus* chi *appears above the picture of a vulture. It is read* ku-ch(i), *"vulture" in Maya dictionaries.*

3. cu *(also in Landa) plus an unknown sign, over the picture of a turkey, must be* cu-tz(u), *"turkey" in Maya dictionaries. The unknown sign is thus* tzu.

4. cu *plus an unknown sign, over a picture of a goddess carrying the god as a burden, must be* cu-ch(u), *"burden" in Maya dictionaries. The unknown sign is thus* chu.

5. chu *plus* ca *(Landa) plus* ah *(Landa), over a picture of a captive God, must be* chu-c(a)-ah, *"captured."*

6. In one place in the Dresden Codex, a defaced sign plus one of Landa's l *signs plus* cu *is equivalent to the Maya bar-and-dot number "eleven,"* buluc *in Maya; the defaced sign must be* bu, *and Landa's second* l *has to be* lu.

7. tzu *plus* lu *over a picture of the Dog God must be* tzu-l(u), *"dog, confirming the readings for these glyphs.*

8. Two ku *signs over a picture of a goddess with a quetzal (a tropical bird), must be* ku-k(u), *"quetzal" in all Mayan languages.*

9. An unknown sign plus two o *signs (in Landa), over a picture of the same goddess with a macaw bird, must be* mo-o-o *(or* mo'o), *"macaw" in Maya dictionaries. The unknown glyph is thus* mo.

—MICHAEL D. COE

very far cry from the hot and humid forests in which the Maya cities had risen and died.

Knorosov is a striking man, with iron-gray hair brushed back severely, and sapphire-blue eyes almost hidden beneath his bushy eyebrows. A formal dresser never to be seen on Leningrad's streets without brown beret, white shirt, and necktie, he wears his World War II battle medals, though he now omits the one bearing Stalin's portrait, proudly pinned to his double-breasted suit. A chain-smoker, Knorosov has a wonderfully ironic sense of humor, like many Russians who have survived the terrible events of this century. He is a mine of information on his beloved city, especially on its history under Peter the Great and his corrupt henchman Menshikov.

Thanks to Knorosov's breakthrough in Maya epigraphy, we can now hear ancient Maya glyphs as the scribes wrote them, and not merely interpret them as soundless visual patterns. Knorosov's great achievement lay in demonstrating that the Maya scribes could, and often did, write syllabically, each glyph standing for a consonant followed by a vowel. Most Maya words are single syllables made up of a consonant-vowel-consonant combination. They were generally written with two glyphs, but the vowel of the second glyph was not pronounced. Basic to Knorosov's approach was his "Principle of Synharmony," according to which the silent second vowel in these combinations often repeats the vowel of the first glyph. Hence, the word for the quetzal bird—a beautiful tropical species highly prized by the Maya for its ornate feathers—is the monosyllabic *kuk*, but was written with two ku glyphs, the second -*u* sound being suppressed.

This approach is universally accepted today by all serious Mayanists, but it was initially rejected by the scholarly establishment here in the West. Indeed, all of Knorosov's work on Maya glyphs came under heated attack for many years from the dean of Maya studies, J. Eric Thompson, whose formidably influential views of the Maya held sway in the Americas for more than a generation. Thompson launched his relentless and often unfair rebuttal in cold war terms in the Mexican journal *Yan* in 1953. Indeed, until his death in 1975, Thompson rejected *all* of Knorosov's work, both in general and in detail. The very vehemence of his attack suggests that he might have had something to fear from Knorosov's quarter.

The critical point in Knorosov's career occurred in 1947, when his teacher, the orientalist and archaeologist Sergei Tokarev, came to him with a proposal. Two years before, the respected German Mayanist Paul Schellhas, then near the end of his long life, had published a very pessimistic article stating that the decipherment of Maya glyphs was an unsolvable problem. Tokarev's challenge to his student was this: "If you believe that any writing system produced by humans can be read by humans, then why don't you try to read the Maya hieroglyphs?" Knorosov took up the challenge and turned it into his doctoral research, which would lead to his degree in historical sciences (*magna cum laude*) in 1955.

The subject of Knorosov's groundbreaking study was the work of Fray Diego de Landa, the fanatical and cruel Spanish Franciscan missionary. Landa, who eventually became Provincial (ruling prelate) in Yucatán, both persecuted the Maya and recorded their customs and history. Famed for his complete mastery of the Maya tongue, he combated what he perceived to be widespread idolatry among his charges in 1552 by conducting an auto-da-fé. In the process, he did massive and irreparable damage to the Maya's written legacy by burning a large number of native Maya texts or codices "because they contained nothing but superstition and the Devil's falsehoods."

Landa was recalled to Spain in 1564 to face charges that he had overstepped his authority in the investigation and torture of native lords and commoners. During his years of exile, he wrote an "Account of the Affairs of Yucatán," which, ironically, is our single most important Colonial-period source on the lowland Maya. The original has been lost, but a seventeenth- century abridgement was discovered in 1862 in Madrid by the Abbe Brasseur de Bourbourg. This precious document not only provided detailed information on all aspects of Maya life on the eve of the conquest, it also— more important in this context—outlined the workings of the Maya calendar and gave the glyphs for the days and the months.

Landa gave us something else that would prove decisive to Knorosov's breakthrough—a description of the Maya writing system itself, albeit one containing a crucial error. From material he had elicited from his informants, Landa pictured 27 signs that, to his mind, formed part of the Maya "alphabet," as well as three additional signs drawn from examples of how signs were strung together in written words and sentences. Early efforts at translating Maya glyphs based on Landa's interpretations ranged from the bad to the ridiculous.

The phonetic approach remained in eclipse for almost a century, until Knorosov published his bombshell in the form of an article written in 1952. The article appeared in *Sovietskaya Etnografia*, a journal in those days otherwise given over to praise of Marx, Engels, and, above all, Stalin. In this article, Knorosov rejected several basic conclusions to which Mayanists had adhered. To begin with, he refuted the evolutionary approach to the development of languages, a position embraced by important Maya scholars like Sylvanus Morley. This approach argued that writing had passed through various stages, beginning with the pictographic, then proceeding through the "ideographic" (in which an idea or object is given by a sign having little or no pictorial reference), and finally moving to the phonetic (in which a sign stands only for a sound). Wrong, said Knorosov. These supposed stages coexist in all early scripts, including Egyptian, Mesopotamian, and Chinese, all of which, like the Maya system, are authentically *hieroglyphic*; they are typical of state societies in which they are maintained as a monopoly by a class of priestly scribes. In such systems, one finds "ideograms" that have both conceptual and phonetic value; phonetic signs; and "key signs" or determinatives, classificatory signs with conceptual value only that remain unpronounced. Knorosov then zeroed in on the Landa "alphabet," which he argued was not an alphabet at all but a *syllabary*—a list of signs standing for consonant-vowel combinations and not individual letters. (Landa himself recorded five of his "letters" as consonant-vowel combinations.) Knorosov claimed, for instance, that the sign given by Landa as the letter *l*

Knorosov in Guatemala

By the fall of 1990 it looked as though Knorosov's long-held dream of actually visiting the Maya cities might at last come true. Yuri Valentinovich had once joked with my wife and me that the problem was not the Iron Curtain, but the "Golden Curtain": to get a Soviet exit visa he was required to put up a prohibitive sum of money, which he didn't have. Now the Guatemalan government had extended an invitation to Knorosov, his Mayanist colleague Galina Yershova, and her Guatemalan husband Guillermo Ovando—an ethnologist specializing in the modern Maya—to spend several months, all expenses paid, in that turbulent country. The invitation had come by courtesy of the wife of President Cerezo (who was soon to leave office), and it seemed God-sent. Exit visas materialized, and the three were off to Guatemala.

Knorosov's party reached their destination by Christmas, and they were welcomed with open arms. Guatemala and the USSR had just established diplomatic relations after a lapse of four decades, and there was much cordiality toward the Soviets. But, as events were to prove, the Cold War wasn't over yet in Guatemala. Yuri Valentinovich was honored with a gold medal by President Cerezo, and Galina was invited to give conferences on Soviet glyphic research (at which, ironically, both she and her mentor rejected most of the recent epigraphic work done by westerners, even though this research had been based on Knorosov's original breakthrough!). And they did manage to visit the great site of Tikal, along with Uaxactún and Mixco Viejo.

Then trouble began. Shortly after the inauguration of the new president in mid-January, a menacing voice on the telephone told Knorosov and his colleagues that they had exactly 72 hours to leave Guatemalan territory or they would be killed. Knowing that Guatemala's right-wing death squads meant business, they hid out with friends for two weeks while awaiting a Mexican visa for Knorosov. Galina and Guillermo had ordinary passports, so their obtaining visas presented no problem; but Knorosov's passport was an official one, which caused the delay.

By February, they had made their way back to the Soviet Union via Mexico and Cuba. The man who had allowed the ancient Maya scribes to speak with their own voice was still unable to walk freely among the cities in which they had lived.

—M.D.C

actually represents the syllable *lu*.

In this and a spate of other articles, Knorosov closely compared the texts with the pictures they accompany in the few surviving Maya codices, especially a manuscript known as the *Dresden Codex;* and he applied the Landa "alphabet" in light of his theoretical system.

Despite the early attacks on his discoveries, Knorosov's logic proved compelling. Linguists and younger colleagues in the United States had a considerably less hostile reaction to Knorosov's work than people like Thompson; and in 1962 the important American epigrapher David Kelley published a paper accepting many, but not all, of Knorosov's readings. Kelley took the Russian's methodology one step further into the inscriptions, and read the syllabically written name of a great leader at Chichén Itzá as *Ka-ku-pa-ca-l(a)* or Kakupacal, "Fiery Shield." It was a first for Maya studies, and the tide has never turned back.

Knorosov's magnum opus, *Pis'mennost' Indietsav Maiia (The Writing of the Maya Indians)*, appeared in 1963. This is an impressive volume covering all aspects of Maya history and anthropology, including a catalog of 540 basic Maya glyphs with their reading (if known) and interpretation. Four years later, Harvard's Peabody Museum published my wife's translation of it, with an appreciative but cautious preface by Tatiana Proskouriakoff. The Russian-born Proskouriakoff had broken new ground in 1960 when she published an article in *American Antiquity* demonstrating that a pattern of dates at Piedras Negras in Guatemala implied that the glyphic inscriptions there, and probably in other Maya cities, recorded *actual human history* rather than just astronomical and religious matters, as Thompson and other Mayanists had long contended. Proskouriakoff's immense prestige assured that this translation would receive serious scholarly attention. The volume was followed by a second major Knorosov work on the four Maya codices, also later published in translation.

Meanwhile, a new generation of Maya epigraphers and linguists had appeared in the United States, Canada, Guatemala, and Western Europe, inspired by Knorosovian methodology, by Proskouriakoff's historical approach, and by the research of Floyd Lounsbury at Yale. Lounsbury set the pace by refining Knorosov's method of glyphic substitution (the search for signs used alternatively in identical contexts), and established new standards of proof for proposed

> Despite the early attacks on his discoveries, Knorosov's logic proved compelling.

new readings. The two new approaches, phoneticism and the historical approach, coalesced in 1973 at the groundbreaking first Mesa Redonda of Palenque. For the first time since the collapse of Classic Maya civilization in the ninth century A.D. the kings of Palenque, including Pakal and his son Chan Bahlum, became real people with real histories.

The final vindication for Knorosov came six years later at a conference entitled "Phoneticism in Maya Writing," attended by no less than 135 participants. Lyle Campbell, one of the organizers, stated in his opening paper: "No Mayan linguist who has seriously looked into the matter any longer doubts the phonetic hypothesis as originally framed by Yuri Knorosov."

Knorosov has not been idle since the days of his early successes. Since then, he and his Soviet colleagues have done important work on those stubbornly recalcitrant writing systems, the Rongo-rongo script of Easter Island and the Indus script, both of which Yuri Valentinovich sees (despite the brevity of the texts and other related problems) as being of the "hieroglyphic" type. Each summer he travels to the distant, windswept Kurile Islands between Siberia and Japan, where he excavates middens left by the ancestors of the Ainu people. Since these disputed islands, seized from Japan at the end of World War II, are in a military zone, he and his fellow archaeologists live under Spartan conditions in army camps and travel around in Red Army armored vehicles. It's quite a change from Maya research.

But Maya epigraphy remains his first love. Along with his young colleague Galina Yershova, who has just completed a biography of Landa, Knorosov has been examining the enigmatic and difficult texts on Maya funerary ceramics. In this area there are outstanding differences of interpretation with Western Mayanists, including myself, that may or may not be reconciled through better lines of communication.

In the meantime, we can only hope that with the demise of the Cold War we may one day greet Yuri Valentinovich Knorosov at the site of those very Maya inscriptions that he has taught us how to read. Ancient Maya rulers would have recognized him as an *ah miats*, "a wise man, cultured, literate," and have accepted him as one of their own. ≞

23

FROM PARLOURS TO PYRAMIDS

Fleeing the "gilded cage of English civilization," artist and adventurer Adela Breton became a skilled copier of Maya murals and reliefs in the early 1900s.

by MARY McVICKER

A T THE AGE OF 50, WHEN MANY OF HER CON-
temporaries were beginning to think of a comfortable retirement, Adela Breton was entering the most
productive years of her career. It was 1900, the place
Chichén Itzá, the Late Classic and Postclassic (ca. A.D.
800–1200) Maya ruin in Yucatán, Mexico. Adela had come
to verify the accuracy of drawings of the renowned British
Mayanist Alfred P. Maudslay. Although she'd already traveled
throughout Mexico, nothing could have prepared her for
the challenge of working at Chichén.

She had spent the first 37 years of her life in Bath,

England. Her schooling included the usual subjects entertained by a Victorian gentlewoman, particularly the study of art. Her mother, who died when Adela was 24, is a shadowy figure, but her father, a retired naval officer with strong interests in archaeology, travel, and exotic places, must have been an important influence. Adela had similar interests, but she bided her time, taking care of her parents, particularly her father. Years later she would refer to this period as "wasting time at Bath."

When her father died in 1887, she inherited sufficient money to give her financial independence. Released from her obligations, she left almost immediately for the Canadian Rockies. The opening of the Canadian Pacific Railroad in 1885 had provided ready access to the area, and women in particular were attracted by opportunities to camp and explore and enjoy a less fettered existence. Some even rode astride—never Adela, however! "The Rocky Mountains were so good, everything perfect except the American women who would ride astride, a sight to make gods & men weep. In all my wild rides it never occurred to me as being possible or necessary," she wrote to Miss Mead, a secretary at Harvard's Peabody Museum, on July 29, 1904.

Adela made her way through the western part of the United States down to Mexico, spending the next 12 years painting and drawing everywhere she went. When she asked Maudslay if there was work she could do while she was in Mexico, he asked her to verify the accuracy of his drawings from Chichén, which he wanted to include in the archaeology section of his great eight-volume work, *Biología Centralia America*. He told her there would be nothing more valuable than a record of the murals at Chichén Itzá.

Her first season at the ruins got off to a bad start. Edward H. Thompson, the United States Consul at Merida, owned a hacienda and the land on which Chichén Itzá was located, and, in a manner of speaking, she was his guest. Excerpts from Thompson's letters reveal irritation and admiration. "Miss Breton is here and I gather from what the tourists say who went with her to Uxmal she's a...Tartar. They say she complained all the way out all the time while she was there and all the way back....," Thompson wrote Frederick Ward Putnam at the Peabody Museum on March 3, 1900.

In the months that followed, matters didn't improve. In an April letter, also to Putnam, Thompson wrote, "Miss Breton returned from Chichén today, I understand. To tell the honest truth she's a nuisance. She is a ladylike person but full of whims, complaints and prejudices.... To my horror I found out the day I left Chichén that she proposes to return to Chichén shortly for another period of time. She certainly is an artist as regards landscapes at least, and she has made one painting in the intervals of her work for Maudslay that is really very nice."

Adela, in her turn, found Thompson irritating, but she was determined. In a May 9, 1903, letter to Alfred M. Tozzer of Harvard University, she wrote that, "It was rather amusing, & very annoying, to stay on by main force as it were, against their will [Thompsons']. But my work became more important as I went on, & I could not be driven away."

Adela's work at Chichén marked her

entry into the professional world of archaeology and anthropology. When Zelia Nuttall, the American archaeologist and ethnohistorian, visited Chichén in 1902, she asked Adela if she could send some of her sketches to Putnam. Impressed by her work, Putnam immediately commissioned Adela to make copies of the site's frescoes.

Adela became good friends with Tozzer, who was also working at Chichén and who wrote his mother regularly, offering the following sketch of "the eccentric Miss Breton" in a February 5, 1902, letter:

She is an English maiden lady of much means.... Her appearance is typical of an independent, unmarried spinster of fully 60 [Adela was 52], tall, thin, and with a long face, grey hair...extremely near sighted, but straight as an arrow. She wore a short skirt, a dark blue shirtwaist with straight collar attached, and brimmed straw hat covered with flowers and planted perfectly square upon her head, but the surprise comes when she starts to talk. She is English...to the very bone and her speech is as exaggerated as any affected English you ever heard upon the stage. She is an artist and a very good one too. She seems to have a special gift of drawing the carvings of the ruins. She has spent many years in Mexico and Yucatán doing this work of copying and drawing the glyphs and sculptures of the ruins. She travels with her inseparable and wonderful servant, Pablo, who cuts paths for her, cooks for her, and makes himself generally useful by tending to her numerous wants.... Her hobby among all the others is this servant.

You look at Miss Breton and set her down as a weak, frail and delicate person who goes into convulsions at the sight of the slightest inconventionality in the way of living. But I assure you, her appearance is utterly at variance with her real self. She seems to court discomfort at any cost....

–Letters to his mother, Letter 12, Tozzer Library.

LIVING AND WORKING AT CHICHÉN WAS difficult; the bugs and the heat, even during the cooler season, added to the strenuous nature of the close, precise work Adela was doing. Light was a problem as well. Details were either exposed to natural light—which visibly hastened their deterioration—or, if they were in an enclosed area, they were badly lit. Recognizing the fragility of the murals and reliefs, she began to copy them inch by careful inch—all the while continuing her work for Maudslay.

> **Adela's original tracings were commissioned by museums and archaeologists.**

Accurate color reproductions required hand copying by someone who combined artistic ability, an exacting attention to detail, and a comprehensive knowledge of the culture that had originally produced the images. Adela's talent made her work highly sought after. Her original tracings and her copies of those tracings, sometimes to scale, were commissioned by museums and archaeologists. "The drawing to 1/4 scale gets on very slowly in these twilight days...." she wrote to Mead in 1906. "Drawing to 1/32 of an inch and correcting to 1/64 is very trying to brain and nerves as well as to eyes and hand...."

These commissions kept her from pursuing her own copying. In a 1913 letter to Professor Bowditch at Harvard, she wrote, "I want very much to get on with my own work & see about publishing my fresco copies & the Acanceh reliefs, & then do some more fieldwork before I am too old." She was 63.

Adela never lost her taste for travel as a release from "the gilded cage of English civilization," as she told Tozzer, a comment strikingly resonant with one made by Gertrude Bell, the Victorian traveler known for her explorations of the Middle East and Arabia: "To those bred under an elaborate social order few such moments of exhilaration can come as that which stands at the threshold of wild travel."

Although she didn't return to Mexico after 1908, Adela continued to study, copy, write articles, and give papers. She was active in the International Congress of Americanists, co-editing the 1912 proceedings with Franz Boas, who would shape the course of American anthropology. In her later years she worked extensively with Maya languages, studying and copying old manuscripts. Although World War I and poor health slowed her down, she worked and traveled until her death in 1923—when she was returning home from a conference in Río de Janeiro.

Her travels and work in Mexico were a source of much reflection in her later years. In a June 5, 1918, letter to George Byron Gordon, director of the University of Pennsylvania Museum, she wrote, "The mornings here [Moncton, New Brunswick] are so like tierra caliente that I often sigh and think of Chichén, and of the wide green ways between the forests of Northern Vera Cruz, with the big blue butterflies and morning glories like bits of sky fallen here and there. I, too, have been in Arcadia." ▲

PART IV:

AN ENDANGERED HISTORY

24

PLUNDERING THE PETÉN

Maya sites in northern Guatemala have been systematically looted for decades. Now the government is fighting back.

by RICHARD D. HANSEN

The Mirador Basin in the far northern Petén region of Guatemala is known for its abundance of sites, many of which are among the largest and earliest in the Maya world. Of 26 known sites, only 14 have been studied; an estimated 30 more await discovery. By the time scholars get there, looters may already have plundered them.

Trafficking in maya artifacts is big business. George Stuart of the National Geographic Society has suggested that 1,000 pieces of fine pottery leave the Maya region each month, not an unreasonable estimate in light of the site damage I have observed. The most sought-after finds are codex-style ceramics, Late Classic (A.D. 600–900) black-line-on-cream pottery depicting mythological and historical events. Looters are often paid between $200 and $500 per vessel. Collectors may pay more than $100,000 for the same pieces in a gallery or at auction. At even minimal prices this amounts to a $10-million-a-month business in stolen cultural property. Collecting Precolumbian art is often viewed as a justifiable means of preserving the past. It is, in fact, a destructive and sometimes violent business, as attested by the recent assassination in Carmelita of Carlos Catalán, a local chiclero who had become a staunch opponent of looting in the Petén.

Since 1989, the University of California, Los Angeles, Regional Archaeological Investigation of the North Petén, Guatemala (RAINPEG) Project has been documenting the extent of the plunder in the Mirador Basin. To date it has conducted major investigations at the large Middle and Late Preclassic (1000 B.C.–A.D. 250) centers of Wakná, Tintal, El Mirador, and Nakbé, all of which have been irreparably damaged by looting. Among sites that have been totally, or nearly totally, destroyed are numerous small, Late Classic (A.D. 600–900) settlements, including Huacute, Porvenir, Pacaya, Lechugal, Ramonal, La Florida, La Manteca, La Muerta, Pedernal, Altamira, La Muralla, Zacatal, El Chiquero, Guiro, and four unnamed sites between Wakná and Nakbé designated 101, 102, 103, and 104. Since Ian Graham of Harvard's Peabody Museum found little if any looting in the area during

his investigations in 1962 and 1970, we know that this destruction has taken place in the past 30 years.

Looters generally are seeking Late Classic period tombs, which are commonly found in smaller residential structures scattered among the ruins of much larger Preclassic centers. These burials provide the jades and fine codex-style pots desired by collectors. Larger structures provide the richest burials, but to reach them requires teams of diggers. Richard E.W. Adams, of the University of Texas, San Antonio, recorded 60-foot-deep looters' trenches at Río Azul, Guatemala, 35 miles east of the the Mirador Basin. Since most looters cannot distinguish between early and late structures on the basis of architectural form, Preclassic buildings are plundered as well. Burials in these structures are more difficult to locate, and looters will dig as many as a dozen trenches in a structure in the course of their search.

We located 103 major trenches and tunnels around the five plaza complexes that form the central portion of a Late Classic settlement known as the Codex Group in the northwestern area of Nakbé. Undoubtedly this area of the site was severely plundered because of the quantity and quality of its codex-style pottery. We know that numerous codex-style pieces in private collections originated there.

Because of the remoteness of the region, site protection programs have been difficult

> ## Looters will dig as many as a dozen trenches in a structure in the course of their search.

to establish. There are 12 guards to protect the sites of El Mirador and Nakbé, currently paid by the Instituto de Antropología e Historia (IDAEH) and the RAINPEG Project. To make the task more attractive to qualified personnel, the pay has been substantially improved over guards' salaries in other parts of Guatemala. To protect the remaining major sites within the Mirador Basin, however, would require an additional 60 guards, as well as horses and mules to ease travel through the region's difficult terrain.

At a symposium on the exportation of Guatemala's cultural patrimony, organized by the Ministerio de Cultura y Deportes and the United States Embassy in Guatemala and held in April of 1997 in Antigua, Guatemala, archaeologists and high-level Guatemalan government officials, including Vice-President Luis Flores Asturias, met to discuss how the country could better protect its cultural patrimony. Among the recommendations made were the establishment of a rotating patrol of armed guards who would move from site to site, an increase in wages for employees of IDAEH, and the levying of additional tourist taxes and site entrance fees to generate revenue for the protection of cultural patrimony. Other suggestions included improved training for customs officials and the expansion of UNESCO emergency import bans on antiquities, such as the one on Maya artifacts from the Petén in effect since 1989. Bilateral agreements between the United States and countries in the region regarding the confiscation of artifacts and prosecution of people responsible for illicit trade in Precolumbian art offer a longer-term and more comprehensive international legal solution. Radio and television efforts to promote the importance of protecting Guatemala's cultural heritage are a local approach worth pursuing. The symposium marked a milestone in the effort to preserve what remains of Guatemala's archaeological heritage. ≜

25

A RUN FOR THEIR LIVES

An archaeologist and his colleagues narrowly escape a mob of angry villagers.

by ANGELA M. H. SCHUSTER

IN 1997, PETER MATHEWS OF THE UNIVERSITY OF Calgary underwent a harrowing ordeal in southern Chiapas, Mexico. Mathews, 46, and ten Mexican colleagues were attacked by villagers living near the Late Classic (ca. A.D. 600–900) Maya site of El Cayo, whose ruins are located on both sides of the Usumacinta River some 80 miles southeast of Palenque. Initial newspaper accounts feared the party dead after its disappearance on June 25, one quoting Yale University's Michael Coe as saying, "It is one of the worst disasters that has ever happened in New World archaeology."

According to Mathews, trouble began on Tuesday, June 24, when his group traveled to El Cayo to make arrangements for the transport of a half-ton Maya altar to the town of Frontera Corozal to protect it from looters. Four feet in diameter, the altar is inscribed with a Maya long-count date of 9.15.0.0.0 (August 18, A.D. 731); its text tells of the reign and parentage of one of the site's rulers.

"When we were in El Cayo in mid-June to plan our upcoming field season, we were told that monuments at the site, particularly the altar that we had found in 1993, were at risk of being stolen," says Mathews. "As it turned out, logistical problems precluded our working at the site, but we thought we should move the altar to safety if the Chol Maya elders and the Instituto Nacional de Antropología e Historia agreed." With appropriate documents in hand, Mathews and his team, along with several Chol officials from Frontera Corozal, went to the site on Thursday, June 26, to reexcavate the altar, which they had buried protectively with fine dirt and a stone cairn the previous season, and crate it for removal by helicopter.

"When we arrived," says Mathews, "some of the protective covering had been removed, and there were three one-foot-long pickax gouges in the altar. We felt that we had gotten to the site just in time." The following morning, however, more than 60 angry villagers demanded that Mathews and his team stop what they were doing, telling them that the altar was to go nowhere. "By midday," says Mathews, "the situation had deteriorated. We told them we would leave the altar right where it was but that it should be reburied to protect it. By this time the group had broken down into different factions with no one in charge. We were held in the main plaza of the ruins near the altar. By nightfall, several men armed with rifles arrived and began dividing up our things. They took our money and anything of value. By this time the altar had ceased to be part of the discussion. We were told to remove our boots and get lost. We fled to the beach. Shots rang out, and we were told to stop in our tracks, leave our knapsacks in a pile, and line up on the bank of the river. We thought we'd be shot, our bodies left to float downstream.

"They preferred to beat us up, hitting us with the butts of their rifles and kicking us. They got me in the eye with a rifle and broke my nose. After the beatings, six of our party fled on foot along the river. The rest of us realized we had to cross the Usumacinta to Guatemala if we were to make it out alive. Two of our party—Martín Arcos, one of the officials from Frontera Corozal, and archaeologist Mario Aliphat—could not swim, so we tried to make a flotation device from a plastic poncho. Martín, who had suffered three broken ribs and a ruptured spleen, walked downstream and tripped over a small canoe at the water's edge. It was just big enough for him and Mario. Three of us swam across the river. The rains had started. We shivered through the night, but we did not want to light a fire and give away our location. We decided to try to make it to Piedras Negras, where Steve Houston [of Brigham Young University] had been working; he would have dry clothes and food and perhaps be in radio contact with the outside world. We hiked Saturday and most of Sunday. Late Sunday afternoon a motor launch supplying the Piedras Negras camp gave us a lift to the site, where we spent the night. The next morning, the boatman took us to Frontera Corozal, where we were met by Mexican government officials, who drove us to Palenque." The fate of the altar is uncertain. ♦

26

PROTECTING THE MAYA PAST

ARCHAEOLOGY news briefs document recent efforts to prevent looting.

Antiquities Scandal
Boston museum under fire
ARCHAEOLOGY, March/April 1998

THE REPUBLIC OF GUATEMALA HAS DEMANDED that Boston's Museum of Fine Arts (MFA) return a number of Maya antiquities, claiming they were looted from archaeological sites within its borders. The richly painted ceramics were given to the museum in 1988 by businessman Landon T. Clay and went on display in a new gallery last December 5. A day before the gallery opened, an article in the *Boston Globe* raised questions about the artifacts' provenience. Guatemala asked for their return, and the U.S. Customs Service began an investigation into how they entered the country. Guatemalan officials have promised they will take the MFA to court if their request is not met.

The MFA has refused to comment, except to say that it reviewed the pieces in 1987, before accepting them, and concluded that they had been acquired legally. Nonetheless, at the time the museum ignored the recommendation of Mayanist Clemency Chase Coggins, now of Boston University, who urged it to decline the offer. According to the *Globe*, it also refused a Guatemalan request for the artifacts' return, even though MFA attorney Weld S. Henshaw, who conducted the review, knew of a Guatemalan law banning the exportation of antiquities without a permit, and no permits had been issued for the items in Clay's collection.

The *Globe* article also cast doubt on the origins of two terra-cotta figures from Mali, loaned to the MFA by trustee William E. Teel and now on display in an adjoining room. Dating from ca. A.D. 1300–1600, the figures probably come from around Djenne, where looters have decimated archaeological sites. The government of Mali, which like Guatemala bans the exportation of antiquities, threatened legal action, and the Customs Service began an investigation. Ironically on September 19, just weeks before the MFA gallery opened, the U.S. and Mali concluded a bilateral agreement barring the importation into the U.S. of artifacts from Mali's Niger River Valley, making a 1993 emergency ban permanent. ▲

—ANDREW L. SLAYMAN

Copán Tomb Looted

Petén sites also ravaged
ARCHAEOLOGY, May/June 1998

THE 1,500-YEAR-OLD TOMB OF A QUEEN at the ancient Maya city of Copán in western Honduras was looted this past February, according to University of Pennsylvania Museum archaeologists. Discovered in 1993 (see page 19, *Who's Buried in Margarita's Tomb*), the tomb is one of the richest ever found in the Maya world, and is believed to be that of the wife of Yax K'uk Mo' (Blue Green Quetzal Macaw), who founded the Copán dynasty in A.D. 436.

"Fortunately, most of the artifacts had already been removed to a conservation laboratory," says the museum's Robert Sharer. "However, the thieves did abscond with at least five carved jades, all of which had been photographed in situ." "The looters appear to have been familiar with the pyramid's tunnel system," adds Jeremy A. Sabloff, director of the University Museum.

The looting at Copán comes on the heels of a wave of site destruction in the area. The Petén region of Guatemala has seen a significant increase in site destruction in the past year (see page 151, *Plundering the Petén*), due not only to looting but to squatters at 13 sites representing some 475 families, many of whom are Guatemalan refugees returning from Mexico in the wake of a December 1996 peace accord signed by the Guatemalan government and guerrilla forces. Some 70 families have moved into the site of Dos Pilas, clearing away monuments and cutting down trees to make room for crops.

In response to the destruction, Guatemalan vice-president Luis Flores Asturias assigned 100 additional guards to the area, bringing the total to 152. The government also pledged 800 more policemen to protect sites and national parks. Juan Antonio Valdés, director of Guatemala's Instituto de Antropología e Historia, has demanded the installation of army posts at threatened sites, but the government is hesitant to take such measures, believing they will be perceived by locals as a military offensive. ≜

–ANGELA M. H. SCHUSTER

Maya Past Protected

El Pilar reserve established
ARCHAEOLOGY, September/October 1998

AFTER MORE THAN TEN YEARS OF NEGO-tiation, a 4,000-acre tract of tropical rain forest straddling the Belize-Guatemala border has been set aside for conservation and preservation. Known as the El Pilar Archaeological Reserve for Flora and Fauna, the park features a 75-acre Maya site occupied between 300 B.C. and A.D. 1000. With 15 plazas and numerous structures, El Pilar, which reached its apogee in the Late Classic period (ca. A.D. 600–900), is the largest site in the Belize River area. An extensive trail system has been developed and visitors can witness traditional farming and craft production by modern-day Maya. "We see the reserve as a living museum," says project director Anabel Ford of the University of California, Santa Barbara, who has led excavations at the site since 1983. It is hoped that the reserve, whose revenues will be derived primarily from ecotourism, will serve as a model for sustainable development throughout the region, which has been losing natural resources to clear cutting and slash-and-burn agriculture in recent years. The El Pilar agreement marks the first time Guatemala and Belize have cooperated on a cultural issue since the latter (formerly British Hon-

duras) achieved independence in 1981. Guatemala has yet to completely abandon its claims to the former crown colony. ≜

–ANGELA M. H. SCHUSTER

Maya Art Return

Carving from the Guatemalan site of El Zotz goes home.
ARCHAEOLOGY, January/February 1999

THE DENVER ART MUSEUM HAS RETURNED a carved wooden lintel taken from the Classic period site of El Zotz in the Petén region of Guatemala, 12 miles northwest of Tikal. One of fewer than a dozen such artifacts known to exist, the lintel, dated stylistically to ca. A.D. 550–650, was stolen from temple I, the northernmost pyramid in the site's main plaza, sometime between 1966 and 1968.

According to Dorie Reents-Budet, visiting curator of the museum's New World section, the lintel depicts a ruler, standing in profile, dressed in war regalia, and holding a knotted staff of war and sacrifice known from stelae at Tikal. The ruler's name is not preserved, and it is unknown whether he was a lord of El Zotz or Tikal. Surviving texts, however, refer to his mother as a "divine," or noble, woman. The glyphs on the lintel representing his father's name also appear on a pottery vessel from Tikal.

The lintel was purchased by the Denver Art Museum in 1973, when the United States had no law prohibiting the importation of Precolumbian art from Guatemala. "When we gathered all of the information surrounding the lintel's acquisition," says Denver Art Museum director Lewis Sharp, "returning it was simply the right thing to do." The lintel, which was welcomed home by Juan Antonio Valdés of the Instituto Guatemalteco de Antropología in a repatriation ceremony this past November, will be displayed alongside a well-known wooden lintel from Tikal in the Museo Nacional de Arqueología e Etnología in Guatemala City. ≜

–ANGELA M.H. SCHUSTER

Maya Stela Fragment Returned
ARCHAEOLOGY, September/October 1999

THE CENTER SECTION OF AN INTRICATELY carved limestone stela taken from the Late Classic (A.D. 600–900) Maya site of El Perú has been returned to the government of Guatemala. Looted from the Petén site sometime in the late 1960s, the monument fragment bears the mask of a deity, possibly the Maya sun god, beneath which is depicted the head of an enemy. According to Ian Graham of Harvard's Peabody Museum of Archaeology and Ethnology, who noted the missing section of the stela when he mapped the heavily pillaged site in 1971, the fragment once formed part of a belt worn by the Maya ruler carved on the stone pillar. Other monuments stolen from the site at approximately the same time include stelae in the collections of the Cleveland Museum of Art and Kimbell Museum in Fort Worth, Texas (now known as stelae 33 and 34); a side panel from stela 33, which was sold as a separate artifact; and possibly an altar now in the collection of the Dallas Museum of Art.

The fragment was brought to Graham's attention shortly before it was to be auctioned at Sotheby's last fall. Sources tell ARCHAEOLOGY that Sotheby's experts suspected the stela fragment was hot and suggested to the owner that they return it as a gesture of good will rather than risk confiscation of the artifact and legal difficulties. The owner agreed, and the stela fragment's return was arranged by the law firm of Herrick Feinstein, which is representing Guatemala in its effort to recover stolen artifacts. ≜

–ANGELA M.H. SCHUSTER

27

MYSTERY OF THE MAYA FACADE

Astute detective work gives new meaning to a looted artwork.

by DAVID FREIDEL

IN 1968, NEW YORK ANTIQUITIES DEALER EVERETT Rassiga arranged a spectacular coup. Looters working in the jungle of Campeche in southeastern Mexico had notified their East Coast contact of the existence of a magnificent painted stucco facade decorated with the well-preserved face of a young Maya king wearing the distinctive flanged crown of royalty (see Plate 7). According to the looters, the facade graced a temple or palace at Placeres, a little-known site some 35 miles southeast of the Late Classic (A.D. 600–900) Maya metropolis of Calakmul. Flanking the king were images of old gods, each of whom held a carved Maya glyph in his left hand. The whole facade had been carefully buried, most likely during what Mayanists call a termination ritual, a ceremonial closing of an important building. Rassiga arranged for an associate to fly to Campeche, cut an airstrip near the site, carve the facade into movable chunks, swathe them in plaster for protection, and fly them to New York for sale (see Plate 4).

The facade entered the art market just as the Metropolitan Museum of Art was planning *Before Cortés*, a blockbuster exhibition of Precolumbian art. Rassiga approached the Met's director, Thomas P.F. Hoving, about acquiring the piece for the exhibition. Hoving turned it down, choosing instead to notify his counterpart, Ignacio Bernal, at the National Museum of Anthropology in Mexico City. Rassiga owned a house in Cuernavaca, and, with the cooperation of Mexican authorities, Bernal made him an offer: give up his house or return the facade. The dealer chose the house, and the looted masterpiece of Early Classic (A.D. 250–600) Maya architectural art was flown to Mexico City, where it was restored and put on display in the museum's Maya hall (see Plate 5).

The man who had been sent to oversee the clearing, cutting, and shipping of the facade to New York had taken a series of color photographs documenting the looting process, including images of the intact facade in situ. In the mid-1980s, I obtained copies of the photographs from a colleague who, as an expert in Mesoamerican art, had been shown the facade when it was for sale in New York. Though my colleague declined to purchase it, he was allowed to retain the photographs for study. My copies, which in time would provide critical information about the meaning of the facade—that it depicted an important meeting between two Maya kings—would languish in a file for more than a decade.

In February 1998, I was preparing a lecture on Maya ideas concerning Tollan, the primordial founding city of Mesoamerican mythology, for a symposium held in honor of Linda Schele at the University of Texas at Austin. Harvard epigrapher David Stuart had argued at a conference at Princeton that *Tollan*, a Nahuatl word, may have been the ancient Aztec name for the site of Teotihuacan (Place of the Gods), in the Valley of Mexico, some 30 miles north of Mexico City. I remembered that each of the old gods carved on the Mexico City facade held a rendering of an upside-down sky glyph represented by a cattail, which Stuart had recently deciphered as Pu. He believes Pu is a Maya translation of the word Tollan, and has made a strong case for the Pu glyph in Early Classic (A.D. 250–600) Maya contexts as being associated with what scholars have termed Teotihuacan symbolism—images of feathered serpents, the water god Tlaloc, speech scrolls, and distinctive "talud-tablero" architecture in which sloped steps are capped by entablatures. It was entirely possible, he surmised, that Pu, like Tollan, referred to Teotihuacan.

Why would the Maya have regarded a city some 700 miles away from their own cultural area as their original homeland? We know that Teotihuacan had strong ties to kingdoms in the Maya lowlands during the fourth and fifth centuries A.D. Stuart and several other scholars have even gone so far as to suggest that Teotihuacan actually conquered the Maya cities of Tikal in the Petén region of Guatemala and Copán in western Honduras, establishing new dynasties at each of them. Evidence for such conquest includes the Teotihuacan-style talud-tablero architecture of the tomb of Copán's fifth-century king Yax Ku'k Mo' (Green Quetzal Macaw).

The hypothesis that it was foreigners in the Maya region who declared their home

crosses the plane of our solar system's planetary orbits (see page 80, *Written in the Stars*). In Maya mythology, it marks the symbolic birthplace of Hun-Nal-Yeh, the Maize God and father of creation.

Guatemalan scholar Enrique Florescano has long proposed that the Feathered Serpent, Quetzalcoatl, the great hero of Tollan, was analogous to the Maya Maize God Hun-Nal-Yeh. Stories recorded at the time of the Spanish Conquest in highland Mexico tell that Quetzalcoatl discovered maize as the critical sustaining food for human beings. The Mexico City facade also suggests the Maya regarded *K'an*, the birthplace of the Maize God, as equivalent to Tollan, the city of Quetzalcoatl.

There are numerous examples of old gods presenting objects in Maya art. In some cases, they hand objects to lords or kings. The portrait at the center of the Mexico City facade is clearly that of a king wearing a royal crown, its flanged form complete with elaborate ear flares, a zoomorphic chin strap, and bird headdress. If, however, both of the old gods were handing Pu-place objects to this Maya king, why did the god on the viewer's right hold his Pu-place object in the wrong hand?

I returned to the photographs for a closer look. To my surprise, several frames showed the crumbling remains of a second large face mask depicting a king on the far right of the facade. It was clear that centuries of erosion and exposure to the elements had taken their toll. Clearly, in the estimation of the looters, it was simply not worth transporting

to be Pu/Tollan, I reasoned, might be tested within the context of the Pu glyph carved on the Mexico City facade. For, unlike examples of this glyph found on Early Classic monuments at Tikal and Copán, the Mexico City facade showed no obvious relationship to Teotihuacan or its associated symbolism. It was purely Maya in style.

So, I dug out the photographs. Examination of the images revealed surprising and critical facts about the Pu glyph and its context. The old god on the viewer's right displays the Pu glyph over the carved profile of a grotesque mask that Mayanists have identified as an effigy incense burner, meaning "throne" or "place of power." It makes sense, then, that the combination of glyphs means "place of Tollan" or "throne of Tollan." The small Pu glyph held by the old god on the viewer's left, however, appeared not with a mask, but beside a large cartouche containing a *K'an* cross. *K'an* means "sky" in Maya, the cross signifying the place in the night sky where the Milky Way to New York. No one ever missed the second mask. Without it, the facade is symmetrical with two old gods flanking a central king, but the Mexico City facade was never meant to be symmetrical. It was radically and wonderfully different. In one corner was an old god, in the other was a king's portrait. Looking at the original building, one would have seen two kings, each in the company of an old god.

While the composition is unique in Maya sculpture, it is common on Late Classic (A.D. 600–900) painted ceramic vases, most of which were crafted more than a century after the Mexico City facade. Mayanists call this scene the "Holmul Dancer," after the site of Holmul in the Petén where a number of vases showing the scene were excavated in the early twentieth century.

In its most common rendering, one or more dancing lords are depicted wearing elaborate costumes that feature feathered bundles on their backs with images of gods. While Karl Taube of the University of California, Riverside, has identified the dancers as impersonators of the Maize God, Yale University's Michael Coe has found that they can also represent royalty from particular cities whose names appear in the glyphic texts framing each figure. Interestingly, the vase Coe used to demonstrate this idea depicted two lords, one from Calakmul, the other from Tikal. The scene on that vase shows each lord dancing, accompanied by a dwarf holding out his hand in the same offering gesture as that of the old gods on the Mexico City facade.

A particularly fine vase showing the meeting of two lords was recently excavated at the site of Buenavista, Belize. Its inscriptions tell us that one lord is from Naranjo, the other from either Dos Pilas or Tikal. We know from inscriptions that the families of Dos Pilas and Naranjo were related, so it is likely that the lords depicted are from these two cities. Given this iconographic tradition, I believe the Mexico City facade shows such a meeting of kings.

Who are they? The answer lies in the *Pu* glyphs held by each of the old gods, which I believe represent each king's ancestral source of legitimate authority.

The old god on the viewer's right holds the combination of glyphs that reads Pu-place or "place of Tollan," which I take to mean Teotihuacan. In the god's other hand is a rabbit head that David Stuart has translated as *bah,* meaning portrait or image. So the king beside him is being identified as a lord of Teotihuacan. The image of the king, however, is not that of a Teotihuacano, but of a Maya king. I believe that this lord, then, is a person who claims ancestry at Teotihuacan.

I believe he is a king from Tikal. Following the work of Stuart, British epigrapher Simon Martin, and Nikolai Grube of the Universität Bonn, we know that Tikal saw the establishment of a new line of kings in A.D. 378, following its military victory over many of the cities of the Maya Lowlands, which had been led by a site represented by a snake-head emblem glyph. The first of these kings, Nuun Yax Ain (Green Crocodile), claimed descent from a Teotihuacan lord that scholars have dubbed Spearthrower Owl, his ancestry evident in portraits carved on Tikal stelae 4 and 31.

Who then is the lord of the *Pu-K'an?* Though *K'an* is generally regarded as a purely mythical location, being the birthplace of Hun-Nal-Yeh, the Maya Maize God, I think that the Lowland Maya had a real geographical place in mind when they referred to it. To identify it, however, one must delve into epigraphy and understand the Maya penchant for outrageous linguistic puns. Such word play served to illustrate natural connections between powerful sacred forces and ideas. The word for sky in Yucatecan Maya, for example, is *ka'an*; the word for snake *kan*. In Maya texts the sky is often shown as a great snake, a practice begun in the Late Preclassic (300 B.C.–A.D. 250). With this in mind, I believe the *k'an* glyph is a representation of the snake-head site thought by many Maya scholars, including myself, to be Calakmul, a massive site in southern Campeche (see page 28, *Maya Superstates*). If this is the case, I believe the lord depicted on the well-preserved portion of the facade is a king of Calakmul.

We know the kings of Calakmul called themselves Holy Snake Lords. It might be taken as a coincidence that they called themselves by a word that sounds like the word for the birthplace of the Maize God. Calakmul was the capital of a widespread and powerful hegemony of Lowland Maya kingdoms during the Late Classic period. Recent excavations at Calakmul, directed by Ramon Carrasco of the Instituto Nacional de Antropología e Historia, have confirmed that it was already a major urban center in the Early Classic period. Just how early Calakmul began to establish its political and military hegemony remains an open ques-

tion since there are so few Lowland Maya centers where archaeologists have conducted excavations of Early Classic structures. Moreover, texts from this early period are relatively rare; those that exist are biased, as they come from Tikal and Copán, enemies of the snake-head site.

What remains problematic for me is the notion of Calakmul as an ancestral city. Even though the site attained some degree of prominence in the Early Classic, I find it unlikely that, being such a newcomer on the Lowland political landscape, it would have been regarded as the city where Maya civilization began.

> ## The Mexico City facade is an extraordinary work of art.

I think we must look for such a city elsewhere, in the geographic center of the Lowland Maya world. Twenty-five miles south of Calakmul lies a city of such vast monuments that they dwarf all later efforts by kings and potentates. It is El Mirador, "the lookout," the most powerful city in the Preclassic Maya world. By the fourth century A.D., however, it had become a ghost town, inhabited by a few intrepid families of master artists who, living in the shadows of the great ruined temples, made El Mirador and nearby Nakbé their home. Some of the finest ceramics ever made in the Maya world were created at El Mirador. Many are executed in the codex style, with scenes and accompanying texts painted in fine black lines on a cream field in a manner similar to that used in Maya bark-paper books.

According to Simon Martin, glyphic texts on some of the codex-style vessels list kings of Kan, a snake-head city. He does not believe they are referring to Calakmul, but to its predecessor, El Mirador. The idea is that Calakmul inherited the mantle of El Mirador and with it the stewardship of the place where humanity was fashioned of the flesh of the Maya Maize God.

I suggest that the facade depicts an encounter between the kings of Calakmul and Tikal, who regarded themselves as the scions of two primordial creation places, K'an and Pu, associated in their time with El Mirador and Teotihuacan. If, in fact, the facade was commissioned as a testament to a detente between Tikal and Calakmul, possibly during the reign of Green Crocodile in the late fourth century, it was short lived. From the fifth century onward, the Lowland Maya world was engulfed by war. Both cities collapsed in the ninth century, in part because of their inability to come to a lasting peace.

What is interesting is that one of the looters claimed that the facade was actually taken from Calakmul. However, this site attribution was probably meant to throw off other looters. The building from which the facade was removed as well as the airstrip used to transport it have been found at Placeres, a relatively obscure center halfway between Calakmul and Tikal's outpost at Río Azul. The facade may have commemorated the most important event ever to happen in that place.

The Mexico City facade is an extraordinary work of art and it is remarkable that, despite the depredations of looters, it has survived. It is also an object lesson that even very large and richly complex examples of Maya art lose crucial meaning when torn from their contexts. If the looters had not recorded their work photographically, no one would have suspected that the composition included a second monumental king mask. That information, in my view, is absolutely vital to a true understanding of the historical and cosmological meaning of the facade. Only time and more research will tell if this interpretation is correct. The Mexico City facade is certain to be a key to understanding the politics of Early Classic Mesoamerica. ≜

28

PIONEERS OF THE BAJO

Jungle surveyors in Guatemala uncover the breadbasket of the Maya world.

by TOM GIDWITZ

THE ABANDONED CITY OF YAXHÁ HAS EVERY-thing you might expect at a Maya site: pyramids and stelae, howler monkeys, and a haunting sense of a tragic past (see Plate 8). At the site's edge is excavation head-quarters, thatch-roofed stucco buildings, a ceramics lab crammed with sherds and pots, and a small army of diggers, masons, and machete-wielding workers.

All this seems as traditional as can be, yet here on a shaded porch, with its view of a sparkling lake and tropical jungle, a revolution is in the making. And it advances a little further each time NASA's Tom Sever and Dan Irwin spread their wares before me.

Sever and Irwin are unrolling photographs as big as bath towels, taken from satellites 400 miles out in space (see Plate 9). These images turn a monotonous swamp, smothered in forest, into a sharply defined landscape, dotted with islands of habitable high ground, ancient reservoirs, long-forgotten causeways, and pyramids that poke above the trees. Never has a research team seen the jungle in so many ways. There is a set of infrared images, a sharply etched mix of scarlet and black that shows almost every tree; a topographic radar map of day-glo lemon, red, and green; and a jumble of turquoise and magenta dots—a 3-D anaglyph image—that, through tinted glasses, morphs into an upland ridge.

Yaxhá is in Guatemala's Petén district, in the heart of the southern Maya lowlands, on the edge of Bajo la Justa, a sprawling 23-square-mile seasonal wetland 18 miles southeast of Tikal. Bajo la Justa is just one of many bajos that make up 40 percent of the Petén landscape. In the rainy season, *bajos* are swampy thickets, great forested tracts of mud that mire any mule or human foolish enough to set foot in them. But this is May, the last weeks of the dry season, and Sever, Irwin, and research partners Pat Culbert, professor emeritus at the University of Arizona, and Vilma Fialko of Guatemala's Instituto de Antropología e Historia have been venturing into this vast wasteland every day. They believe that the *bajos*, once ringed by Maya cities but long ignored by archaeologists, were the breadbasket of the Maya world.

Some 1,300 years ago, after centuries of exponential growth, the southern Maya lowlands in present-day Belize, Guatemala, and southern Mexico were home to what Culbert terms "one of the most densely populated areas in the preindustrial world." The Maya city-states had populations of astonishing size; their magnificent pyramids towered over tens of thousands of dwellings. In the Late Classic period (A.D. 600–900), the Maya averaged more than 500 people per square mile, totaling many millions of people in an area the size of Maine; but disaster soon followed. In one of history's most puzzling demographic mysteries, Maya civilization collapsed. By A.D. 950, the lowland cities were largely deserted.

There are many explanations for this catastrophe. War, drought, and disease are the most commonly given, but Culbert and his associates find these explanations incomplete. In fact, they say that searching for a single cause for the collapse is misguided. The key to the Maya fall, they claim, lay in the mechanism that spawned the civilization's long period of growth, in the finely tuned agricultural system that the Maya created to feed themselves.

They are convinced that the Maya tamed the *bajo* wetlands with dams and canals, turning the swamp into farmland, and establishing villages and administrative centers on higher ground. "The fields must have been crammed with workers, laboring from dawn till dusk," says Culbert, who envisions a resource-hungry Maya barely one step ahead of the demands of the day.

Study the *bajos*, they say, and you'll understand how war may have been just a symptom, how a Maya drought may have been manmade, and why the Maya could not save themselves forever. The team has embarked on a campaign to reconstruct what Culbert calls "an extinct agricultural system," to pull back the jungle's thick green curtain with machetes, pack mules, state-of-the-art satellite imaging, and information gleaned from ceramics, soil cores, NASA computers, and local farming techniques,

They're also working with a sense of urgency, certain that the past holds lessons for today. Stand atop Yaxhá's pyramids and your heart sinks: not 20 miles away, walls of smoke rise in the sky. Settlers are swarming into the Petén, slashing and burning the rain forest, clearing cornfields and cattle pastures. The Mexican lowlands have been almost entirely deforested; the Guatemalan jungle is not far behind. "There's a modern collapse in the making," says Culbert. "The ancient Maya may help us avoid that." The researchers believe they can uncover how the Maya successfully farmed in this area, and then take those techniques and use them today. The goal is to adopt what worked for the Maya, but stop short of their excesses.

TO EXPLORE THE *BAJO* IS TO EXPERIENCE sweltering heat, impenetrable thickets, shrubs that ooze burning sap, four-inch-long wasps, lethal snakes, killer bees, and ants everywhere you sit. But it is also a place of beauty. "I adore the jungle," says Culbert. "Every day there's some little marvel." On our walks into the bajo, he inspects sprays of red orchid, orange mushrooms covering a log, and glistening blue butterflies whom he woos with gentle words.

At 71, Culbert is one of the grand old men of Maya studies. Visit the Tikal museum and you'll see his photo on the wall, in a group shot from the 1960s. His tall, lanky figure, broad glasses, and beard (although not then white) are instantly recognizable. In 1960, he began ten years of work as the ceramics expert at the University of Pennsylvania's Tikal excavation. He wrote the first complete description of the Tikal ceramic sequence, and his books are required reading for Mayanists. He insists he's trying to spend less time in the jungle, though he's already

planning his next two years of field research.

Culbert has a fondness for melodrama, and he loves to play a hunch. He bets on sports and poker slots, and in his research he has combined a gambler's instincts with a marathoner's tenacity. Twenty-five years ago he sensed conventional wisdom about the Maya was wrong. As Tikal's ceramics specialist, Culbert scrutinized every sherd of the site's pottery, at first from the elite's temple tombs, then those from an ever-growing number of house mounds discovered in 50 square miles around the city.

The large number and dates of the house mounds revealed a paradox in terms of population growth and subsistence. In the 1960s, the Maya were thought to have gotten by on slash-and-burn agriculture, as they did during the Preclassic (2000 B.C–A.D. 250), when their population was no more than 100 people per square mile. But by A.D. 400, in the middle of the Early Classic era, Tikal's population had reached more than 250 per square mile in the city center. The city would eventually house 60,000 people. Slash-and-burn farming could never have supported so many.

In the 1970s, researchers were finding evidence of Maya wetlands agriculture in the Yucatán Peninsula. It was said that raised fields in permanent wetlands—relatively few compared to the ubiquitous *bajos*—along with extensive root crop cultivation, kitchen gardens, multiple crops on terraced highland fields, and dry season plantings in river floodplains would have filled any subsistence shortfall.

Culbert was not convinced. If the Maya relied solely on these sources, the largest Late Classic Maya city-states would have had to

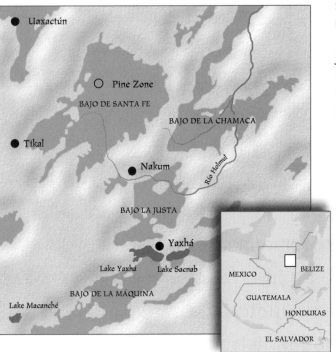

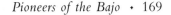

for the harvest of two dry season crops.

In the late 1970s, Culbert joined a team that used airborne radar to pierce the forest canopy and survey the *bajos* for proof of widespread cultivation (see Plate 10). But no sooner were their data published, than critics began to tear them apart. Their canals and wetland fields were phony signals spawned by system noise, false echoes, and cracks in the limestone bedrock. But Culbert pressed on, and in 1989, he discovered drainage canals cut into a *bajo* near Río Azul in northeastern Guatemala. It was the first drained field system found in the Petén.

import food from as far as 50 miles away. And he kept bumping up against the fact that most of the region's major sites border on *bajos*. For example, Tikal is on the edge of Bajo de Santa Fe, Calakmul borders Bajo el Laberinto, Yaxhá and Nakum flank Bajo la Justa. How could the Maya dismiss a resource so close at hand?

"You can't have a population density of 500 people per square mile and ignore 40 percent of the landscape," says Culbert. He maintains that the Maya not only planted two crops during the rainy season on elevated ridges but used the *bajos* during the dry season as well. Canals cut into the *bajos* could have sped drainage of the rainy season's floods. This would have allowed earlier planting, at the dry season's onset, and extended the growing season long enough

A SUCCESSFUL AGRICULTURAL SYSTEM requires fertile ground to farm, people to work and manage it, and water. Skeptics have long doubted the *bajo* has any of these things. But smack in the middle of Bajo la Justa, between Yaxhá and Nakum, is a site that has all three. Known as Poza Maya, it sits atop a ridge that the Maya modified to form a sheer bluff 90 feet high. It has 40 large structures—palaces, temples, and 60-foot pyramids—arranged around nine courtyards, built upon floor after floor of older, buried plazas. There's a squarish, artificial *aguada*, a waterhole or reservoir, known as Maya Aguada, half a mile away. Bermed with walls more than six feet high and two-hundred-fifty yards on a side, Maya Aguada appears to have been carved out of the bajo with a giant knife; its size and depth make it easily identifiable in satellite images.

First described in the 1970s, Poza Maya is an enormous site to be in a *bajo*, undoubtedly an administrative center and a place of wealth and power. Then in the early 1990s came a new discovery, one that intrigued Vilma Fialko as few had before. In the bottom of a looters' trench sliced deep into a pyramid, archaeologists discovered a broken pot, part of a sacred offering. Inside was a tiny ear of ancient corn.

Fialko, 47, is director of intersite surveys for Project Triangle, the most ambitious archaeological research effort in the history of the Petén. Sponsored jointly by Guatemala and Germany, the project is excavating and restoring the Maya cities of Yaxhá, Nakum, and Naranjo, and exploring the jungle in between. Its ultimate goal is to create a national park to serve as a buffer between existing bioreserves and the encroaching deforestation.

A handsome woman with high cheekbones and thick black hair, Fialko spends two weeks a month, six months a year, deep in the rain forest. Since 1994 she has been leading a team of 24 archaeologists, topographers, and laborers on grueling 12-hour days. They cut trails over ridges and highlands, across rivers and through the *bajos*. They survey the land, map ruins, dig test pits, and analyze unearthed ceramics across a swath of jungle a half-mile wide. It's brutal, exhausting work: the 14-mile survey between Nakum and Tikal took her a year and a half. But Fialko thrives on it, and the jungle has worked itself deep into her bones. In 1999, when she was a scholar in residence at Dumbarton Oaks in Washington, D.C., she felt homesick. "It wasn't Guatemala homesick," says Fialko. "It was jungle homesick." She papered her office with huge photographs of the rain forest. "It was solid green. But I felt much better."

Fialko has long been fascinated with how the Maya adapted to different environments. Her surveys for Project Triangle span unmapped jungle and cross a spectrum of habitats and ancient communities, large and small. On her *bajo* transects, Fialko found remains of residential structures on "islands" of high ground above the level of the rainy season floods. Ceramic chronologies showed their occupation mirrored that of the larger Maya lowlands—beginning in the Preclassic and ending with the Late Classic collapse.

In 1993, Fialko met Culbert at the Guatemala national archaeological meetings, and invited him to join her study. Soon after, she sent him the sample of Poza Maya corn. Culbert had it radiocarbon dated—it was the fruit of a Maya harvest in approximately A.D. 500.

> Poza Maya is an enormous site to be in a *bajo*, undoubtedly an administrative center and a place of wealth and power.

Corn at Poza Maya. Could it have come from the *bajo* itself? Skeptics say the dry season soil is too parched to be cultivated. To find out, Culbert and Fialko turned to local experts who know the *bajo* plants and soil best: *milperos*, who farm milpas, or cornfields; gum tapping *chicleros*, who harvest sap from chicle trees; and *xateros*, who collect wild sprays of xate palm for international export to florists. The locals told them the bajo soil varies, with some areas useless for farming, others highly prized.

The most desirable land is dominated by palm trees, indicating soil that is well drained, yet sufficiently moist. Culbert and Fialko once again walked the transects and

Mundo Maya

Mexico and four Central American nations have joined forces to promote and preserve their shared Maya heritage. The multimillion dollar project, known as "Mundo Maya," or "Maya World," intends to showcase the history and culture of the entire region as "one entity without borders," according to Mexico's Minister of Tourism, Pedro Joaquin Coldwell.

The first infusion of funds for the project, a gift equivalent to $1 million for planning and feasibility studies, has come from the European Economic Community, itself about to become an entity without borders. While the boundaries of Mexico and the other participating countries, Belize, Guatemala, El Salvador, and Honduras, will remain secure, every effort will be made, according to project planners, to facilitate travel to and within the region.

Travelers flying from Guatemala City to Mérida, for instance, will no longer have to go to Mexico City first; tourists en route from Belize City to Mexico City will not have to touch down in Miami. Bus travel throughout the region will also be simplified, with travelers no longer required to change buses when crossing into Mexico from Guatemala.

Cancun will serve as the "gateway" to the Mundo Maya, according to project promoters, who hope to lure some of that resort's two million annual visitors into the Maya heartland. By developing or improving local and regional museums and by providing tourist facilities at some of the smaller,

more remote archaeological sites Mundo Maya developers hope to spread the touristic wealth. At present, of the 106 archaeological sites open to the public in the five-country region, eight of them receive 85 percent of the annual influx of tourists. One million people, for instance, visited Mexico's Tulum last year. "If so many people are going to visit so few sites," says one anguished Mexican tourist official, "they are going to destroy them."

The EEC's investment will be used to develop marketing studies, train personnel, create promotional materials, and provide logistical support for archaeological projects in El Salvador and southeastern Mexico. Mexico is already providing technical assistance and tourism development programs in both Belize and Honduras. Meanwhile, there are plans to build a marina at Belize City, a museum in Belmopán, Belize, and an airport at the site of Copán, in Honduras, where some of the region's most exciting archaeological fieldwork is now in progress.

"We still have a lot of work to do with our own people in this region," cautions Rodolfo Lobato Gonzales, Mexico's Mundo Maya high commissioner. "We still have roads running through sites, urban sprawl, jungle encroachments, and a lack of proper tourist facilities. Improving what we have has got to be a grassroots effort. Our people have to become aware of what they have to offer. Once we convince them, it won't be too difficult to convince the rest of the world."

—PETER A. YOUNG

bajo roads. They counted plants and tested the soil. Palm *bajo*, its fertile, moist dark soil more hospitable to farming than even that of upland forests, was found along one-third of the transects and two-thirds of the bajo road they surveyed.

But these transects were just two narrow samples. To prove the potential of the entire *bajo*, Fialko and Culbert could cut more survey transects, but it would take them years to achieve a systematic overview. They needed another technique to investigate the *bajo*, a method that would let them study the whole region, rather than one site, or one strip of land, at a time.

THE MAYA LIVED IN A TRIPARTITE UNI-verse—below was Xibalba, the watery home of the Lords of the Dead; in the middle was our material world, borne on the back of a giant turtle; in the sky above, the sun and planets followed the long, scaly body of the Cosmic Monster, a two-headed beast represented by the Milky Way. Maya kings, queens, and high priests communicated with the lords of Xibalba and the heavens through vision serpents—giant, twisting, hallucinatory snakes that appeared to the elect when they pierced their tongues or penises and shed their sacred blood.

Fortunately, communicating with the sky is a bit easier these days, and it's essential to Tom Sever and Dan Irwin's work. As we stand in a cool grove of corozal palms, beneath the arching domes formed by their long, feathery leaves, Sever and Irwin are capturing satellite signals with their global positioning system receiver. Their aim is to pinpoint this grove's exact latitude and longitude, find it on their high-altitude images,

and use its characteristics to locate and measure the extent of similar groves that grow throughout the *bajo*.

Sever and Irwin have been working together for three years, and it's hard to imagine a more tightly meshed partnership. At 52, Sever is NASA's only staff archaeologist, an expert in ancient astronomy and modern-day space science. Although it may seem odd for an archaeologist to be on NASA's roster, Sever plays an important role in the agency's efforts to understand planet Earth. He virtually invented the methods of using airborne or satellite data—remote sensing, or RS—to interpret archaeological sites. Irwin, 33, is one of a new generation of RS specialists who are expanding the field's horizons.

Culbert and Fialko asked Sever to join their project in 1995 in the hopes his high altitude images could help them quantify *bajo* vegetation. They soon saw that his imagery could do what Culbert's own pioneering radar survey could not: reveal the canals, causeways, and structures hidden beneath the forest canopy.

A tall, athletic man with a trim moustache and a ready laugh, Sever has a relentless devotion to the potential of RS, though his passion has not come cost free. On one mission he contracted chronic malaria, and once a band of left-wing Guatemalan guerrillas captured and held him at gunpoint for ten hours. When I first met him at his office at NASA's Marshall Space Flight Center at Huntsville, Alabama, I was taken in by his languid Missouri Ozark drawl, but Sever is hardly laid-back. His mental engines run at light speed, and he likes to keep them stoked. His dream, he half jokes, is to become a short-order breakfast cook, thriving on the frenzy of shouted orders.

In his teens, unhappy at seminary school, Sever "fell in love with the sky." Escaping his dorm after dark he found solace in the stars and filled the night with invented constellations like the Tugboat, the Robot, and the Baseball Bat. For his master's in archaeology and astronomy at the University of Illinois, he studied Anasazi astronomy and their observatories at Chaco Canyon, New Mexico, and Mesa Verde, Colorado. He spent a summer in Peru, mapping the Quechuan Inka's ceques, sacred lines that radiate from Cuzco's Temple of the Sun. There are 42 of these lines inscribed in the ground that fan out for miles into the mountains; in three months Sever and his colleagues could trace just two and a half. "I felt there just had to be a better way than walking through the Andes in this tedious, laborious, intensive activity," he recalls. The better way was a satellite high in the sky.

Remote sensing is the observation of objects and phenomena from a distance. The human eye is one kind of remote sensor, sensitive to the energy of visible light. But visible light is just a narrow sliver of the entire electromagnetic spectrum. By using coated films or electronic sensors sensitive to, say, near infrared or thermal radiation, remote sensors can detect the energy humming from objects all around us and pluck out information we would otherwise be unable to see.

Every substance has its own spectral signature—it emits or reflects energy at a number of characteristic wavelengths. Remote sensors reading these spectral signatures can distinguish oak from maple trees, granite from sandstone, a clear spring from a muddy pond. In fact, spectral signatures can be so distinct that satellites can identify disturbed soil over gravesites, a buried wall releasing the sun's warmth at night, or a distinct crop of plants growing on an irrigation ditch now filled with sediment. These spectral signatures, assigned false colors with computers, make hidden features leap to the eye.

RS satellites, however, do not free researchers from investigations on the ground. When satellites pass over fresh territory, or when a new generation of remote sensors flies aloft, they detect undefined spectral signatures. Scientists must link these to corresponding material in the field by visiting suspected ruins or other features to find out exactly what they are. This process is called "ground-truthing." "Without it," says Sever, "we'd just see chaos."

The first generation of remote sensors—cameras sent aloft in hot air balloons—took pictures for archaeologists as early as 1891. But 25 years ago, when Sever first tried to convince colleagues that satellite RS could change their world, his message went unheeded. The 1970s Landsat satellite could not detect any object smaller than 250 feet across; data processing was expensive; and there was an aversion to mathematics in what was, essentially, a conservative branch of the humanities. "Computers, RS, and multivariate analysis were not the typical things archaeologists were used to," he says.

In 1978, Sever quit his high-school teaching job to crunch numbers at NASA's RS laboratory, the John C. Stennis Space Center in Mississippi. He spent years mastering the computer algorithms that turn spectral signatures into useful images. In 1982, his NASA colleagues flew over Chaco Canyon

Maya King Unearthed

The tomb of a fifth-century A.D. Maya king has been found at La Milpa in northwestern Belize. Discovered within a stone vault built into a rock-cut chamber six feet wide, ten feet long, and six feet high, the remains are those of a male 35 to 50 years old. A little more than five feet tall, he had no teeth, a possible indication of disease or poor nutrition, and his neck vertebrae showed signs of trauma. The king was found lying on his back, adorned with a green jadeite necklace bearing the carved head of a vulture, and ear spools inlaid with obsidian. A jadeite bead the size of a cherry was found in the king's mouth. The green stone was an ancient Maya metaphor for life and breath.

"The jadeite vulture pendant is particularly significant," says Boston University archaeologist and site excavator Norman Hammond. "The bird is the quintessential sign of kingship in the ancient Maya world. We also believe that this is a royal tomb from the sheer complexity of the burial ritual." Unlike most royal burials, however, the La Milpa tomb was not built within a pyramid, but dug into the site's main plaza. Because of its location the tomb escaped the notice of looters who ravaged the site in the 1970s.

Although no inscriptions have been found within the tomb that would identify its occupant, Hammond believes the remains may be those of Bird Jaguar, whose name appears on an early fifth-century stela discovered at the site in 1993 and recently translated by epigrapher Nikolai Grube of the University of Bonn.

La Milpa, whose ruins include 11 plazas and some 50 masonry structures, flourished in two periods the first between ca. A.D. 1 and 450, the second between ca. 750 and 900—between which the site was abandoned. The newly discovered king was among the last to rule during the site's first occupation.

—ANGELA M.H. SCHUSTER

and scanned its prehistoric Anasazi Indian villages with a new type of sensor, the Thermal Infrared Multispectral Scanner (TIMS). The TIMS has 16-foot resolution and is so sensitive it can measure temperature differentials of a tenth of a degree. Sever massaged the data for months, bringing to light building foundations, fields, and 1,000-year-old roads. Eventually, with the help of Boston University's James Wiseman, he cosponsored a landmark 1984 conference where he presented his findings to two dozen of the United States' leading archaeologists and won them over.

In the years since, Sever has used remote sensors on satellites, the space shuttle, jets, prop planes, and helicopters. He has found ancient biblical watchtowers, prehistoric footpaths buried in volcanic ash (see ARCHAEOLOGY, November/December 1988), and features associated with the long-sought Maya Site Q.

In Central America, Sever's impact has been profound. In 1988, he studied a proposed hydroelectric dam project on Guatemala's Usumacinta River that threatened to submerge dozens of Petén villages and some of the region's most important Maya sites. Sever produced a startling Landsat image—the river's Mexican side was almost totally deforested; in Guatemala, the land was still thick with trees. When Guatemala's president saw the picture he halted the project and convinced the presidents of Mexico and the other Central American countries to pledge to protect the environment.

One result of this work was the Mesoamerican Biological Corridor, a continuous green belt of parks and nature reserves that will eventually stretch from southern Mexico to Panama. Sever shares responsibility for mapping and monitoring the corridor, and he hired environmental scientist Dan Irwin to help.

Irwin is a short, spirited, gregarious man, and he seems to know every laborer, driver, *chiclero*, and scientist in the Petén. He worked for four years in the district as a remote-sensing specialist for Conservation International, a nonprofit environmental conservation agency, and spent weeks at a time conducting vegetation surveys in the jungle. In 1996, he married a woman from rural San Andrés, a village of *chicleros* and *xateros* who depend on the forest for survival.

The Petén's future weighs heavily on Irwin. In San Andrés, now his second home, he has built a children's library and a handful of businesses—a ferryboat service, a family billiard parlor, an ironworks, and an internet café—to provide employment alternatives to slash-and-burn farming. He has brought generators and slide projectors to isolated jungle villages, where excited crowds turn out to see his aerial images. At first, no one knew what they were looking at, and Irwin had to teach them how to read the pictures. "They started seeing a road they knew, a lake, and then the forest boundaries," he recalls. "Their mental light bulbs went on, and I'll never forget it—they started to realize they'd better take these conservation projects seriously."

Fialko and Culbert have used the RS imagery to locate elevated ridges and *bajo*

Drought and the Maya Demise

A 200-year drought beginning ca. A.D. 800 may have played a substantial role in the decline of Classic Maya civilization in the Lowlands of the southern Yucatán Peninsula, according to geologists David A. Hodell and Jason H. Curtis of the University of Florida, and Mark Brenner of the university's Department of Fisheries and Aquatic Sciences, who studied core samples from the bed of Lake Chichancanab in the Yucatán Lowlands. Chemical analysis of shell carbonate and gypsum, burned grasses, and root fragments from the samples indicated that the driest period in the region since the lake's formation 8,000 years ago coincided with the ninth-century collapse of Classic Maya civilization in the area. Moreover, evidence of low lake levels elsewhere in Mexico and of increased forest fires in Costa Rica suggests that the drought was widespread. While the drought may have marked the end of Classic Maya civilization at many cities to the south, others

such as Chichén Itzá, Uxmal, Kabah, and Sayil in the northern Yucatán continued to flourish.

Theories about the collapse of the Classic Maya have included overpopulation, inter-city wars, and environmental degradation such as forest clearance, soil depletion, and erosion. While these factors certainly contributed to the collapse, the drought, which probably lasted at least two centuries, may have brought the region to its breaking point. According to Mayanist Jeremy Sabloff, director of the University of Pennsylvania Museum of Archaeology and Anthropology, "The arrival of a drier regime would have exacerbated the perilous situation, ultimately causing the demise of elite power, the abandonment of many urban centers, and important demographic and economic shifts from the southern to northern Lowlands."

—MARC S. PERLMAN

islands, and virtually every one they visit has a site. They have discovered settlements dating as far back as 500 B.C. and occupied for generations, some with hundreds of structures and elite residences yielding sherds of painted pots. With RS, they can find old roads and trails and pinpoint the most promising sites for their excavations.

Deep in Bajo de Santa Fe, Fialko has discovered a 1–1.5-mile-wide forest of Chiapas white pines growing in the scrub, the only pines for 100 miles. The satellite images led her to a 50-foot-wide *bajo* island in its midst, where she and Liwy Grazioso, her field director, have excavated a curious square building. Its quarried stone was brought from three miles away, and it held artifacts of the elite: elaborately worked obsidian pieces, polished stone ear plugs, and a bracelet of tiny, carved shell figures, their hands clasped as if bound.

> # Archaeologists discover a saga of ecological exploitation, change, adapation, and defeat.

IN A LAND WHERE 90 PERCENT OF THE rain falls between May and December, where the porous limestone bedrock sucks away water like a sponge, the Maya made extraordinary efforts to save every drop. Satellite pictures show canal networks and miles of grand causeways that may have been aqueducts. Fialko has found dams and weirs on *bajo* streams. She has discovered that the floodplain of the Holmul River, once a year-round *bajo* river linking many of the area's largest cities, is peppered with reservoirs and

chultuns, the Maya's bottle-shaped, underground storage pits that may have been dug to catch water.

The team asked Nick Dunning, a University of Cincinnati environmental archaeologist, to take a look at the *bajos'* soil history. In corings from upland lakes and trenches in dry dirt from several *bajos,* he found that the Maya's environment underwent a drastic change midway through their tenure. Beginning around A.D. 100, most of the area's surface water disappeared. Several feet below the *bajos'* surface is a layer of what was once moist, wetland peat, rich with pollen from trees, aquatic plants, and corn; at the end of the Preclassic era, and for the next 500 years, this soil was buried in successive layers of water-borne limestone clay.

These strata tell a story. When paired with the *bajos'* archaeological evidence, and the findings of other researchers throughout the lowlands, the history of the Maya environment becomes clear. It is a saga of ecological exploitation, change, adaptation, and defeat.

The Maya first took up residence in the lowlands around 2000 B.C. The *bajos* were then year-round wetlands or shallow lakes fringed with water lilies, cattails, and grassland. The Maya prospered on their shores. They were soon sowing seed in their marshlands, and clearing the forests in adjacent uplands to farm.

As the Maya population grew, slash-and-burn farming chewed through the upland forests. Ultimately, virtually every tree in sight was cut. Erosion and evaporation quickened. Rain scoured away the upland's fertile soil and wore at the limestone beneath. The rock, eroded to powder, washed downhill, filling the *bajos'* shallow basins with fine-grained clay.

By the end of the Late Preclassic era, ca. A.D. 250, the Maya had transformed their environment. The *bajos* had silted up. The permanent wetlands were gone. Rain ponds and puddles now lingered in the *bajos* only into the dry season's first sun-baked weeks. For five months a year, water was scarce.

The Maya had to adapt. Nakbe and Mirador, large urban centers that once thrived on the *bajos'* edge, were abandoned. At other cities, water control grew paramount; the Maya built large reservoirs at Calakmul, Uaxactún, La Milpa, and other urban centers. At Tikal alone, there is evidence of ten reservoirs with a 40-million-gallon capacity, built to capture the runoff from the city center's paved plazas.

For food they farmed the *bajos*, cutting irrigation ditches into the limestone clay and building up mounds beside them for planting. They built a network of administrative settlements on *bajo* islands. They dammed arroyos and bled water from the rivers. The population doubled, then doubled again.

Adaptation was successful—for a time. The cities grew more crowded, the elite more numerous, the temples and palaces grander still. But by the Late Classic, around A.D. 750, the system's capacity had been reached. Human skeletal remains from the last decades of Maya rule unearthed at the sites of Tikal, Altar de Sacrificios, and Copán suggest a decline in stature and show an increased number of scars from malnourishment. The soil was exhausted, the farming infrastructure weak. Warfare increased. Polities fractured. The end had come.

ON ONE OF MY LAST AFTERNOONS IN the area, I dragged the team to the top of Yaxhá's Temple 216 for a picture—even Pat Culbert, who abjures pyramids and hates heights. The sun was brutal, and we were tired. We had hiked much of that morning, journeying to ground-truth a strange feature revealed in the images, only to be chased from the site by killer wasps.

Temple 216 is a towering pyramid that overlooks Lake Yaxhá and a panorama of jungle. But the view that day was sobering. The sky was hazy with the ash of smoking rain forest. To the east, a dozen fires burned.

The Petén landscape is undergoing its greatest transformation since the Maya stripped it bare. In the last 40 years it has lost half its forest as its population has shot from 20,000 to 400,000. By the year 2020, even if current laws protecting the Guatemalan rain forest are strictly enforced, only 16 percent of its original coverage will remain; if deforestation continues without enforcement of the laws, only two percent will survive.

As roads slice the jungle open and a quilt of farmland spreads, the soft limestone Maya ruins, stripped of shade, fall prey to heat and rainfall and crumble in the sun. Looters rush in, trash tombs, and buzz-saw sculpture. Many ancient buildings are so perforated with holes they are in danger of collapse.

Says Sever, "We're literally in a race against time." ≜

29

ON THE HEALER'S PATH

A journey through the Maya rain forest

by ANGELA M.H. SCHUSTER

There is in this land a great quantity of medicinal plants of various properties; and if there were any person here who possessed a knowledge of them, it would be most useful and effective, for there is no disease to which the native Indians do not apply the plants.
—DIEGO DE LANDA, *Relación de las Cosas de Yucatán,* 1566

WHACK-ACK-ACK-ACK. EACH STRIKE OF THE machete echoes through the rain forest, setting off a cacaphonous response from all manner of birds and monkeys. A clean cut in a tree trunk begins to ooze a blood-red sap. "K'ik'-te, the blood tree," explains our guide Leopoldo "Polo" Romero. "We use it to treat open sores and chronic skin conditions." For Polo, a 56-year-old Yucatec Maya, the bewildering tangle of vines and trees through which we have been hiking for the past several hours is a jungle pharmacy rich in prescriptions for every known human affliction. Polo is a bush doctor and treater of snake bites. He is also one of a handful of curanderos, traditional Maya healers, who has come to the 6,000-acre Terra Nova Medicinal Reserve in western Belize to share his knowledge of the rain forest and the curative properties of its plants with scientists from the New York Botanical Garden and the National Cancer Institute. Established in 1993, Terra Nova is the world's first ethnobiomedical forest reserve and the brainchild of Rosita Arvigo, a Chicago native and Maya-trained healer.

For nearly three millennia the Maya flourished in the rain forests of Guatemala, Mexico, and Belize, harvesting roots, fruits, and foliage for food, fuel, fiber, construction materials, and, perhaps most important, medicine. Even with the advent of European medical practices following the Spanish conquest of the region in the sixteenth century, traditional ways survived and, in some areas, continue to be the sole source of healthcare. "As my mentor, Don Elijio Panti, would tell me," says Arvigo, "for every ailment on Earth, the spirits have provided a cure—one just has to find it."

A professional herbal healer, Arvigo, 60, of Italian-Syrian descent with deep-set eyes and narrow features, spent seven years among traditional Nahuatl healers in Mexico's Sierra Madre Mountains. She came to western Belize in 1976, believing that, with its rich heritage in traditional medicine, it would be an ideal place to both practice and learn. "I also had two small children and I wanted to bring them up in a fresh, natural environment rather than in the hustle and bustle of Chicago."

With her then husband, fellow healer Greg Shropshire, Arvigo purchased a small plot on the bank of the Macal River just outside San Ignacio and set up a clinic in town.

"It was a warm June day in 1983, and this elderly man, his slight, sinewy frame bent by time, came and sat on our clinic porch," says Arvigo, recounting her first meeting with Don Elijio. "I invited him in and we began to talk. The old man asked me what was in the glass jars on the clinic shelves and I began to explain their contents and the principles of herbal healing. Greg and I had brought a large supply of healing herbs from the States, but found that they were beginning to mold and rot in the humid tropical environment. Don Elijio was quick to notice the poor condition of the plants and immediately began telling me how to care for natural pharmaceuticals in a tropical environment. When he told me his name I suddenly realized that I had been giving a lecture on herbs to one of Central America's most revered *h'men* [doctor-priests]."

"Great and terrible stories had circulated about this old Mopan Maya," she continues. "Some people spoke of near miraculous healings, cured diseases, and numerous lives clutched from death's bony hand. Others, however, claimed he was nothing more than a lecherous old drunk and a witch who cast evil spells on innocent people." Rumors had circulated that Panti was from a family of sorcerers, his father a hechisero, a practitioner of black magic who enchanted women and was believed to have been responsible for a number of unexplained deaths.

Little did Arvigo know that her meeting with Don Elijio would lead to an apprenticeship lasting until his death at the age of 103 in 1996. During more than a decade of study, the Maya *h'men* taught her about the curative properties of the rain forest and the spiritual tools needed to use it. "Don Elijio's knowledge of the plants was staggering. He regularly used nearly 200 of them to treat patients from as far away as the northern Yucatán," she says. "I cannot tell you how often I wondered whether, as a non-Maya, I even had the capacity to learn it all. In time, the dark, mysterious forest of trees and lianas suddenly became a familiar place of knowledge and healing."

Like traditional healers worldwide, Maya curanderos operate by what is known as a doctrine of signatures—that is, many plants tell you how they should be used. Those that are red or bear red fruit or flowers are for blood-related conditions or burns and rashes; yellow plants—the color of pus and bile—are for infections and ailments of the liver and spleen; blue plants tend to contain sedatives and are used to treat the nervous system; white plants signal death and are often poisonous.

There are a variety of traditional healers in Belize, each with their own specialty or level of learning. A granny healer, for example, is a man or woman who has raised a sizable brood of children, grandchildren, and even great-grandchildren, using only home remedies to treat common household ailments such as diarrhea, cramps, skin diseases, and nervousness. Granny healers are well versed in rain forest medicine, but tend to care for only their immediate families. A village healer is essentially a granny healer whose practice has grown beyond his or her immediate family to include an entire village. Aiding granny and village healers are midwives, often trained by a parent or

grandparent to deliver babies in rural areas and to treat children using an array of herbal teas, poultices, and powders. The massage therapist, or sobadera, treats muscle spasms, backaches, sprains, stress from overworked muscles, and general aches and pains using herbal baths, poultices, teas, and oils to massage painful areas. "This knowledge," says Arvigo, "is passed down from generation to generation and is often considered a divine gift."

The bone setter, *kax-bac* or *guesero*, specializes in sprains, fractures, broken bones, and pulled ligaments, using manipulation techniques along with a type of acupuncture known as pinchar, in which stingray spines are used to relieve pain. Snake doctors treat venomous or infectious bites caused by snakes, spiders, scorpions, bats, rats, and rabid dogs, as well as puncture wounds from rusty implements. In areas infested with poisonous snakes and insects, these doctors are often a patient's only hope since most hospitals are far away and many do not have the proper antivenin. Treatment often consists of puncturing a patient's skin in the affected area with stingray spines or thorns. The snake doctor's practice and formulas are secret and usually passed on to only one person in a generation, but according to Polo, one must chew tobacco while sucking out toxins in order to avoid being poisoned himself.

The most experienced healers, however, are the *h'men* (literally, "he or she who knows"), doctor-priests who have the experience, power, and mandate to deal with both physical and spiritual ailments. They are believed to have the ability to contact the spirit world and ask for assistance in the diagnosis and treatment of ailments. A traditional healer would never embark on a course of action for a patient without first attempting to determine whether an ailment was of physical or supernatural origin.

"In Western medicine," says Arvigo, "we separate the physical from the mental or spiritual, seeing M.D.s for sickness; psychiatrists for mental problems. For the Maya, there is no such separation between the physical and mental or spiritual. Stress, grief, or other mental ailments bring on disease and vice versa." It is the shaman's job, she says, to heal the mind, body, and soul by physical and spiritual means—the physical with plants, the spiritual with incantations and prayers.

The incantations and prayers that accompany treatment are invocations of both ancient deities—the Nine Benevolent Maya gods, especially Ixchel, goddess of healing and weaving—and Christian saints. Use of such invocations is well known from antiquity, having been documented in one of the earliest surviving treatises on New World medicine. Written in Yucatec Maya using European script, the manuscript, which is known as the Ritual of the Bacabs, contains 46 medicinal incantations and prescriptions. Though it dates to the late eighteenth century, it is clear from the archaic nature of the language used in the manuscript, which is currently in the collection of the Princeton University Library, that it was copied from a much earlier document.

In Maya medicine, says Arvigo, diseases are regarded as semipersonified beings that can be controlled or ordered about by a shaman. Medicinal plants provide the cure, she says, but healers often rely on supernatural forces for guidance in determining precisely which plants or parts of plants to harvest and how to prepare them. Crossing the divide between the physical and spiritual worlds, however, requires a *sastun* (sas means "light" or "mirror"; tun, "stone"), usually a small, glistening, translucent stone. By peering into it, a shaman can determine the source of an illness or divine answers to questions, communing with the spirits as if they were close friends.

"One can not simply acquire a *sastun*," she explains. "A *sastun* must be sent by the Maya spirits. Sometimes, a healer may wait years for one to arrive, if, in fact, it ever does." Don Elijio had asked the spirits for a *sastun* for two years, she says, setting up what is known as a *primicia* altar in his cornfield nine times a year. The altar, adorned with nine gourds filled with atole (a sweetened corn beverage), one for each of the Maya gods, is used on feast days to conduct a ceremony in which one can commune with spirits and ancestors. One day, having just completed a *primicia* ceremony, Don Elijio was suddenly overtaken by a feeling of joy and happiness and found himself skipping back home like a young boy. When he arrived, his wife presented him with a luminous green stone, saying, "Look what I found on the floor today. A child must have left it here. Isn't it pretty?" And that was how he received his *sastun*. Arvigo now possesses Don Elijio's *sastun*, which he gave to her shortly before his death.

Realizing the richness of Maya traditional medicine and the importance of recording practices that had been handed down for generations before they disappeared, Arvigo founded the Ixchel Tropical Research Foundation in 1986. "I knew that the ways of traditional healers like Don Elijio were being eclipsed by Western medicinal practices, and that, like other fragile vestiges of Prehispanic culture, they would soon disappear without a trace. People, especially in developing countries like Belize, don't want to appear backward by associating with traditional healers. They would rather see Western doctors in starched white lab coats who dole out synthetic drugs. Some drugs, such as cortisone, which comes from dioscorea, and vincristine, which is used to treat Hodgkins disease and comes from the rosy periwinkle, are extracted from the very plants growing in a patient's backyard."

In an effort to preserve what remains of traditional Maya medicine, Arvigo embarked on a campaign to interest the scientific community in its extraordinary potential. "Can you imagine, here I am, witnessing what may be the last traces of Prehispanic

> ### The dynamic between researchers and traditional healers has changed in recent years.

medicinal knowledge in one of the last contiguous stands of old-growth rain forest in Central America, which is gradually being destroyed for farming and development, and I'm wondering whether Don Elijio's profession is going to die with him and the rain forest. Had any of his plants been studied by modern science? Was he all that was left of the medical system of the ancient Maya, the last thread dangling from a once glorious tapestry of healers who were revered, perhaps even deified by their society?"

"I began a vigorous letter-writing campaign to scientists around the world. One day, a friend passed along a newspaper article about a worldwide search for medicinal plants bearing anti-cancer and anti-AIDS compounds. The scientist in charge of collecting Central American specimens was ethnobotanist Michael Balick of the New York Botanical Garden."

"We get numerous requests for research support," says Balick, 48, whom I visited in his New York Botanical Garden office, "but we are only able to pursue a few of them. When I received Rosita's letter back in '86, I thought this would be an ideal project for us. We had just received a grant from the National Cancer Institute to screen Central American plants that had the potential for providing cures for two diseases for which modern medicine has only limited therapies—cancer and AIDS."

"Less than 1/2 of one percent of the planet's 265,000 species of higher plants has been exhaustively analyzed for their chemical composition and medicinal properties," he says. "From that 1/2 of one percent comes some 25 percent of all prescription pharmaceuticals that have been developed to date, drugs such as the heart medication digitalin from foxglove and the anti-inflammatory cortisone from dioscorea. As you can see, we have a long way to go."

"Given the number of plants out there, we simply do not have the resources to study them all. So, as scientists, how do we go about narrowing our research and increasing our chances of collecting the plants with the greatest curing potential? One way is to talk to the people who use them. We call this technique ethno-directed screening."

Balick and his team took to the field with Arvigo and Panti, collecting more than 3,000 specimens for testing and interviewing local healers about their use. After being properly pressed and dried, duplicate sets of specimens—stems, leaves, fruits, flowers—were sent to herbaria in both Belize and the United States, the latter being studied at the New York Botanical Garden.

In addition to its collection of rare medicinal trees, vines, and herbs, Terra Nova is home to seedlings rescued from tracts of rain forest that have given way to development, guaranteeing that future generations of healers and scientists will have plants to harvest. In addition to Terra Nova, Arvigo founded the Rainforest Medicine Trail at her farm just outside San Ignacio. The trail, which is open to the public, exhibits 50 of the most commonly used medicinal plants in the Maya world. Her farm also functions as a research station and a base of operations for a commercial enterprise that produces and sells a variety of tinctures made from Maya medicinal plants.

Arvigo and Balick note that the dynamic between researchers and traditional healers has changed in recent years. "We no longer simply go and observe," says Balick, "we form research partnerships. Most traditional healers with whom we have worked are elated that science is incorporating their knowledge rather than ignoring it. Should any drug come as the result of their traditional knowledge, the traditional healers will profit from it." Both the Botanical Garden and the National Cancer Institute have an agreement with the Traditional Healers Foundation, established to ensure the curanderos share the proceeds from any drug development.

Whether the plants will ultimately yield treatments for diseases such as cancer and AIDS remains to be seen as it will be some years before the Belize botanical collection has been exhaustively analyzed. "Our goal," says Arvigo, "has been simply to document the remnants of what once existed and to make it freely available to all who wish it." ≜

The author would like to thank the Traditional Healers Foundation of Belize, The New York Botanical Garden, and the Department for Middle American Research, Tulane University, for their assistance in the preparation of this article.

30

THE ENDURING MAYA

Henequen plantations like Yaxcopoil in the northern Yucatán attest a peoples' indomitable spirit.

by MARK ROSE

OT ALL MAYA RUINS ARE ABOVE GROUND, NOR ARE they all Prehispanic in date. I had spent the first few days of a week-long tour of archaeological sites in northwestern Yucatán wandering among the majestic ruins of Uxmal, Kabah, Sayil, and Labná, which flourished around A.D. 900. Then I visited the the spacious cavern of Loltún, with its stalactites and stalagmites and a scattering of painted Maya glyphs. What intrigued me most at Loltún were the stone walls built by the Maya to fortify the cave's entrances during the Caste War of 1847 to 1852. Rebelling against harsh conditions in the sugar plantations of the southern Yucatán, the Maya had overrun the peninsula. At the height of the insurrection only the cities of Mérida and Campeche held out against them. Mexico was slow in sending aid, perhaps because Yucatán had defied Mexican authority in 1838 by signing an alliance with the independent Republic of Texas, and had declared itself neutral in the Mexican-American War (1846–1848). In desperation, the government in Mérida appealed to Spain, Great Britain, and the United States for help, offering them sovereignty over Yucatán in exchange for assistance. Ultimately, the besieged cities survived only because the Maya army dispersed at the start of the planting season. But the war and its aftermath cost Yucatán half its population. The stone walls at Loltún are a testament to the bitter struggle.

Nearly three centuries before the Caste War, in July 1562, Fray Diego de Landa had torched the Maya books at Mani, a few miles northeast of Loltún. "Since they contained nothing but superstitions and falsehoods of the devil," de Landa wrote, "we burned them all." I visited the church at Mani, a fortress-like sixteenth-century structure with thick, high walls pierced by narrow windows, but it was closed and I could only walk about on the grounds where de Landa had conducted his auto-da-fé.

The next morning I went north to Yaxcopoil (the Maya name means "place of the green alamo trees"), a hacienda on the road between Mérida and Uxmal. I strolled through the quiet tree-shaded gardens and ornate eighteenth-century arch that marks the entrance to the hacienda. Overlooking the main hall of the owner's residence, or *casa principal*, are portraits of Don Donaciano Garcia Rejon and his wife Doña Monica Galera, who in 1864 acquired Yaxcopoil and whose descendants own it today. Beyond the casa are Yaxcopoil's Renaissance-style work buildings, adorned with graceful classical sculptures.

In the nineteenth and early twentieth centuries Yaxcopoil's wealth came from henequen, whose fleshy gray-green leaves contain strong fibers used in the manufacturing of twine and rope. Today the hacienda is a museum. Among the items for sale in its small gift shop are brass tags, about the size of large postage stamps, that have various numbers on them—500, 1,000, 1,500, etc. My guide explained that the tags were used to keep track of the number of henequen leaves each man harvested.

In the forward to his translation of de Landa's *Relación de las Cosas de Yucatán*, William Gates labeled henequen the "green gold...that with cattle and sugar turned the last screws on Indian independence." Gates was probably influenced by the journalist John Kenneth Turner, who in 1908 posed as an investor to make first-hand observations of the haciendas. Turner's dramatic account, published in his book *Barbarous Mexico*, was an uncompromising attack. The hacienda owners, he wrote, were "a company of little Rockefellers" who formed a "slave-holders' club." The slaves, he said, included "8,000 Yaqui Indians imported from Sonora, 3,000 Chinese and between 100,000 and 125,000 native Mayas, who formerly owned the lands that the henequen kings now own."

Henequen workers were kept on haciendas by means of debt peonage. Slavery was illegal, but the debts of individual workers could be purchased. The workers were unable to leave unless they repaid their debt, and they were paid so little that repayment was virtually impossible. On average, 1,000 leaves were harvested each day, but as many as 2,000 might be demanded. Beatings, malnutrition, and inadequate medical care were the lot of the workers.

Henequen was not cultivated commercially during the colonial period because the fibers had to be extracted from the leaves by hand. But the invention of the mechanical rasper, or *desfibradora*, during the 1850s was a breakthrough. With the introduction of steam power in 1861 and the invention of the mechanical binder in 1878, henequen production soared to meet the demands of North American farmers for inexpensive twine to bind their wheat sheaves and hay. By 1900 more than 85 percent of North American binder twine was manufactured with Yucatecan fiber.

The beneficiaries of the henequen boom were the 30 or so close-knit families who controlled the land, labor, and capital. Haciendas that had raised corn and cattle were replaced by henequen plantations. Maya peasants weeded henequen fields and harvested leaves or stoked boilers and ran the desfibradoras.

Turner concluded his account with a scathing description of Mérida and its henequen-based wealth. "I shall never forget my last day in Mérida. It might even challenge comparison in its white prettiness with any other [city] in the world…. My last afternoon and evening in Yucatán I spent riding and walking about the wealthy residence section of Mérida. Americans might expect to find nothing of art and architecture down on this rocky Central American peninsula, but Mérida has its million dollar palaces like New York, and it has miles of them set in miraculous gardens. Wonderful Mexican palaces! Wonderful Mexican gardens! A wonderful fairyland conjured out of slavery—slavery of Mayas and of Yaquis."

Allen Wells, author of *Yucatán's Gilded Age*, dismisses Turner as a "militant socialist journalist writing during the heyday of the muckrakers." While not defending the abuses, Wells sees the transformation of self-reliant cattle and corn haciendas of the early nineteenth century to henequen plantations dependent on world markets as the result of the complex relationships among local oligarchies, evolving Mexican political policies, and North American business interests. In *Agrarian Reform and Public Enterprise in Mexico*, Jeffrey Brannon and Eric Baklanoff note that where 95 percent of cultivated land in the Yucatán was producing corn before the Caste War, by 1910 henequen accounted for 70 percent of the land. But the boom times did not last. The market and prices collapsed when new plantations in Africa and Java undersold the Yucatecans, and again when synthetic fibers were introduced. Were the henequen plantations and system of debt peonage the last stage in the subjugation of the Maya as Gates suggests? Following hard on the heels of the Caste War the henequen boom had that effect, whether or not it was intended.

Most tours in the Yucatán focus, understandably, on the spectacular ancient ruins. But Maya culture did not end with the fall of Uxmal, or the arrival of the Spanish, or even the Caste War. Turn-of-the-century Mérida and henequen plantations like Yaxcopoil, for all the suffering they represent, are no less a part of Maya history and as moving a tribute to the indomitable Maya spirit. ♨

ABOUT THE
AUTHORS

ANTHONY F. AVENI is Russell B. Colgate Professor of Astronomy and Anthropology at Colgate University. The text of "Mediators in a Universal Discourse" is adapted from *Conversing with the Planets* (New York: Times Books, 1992).

ARLEN F. CHASE and **DIANE Z. CHASE**, professors in the department of sociology and anthropology at the University of Central Florida in Orlando, have been directing excavations at Caracol since 1985. Project funding has been provided by the Dart Foundation, the government of Belize, the Harry Frank Guggeheim Foundation, the Institute of Maya Studies, the National Science Foundation, the University of Central Florida, the United States Agency for International Development, and donations to the University of Central Florida Foundation, Inc.

MICHAEL D. COE is Charles J. MacCurdy Professor of Anthropology at Yale University. Coe received his graduate and undergraduate degrees from Harvard University where he specialized in Mesoamerican archaeology, concentrating on the Olmec and Maya civilizations. His research has led him to Precolumbian sites in Belize, Costa Rica, Guatemala, and Mexico and he is now writing a history of the decipherment of Maya glyphs.

T. PATRICK CULBERT is a professor of anthropology at the University of Arizona.

JOHN DORFMAN is on the staff of the *New Yorker.*

WILLIAM L. FASH, Jr. worked at the ruins of Chalcatzingo, Mexico (in 1974 and 1976) and in the southwestern United States (1975) before focusing on Maya archaeology as an assistant to Gordon Willey on his settlement surveys and excavations in the Copán Valley in 1977. He received his Ph.D. from Harvard in 1983.

BARBARA W. FASH has been an artist and illustrator for a variety of archaeological projects since her introduction to fieldwork in Mesoamerica at Chalcatzingo, Morelos, Mexico, in 1976. In 1977, she began drawing the monumental art and inscriptions of the ruins of Copán. She now serves as sculpture coordinator and chief artist on the Copán Mosaics Project.

DAVID FREIDEL of Southern Methodist University co-authored *Forest of Kings* and *Maya Cosmos* with the late Linda Schele. With Charles Suhler, he directs the Selz Foundation Yaxuná Archaeological Project.

TOM GIDWITZ is a freelance writer specializing in the earth sciences and archaeology.

IAN GRAHAM is director of the Maya Corpus Program at Harvard's Peabody Museum of Archaeology and Ethnology.

GILLETT GRIFFIN teaches Precolumbian art at Princeton University. Born in Brooklyn in 1928, he grew up in Connecticut and studied painting and graphic design at Yale University. In 1966 he resigned from the position of curator of graphic arts at the Princeton University Library to return to his painting and to explore Mexico's Precolumbian ruins. That year he and an associate identified the earliest datable mural paintings in Mesoamerica at Juxtlahuaca Cave in Guerrero, Mexico.

NIKOLAI GRUBE is an anthropologist at the University of Bonn and epigrapher for the Caracol Project, Belize, and Proyecto Yaxhá, IDEAH, Guatemala.

RICHARD D. HANSEN is an assistant research scientist at the Institute of Geophysics and Planetary Physics, University of California, Los Angeles. He directs the RAINPEG Project.

PAUL F. HEALY was looking for data on farming techniques when he accidentally stumbled on a grave containing rare Maya musical instruments. "It was a simple case of luck," says Healy, who for the past decade has been conducting fieldwork in Belize, where he is investigating ancient Maya agricultural methods. Healy, who graduated from the University of California at Berkeley and holds a Ph.D. from Harvard University, is a full professor in the Department of Anthropology at Trent University, Peterborough, Ontario.

He is the author of many publications on Maya and Central American archaeology, including *Archaeology of the Rivas Region, Nicaragua* (Waterloo: Wilfrid Laurier University Press, 1980). Healy wishes to acknowledge the financial support of the Social Sciences and Humanities Research Council of the government of Canada, Trent University, and the cooperation of the Belize Department of Archaeology.

SIMON MARTIN is epigrapher for the Proyecto Arqueológico de la Biosfera de Calakmul, INAH, Mexico, and an honorary research fellow of the Institute of Archaeology, University College, London.

MARY McVICKER, an independent scholar, writes about the history of archaeology in Mesoamerica. She has co-edited catalogs for two exhibitions of Precolumbian art, and is the author of a biographical sketch of Adela Breton for The Art of Ruins. She is also completing a full biography of Breton.

MARY MILLER, a professor of art history at Yale University, leads the Bonampak Documentation Project. Data gathered from this research will be used by the Proyecto Pintura Mural (PPM), an interdisciplinary Mexican endeavor under the direction of Beatríz de la Fuente, which has undertaken the complete documentation of all Prehispanic paintings in Mexico.

MARK S. PERLMAN is a former editorial intern at ARCHAEOLOGY.

COLLEEN P. POPSON, formerly associate editor of ARCHAEOLOGY.

MARK ROSE is executive editor of ARCHAEOLOGY.

ANGELA M.H. SCHUSTER, formerly senior editor of ARCHAEOLOGY, is now with the World Monuments Fund.

PAYSON D. SHEETS is professor of Anthropology at the University of Colorado in Boulder.

ANDREW L. SLAYMAN is a former senior editor of ARCHAEOLOGY.

CHARLES SUHLER of Southern Methodist University, with coauthor David Freidel, directs the Selz Foundation Yaxuná Archaeological Project.

DENNIS TEDLOCK, professor of English and anthropology, and **BARBARA TEDLOCK**, professor of anthropology, are both on the faculty of the State University of New York at Buffalo.

GENE WARE is chief technical specialist, College of Engineering and Technology, Brigham Young University.

RICHARD A. WERTIME, received a faculty development award from Beaver College in Glenside, Penn., which funded his travels to study the Maya.

JAMES WISEMAN is a contributing editor to ARCHAEOLOGY and a professor of archaeology, art history, and classics at Boston University.

PETER A. YOUNG is the editor-in-chief of ARCHAELOGY.

BOOKS FOR FURTHER READING

Chase, Arlen F. and Chase, Diane Z., eds., *Mesoamerican Elites: An Archaeological Assessment* (Norman: University of Oklahoma Press, 1992).

Coe, Michael D., *Breaking the Maya Code: The Last Great Decipherment of an Ancient Script* (Thames & Hudson, 1999).

Culbert, Patrick T., *The Ceramics of Tikal: Vessels from the Burials, Caches and Problematic Deposits* (Philadelphia: University of Pennsylvania Press, 1993).

Culbert, Patrick T., *The Lost Civilization: The Story of the Classic Maya* (New York: HarperCollins, 1974).

Culbert, Patrick T., *Maya Civilization* (Washington, D.C.: Smithsonian Books, 1993).

Fash, William, and Fash, Barbara, *Scribes, Warriors and Kings: The City of Copán and the Ancient Maya* (New York: Thames and Hudson, 2001).

Fash, William L., *Aztec Ceremonial Landscapes*. Edited by David Carrasco. (Niwot, Colorado: University Press of Colorado, 1998).

Freidel, David, L. Schele, J. Parker, J. Kerr and M. Everton, *Maya Cosmos: Three Thousand Years on the Shaman's Path*. New York: William Morrow, 1995.

Freidel, David, Cozumel: *Late Maya Settlement Patterns*. Edited by Jeremy A. Sabloff. (Academic Press, 1997).

Healy, Paul, *Archaeology of the Rivas* Region, Nicaragua (Waterloo, Ontario: Wilfrid Laurier University Press, 1980.)

Graham, Ian, *Corpus of Maya Hieroglyphic Inscriptions*. (Cambridge, Massachusetts: Peabody Museum of Archaeology and Ethnology, Harvard University, 1975).

Graham, Ian, *Alfred Maudslay and the Maya: A Biography* (University of Oklahoma Press, 2002).

Grube, Nikolai, Maya: *Divine Kings of the Rainforest* (Konemann, 2001).

Houston, Stephen, Mazariegos, Oswaldo C., and Stuart, David, eds., *The Decipherment of Ancient Maya Writing* (University of Oklahoma Press, 2001).

Knorosov, Yuri, *Maya Hieroglyphic Codices*. Translated by Sophie D. Coe. (Albany: Institute for Meso-American Studies, State University of New York at Albany, 1982).

Martin, Simon and Nikolai Grube, *Chronicle of the Maya Kings and Queens: Deciphering the Dynasties of the Ancient Maya*. (New York: Thames and Hudson, 2000).

Miller, Mary E., *Art of Mesoamerica: From Olmec to Aztec*. (New York: Thames and Hudson, 1996).

Miller, Mary E. and Karl Taube, *The Gods and Symbols of Ancient Mexico and the Maya: an Illustrated Dictionary of Mesoamerican Religion*. (New York: Thames and Hudson, 1997).

Miller, Mary E., *Maya Art and Architecture*. (New York: Thames and Hudson, 1999).

Miller, Mary E., *Murals of Bonampak*. (Princeton: Princeton University Press, 1986).

Robertson, Merle Green, *Ancient Maya Relief Sculpture: Rubbings by Merle Green Robertson* (Greenwich, Connecticut: New York Graphic Society, 1967).

Robertson, Merle Green, *The Sculpture of Palenque*. (Princeton: Princeton University Pres, 1983).

Schele, Linda, *The Blood of Kings: Dynasty and Ritual in Maya Art*. (New York: George Braziller, 1992).

Schele, Linda and Peter Matthews, *The Bodega of Palenque, Chiapas Mexico* (Washington D.C: Dumbarton Oaks Pub Service, 1978).

Schele, Linda, P. Matthews, and J. Kerr, *The Code of Kings: The Language of Seven Sacred Maya Temples and Tombs*. (New York: Scribner, 1999)

Schele Linda, J. Perez De Lara, R. Pina Chan, and P. De, *Hidden Faces of the Maya*. (Poway, California: Alti Pub, 1998).

Schele, Linda. *Maya Glyphs: The Verbs*. 1982. Austin: University of Texas Press.

Schele, Linda and Jeffrey H. Miller, *The Mirror, the Rabbit, and the Bundle: (Accession) Expressions from the Classic Maya Inscriptions (Studies in Pre-Columbian Art and Archaeology)* (Washington D.C: Dumbarton Oaks Pub Service, 1983).

Sheets, Payson D., ed., *Before the Volcano Erupted: the Ancient Cerén Village in Central America* (Austin: University of Texas Press, 2002).

Reents-Budet, Dorie, L. Schele and M. Mezzatesta, *Painting the Maya Universe: Royal Ceramics of the Classic Period* (Durham: Duke University Press, 1994).

Popol Vuh-the Mayan Book of the Dawn of Life. Translated by Dennis Tedlock. New York: Simon and Schuster, 1996).

Whittington, Michael, ed., *The Sport of Life and Death: The Mesoamerican Ballgame* (New York: Thames & Hudson, 2001). Visit www.calstatela.edu/academic/anthro/jbrady/ulama/proyectoulama.htm to see the most recent photographs and reports from the *ulama* research team from California State University, Los Angeles.

INDEX